The Peculiarities of Liberal Mod
in Imperial Britain

THE BERKELEY SERIES IN BRITISH STUDIES

Mark Bevir and James Vernon, University of California, Berkeley, Editors

The Peculiarities of Liberal Modernity in Imperial Britain

Edited by

SIMON GUNN AND JAMES VERNON

Global, Area, and International Archive
University of California Press

BERKELEY   LOS ANGELES   LONDON

The Global, Area, and International Archive (GAIA) is an initiative
of the Institute of International Studies, University of California,
Berkeley, in partnership with the University of California Press,
the California Digital Library, and international research programs
across the University of California system.

University of California Press, one of the most distinguished
university presses in the United States, enriches lives around the
world by advancing scholarship in the humanities, social sciences,
and natural sciences. Its activities are supported by the UC Press
Foundation and by philanthropic contributions from individuals
and institutions. For more information, visit www.ucpress.edu.

University of California Press
Berkeley and Los Angeles, California

University of California Press, Ltd.
London, England

Library of Congress Cataloging-in-Publication Data

A catalog record for this book is available from the Library of Congress

20 19 18 17 16 15 14 13 12 11
10 9 8 7 6 5 4 3 2 1

To Patrick Joyce, friend, mentor, historian

Contents

Acknowledgments

This volume had its origins in the conference "Liberal Subjects: The Politics of Social and Cultural History since the 1970s," held at the University of Manchester in March 2008 to honor Patrick Joyce on the occasion of his retirement. As the dedication to this book indicates, we both owe Patrick a good deal. As an adviser he was a constant catalyst for thought and conversation, and his scholarship continues to inform our work as well as that of many others far beyond the sometimes parochial world of British social and cultural history.

We would like to thank all those who participated in the conference, especially Harry Cocks, Francis Dodsworth, Anindita Ghosh, Rosaleen Joyce, Frank Mort, Frank O'Gorman, Carolyn Steedman, and William Sewell. Penny Summerfield and Mike Savage were instrumental in ensuring that the conference was held in Manchester. The event was funded by the ESRC Centre for Research on Socio-Cultural Change (CRESC) and the School of Arts, Cultures, and Humanities at the University of Manchester, as well as the British Academy and the Center for British Studies at the University of California, Berkeley. We are very grateful for the generous support of all these organizations. This volume bears only a passing resemblance to the original conference, and we are indebted to all the contributors for their willingness to revise and reframe their essays, sometimes under a rather heavy editorial hand. We are enormously grateful to the two readers for the Press (one revealed herself to be Jordanna Bailkin), who provided such incisive and trenchant comments that we restructured the collection and engaged in another round of revisions. Thanks to Penny Ismay for the index.

James Vernon thanks the participants of his graduate classes for their help thinking through the nature of modernity in imperial Britain. I

/   *Acknowledgments*

am honored to work with such talented people. The Andrew W. Mellon Foundation generously funded a collaborative program between UC Berkeley's Center for British Studies and the University of Chicago and Yale University reexamining Britain's transition to modernity in which Steven Pincus has proved a fine interlocutor. Last, but by no means least, my thanks to Ros, Jack, Mischa, and young Alf—the next one is for you.

Simon Gunn wishes to thank colleagues and graduate students at the Centre for Urban History, University of Leicester—a good place to think about the micro-dimensions of liberal modernity, from street numbering to water closets. At Leicester I have benefited especially from conversations with Robert Colls and Prashant Kidambi. My biggest debt, though, is to Gabriele Griffin, not least for her periodic reminders that there is always another way of seeing things.

s. g. *and* j. v.

Foreword

How shall the history of Britain be written? Obviously, there are many answers to this question. This book proposes two, in the shape of the ideas of liberalism and modernity. These answers are powerful ones, for both concepts are indeed central to an understanding of Britain. As the editors argue in their introduction, these concepts are central because they pose the most searching questions, both about how historians have understood the course of British history in the past and how they have come to view it now, over the past three or four decades. Looking back over the past couple of generations of British experience and how historians have responded, the changes have been considerable. In the 1960s and into the 1970s Britain was seen as the exemplary case of modernity. It was in Britain, so it was held, that the conditions of a liberal economy and polity were historically most developed, and alongside them industrialization and urbanism.

Since then much has happened to alter this view. Economic globalization, European integration, and the information revolution have been among the forces for change. These changes have in turn led to changes in the nature of the nation-state, apparent in a lessening of its power and a questioning of what it now means to be a member of a nation-state. In turn, therefore, comes the question, what does it mean to write "British history" now? The chapters that follow offer a fascinating, original, and important answer to this question. In their various ways the contributors connect to the different intellectual perspectives that have resulted from the great social, economic, and political changes that have occurred. The intellectual agenda that follows embraces postcolonial and post-Foucault governmentality perspectives, for instance, and a new awakening of interest in the nature of materiality in relation to power. Along with this, the introduction offers a rigorous analysis of the central terms of the book, *liberal* and *modernity*, both of which, but especially the latter, are notoriously fluid and varied. What the volume does is to renovate these terms and return them to intelligent discourse.

There has been a remarkable turning outward from the insularity of previous times, when the history of Britain could be written in terms of competing and narrow political "interpretations," Tory, Whig, and liberal-left. When attention was lifted from Britain (for which England often stood proxy) insularity manifested itself in another kind of way: understanding Britain as the exemplary case of liberal modernity involved corroborating a particular kind of Anglo-American liberalism, in large part shaped by the Cold War. Instead of this we now have a much more outward-looking academic history, concerned with connections and translations of all sorts, so that British history is now seen to be inseparable from imperial history, transnational and global history.

What has become apparent is just how rapid and important was the diffusion of the intellectual and material components that made up liberalism and modernity. In these processes Britain in some versions of events is seen to be as much a product as a creator of modernizing dynamics,[1] which came from earlier periods and spaces of modernity, including those outside the British empire. Critiques of Eurocentrism such as that of Jack Goody have alerted us to how many of the characteristics of "modernity," including capitalism, urbanization, science, and individualism, are to be found before the eighteenth century and outside Europe.[2] The less polemical work of historians in world/global history, especially global economic history, poses the radical question as to whether Eurocentrism itself is responsible for the concept of modernity in the first place.[3] However, as the editors so rightly say, while "going global" means that Britain and the West are now seen as the result of world historical processes, the larger picture in turn has produced its own limitations. And an emphasis on convergence should not displace comparison and recognition of locally specific responses to general, shared historical processes. In short, there *was* something "peculiar" about Britain. This peculiarity, especially as it was centered on liberalism and ways of being modern, was importantly about empire, but it was not only about empire. It had to do with a particular set of historical conditions, shaped by the exigencies of empire but also those of state form, and of the dynamics of nation, region, and locality within the United Kingdom.

Out of these conditions and peculiarities therefore begins to emerge a new emphasis on the significance of Britain in developing distinctive and important ways of being modern, to which liberalism, in the larger sense used in this volume, was central. These ways, as the editors explain, by no means exclude the possibility of a modernity that was both conservative and liberal, as the British experience so clearly was. This recognition of Britain's complex ways of being modern has dealt a death blow to the historical orthodoxy of the 1970s and 1980s that Britain was never really a country that had been modern in the first place (or at least was not modern until Thatcherite neoliberalism had done its work). In short, Britain is seen to matter again, in a new way.

This volume does not take the direction of systematic cross-nation comparison, something needed at the level of the empire-state as well as the nation-state, as the editors recognize. Even at the nation-state level comparison is still relatively undeveloped, especially work that builds in the contribution of the cultural turn. What this collection does is to prepare the ground for comparative work while at the same time deepening understanding of the complexity of the British case, both in its home and in its colonial dimensions. There is also in this volume a concentration on the nineteenth and twentieth centuries, but this is not to the detriment of the importance of previous developments, again as the editors recognize. Rather than the post-1800 emphasis of the volume foreclosing discussion of the question, When were liberalism and modernity? it opens up questions about the temporalities of liberal modernity in a new way. It helps us understand the nature of British history not only by posing new questions but also by applying new intellectual tools. In the conference from which this volume is derived, as indeed in the discipline of history more broadly, it is evident that conversations between different theoretical and disciplinary approaches are undergoing a revival,[4] and this volume is an important contribution to these ongoing conversations as well as to the central question of Britain's peculiar kind of modernity and of liberalism.

Patrick Joyce

1. Introduction

What Was Liberal Modernity and
Why Was It Peculiar in Imperial Britain?

Simon Gunn and James Vernon

This book is about the nature of modernity in imperial Britain and whether it can be characterized as liberal. Historically, liberalism and modernity are often seen to be so intimately entwined that they appear symbiotic. From the early nineteenth century to the late twentieth century many prominent intellectuals and overseas observers credited the apparent miracle of Britain's modernity—the combination of rapid industrialization, imperial expansion, and relative political stability in the transition to democracy—to a liberalism it had created.[1] By the 1950s, when Britons were rapidly losing confidence in the modern and civilizing characteristics of their trade, empire, and political institutions, modernization theorists once again valorized Britain's liberal path of development as an exemplary world historical model. This volume critically engages with these accounts. It examines the apparently miraculous and exemplary nature of imperial Britain's historical experience over the past two centuries and asks how useful the terms *liberal* and *modernity* are in helping us understand it. In doing so, it reopens discussion about the peculiar ways in which Britain became modern, how liberal interventions seeking to create new and modern conditions occurred at different historical periods, unfolded at various rhythms, and were often compelled to combine with the very customary forms and practices they were assumed to displace. And finally, this volume insists that the peculiar nature of Britain's liberal modernity was, paradoxically, also often an imperial and transnational formation.

In the interdisciplinary field of British studies, and indeed far beyond it, few terms are as promiscuously used as *liberalism* and *modernity*. We are not suggesting that they are the most frequently deployed terms. In his analysis of the most widely used keywords in the humanities and

TABLE 1.1 Keywords in Humanities and Social Sciences, 1980–2009

| | Keyword | | | |
Date	Identity	Globalization	Modernity	Liberalism
1980–84	19	0	1	0
1985–89	33	1	4	0
1990–94	3,091	253	581	453
1995–99	6,803	1,423	1,344	810
2000–2004	11,623	4,754	2,278	934
2005–2009	13,110	4,415	2,351	937

SOURCE: OCLC ArticleFirst database, http://firstsearch.oclc.org. Accessed 1 October 2009.

social sciences after the cultural turn, Frederick Cooper demonstrated the ubiquity of the term *identity* during the 1990s, with *globalization* and *modernity* following some way behind, trends that appear to have continued over the past decade (see table 1.1).[2] Similarly, in British studies the impact of the cultural and imperial turns has been no less marked over the past two decades (see table 1.2). While the debate about the utility of *class* as an analytical category partly helps explain its prevalence during the 1990s, it is the increasing frequency of *identity, empire, gender,* and *race* that stand out. Given the well-established prominence of political and imperial history in British studies, it is unsurprising that *liberalism* has remained a constant presence, while *modernity* appears to be growing in importance. However, despite the consistent use of *liberalism* and the novelty of *modernity*, there remains a fundamental ambiguity in their use and meaning. Indeed, they are so variously defined as terms of description and analysis that some now consider them irredeemable and useless.[3]

A key task of this volume is to put analytical pressure on the categories of liberalism and modernity so that we can assess their utility in making sense of the historical experience of imperial Britain over the past two centuries. In this introduction we explore how scholars conceptualize *liberalism* and *modernity* in contrasting or complimentary ways, as well as their differing investments in these terms as ways of understanding the historical transformation of imperial Britain. The aim is to generate a richer understanding of what it is we mean by liberalism and modernity, how it is they might be

TABLE 1.2 Keywords in British Studies, 1980–2004

	Keyword						
Date	*Identity*	*Empire*	*Modernity*	*Liberalism*	*Class*	*Race*	*Gender*
1980–84	87	107	3	48	214	72	7
1985–89	135	155	11	77	274	99	48
1990–94	199	150	27	57	306	117	138
1995–99	282	194	67	60	329	155	213
2000–2004	295	204	78	68	326	167	215

SOURCE: Search of JSTOR database, British Studies subject area collection (www.jstor.org/action/showJournals#359817624), accessed 1 October 2009. We searched seven prominent journals, including the *English Historical Review*, *Victorian Studies*, and the *Journal of British Studies*. Indexing for all journals ended in 2004 at the time of search, with most stopping in 2003; the *English Historical Review* ended in 2001.

said to "fit"—or not fit—together in specific historical contexts—in short, to explain in what ways imperial Britain's modernity was liberal.

First, let us deal with modernity. Cooper rightly attaches significance to *modernity* having surpassed *modernization* in 1995 as the way to describe a condition or process of becoming modern.[4] His point is that when scholars spoke of modernization we knew what they were talking about: they described a progressive and totalizing process toward the telos that was the modern condition. The process of modernization was held to be not only irresistible but also universal, that is, applicable to all populations across the globe. Britain held a privileged place in modernization theory.[5] It was the first modern nation and one whose historical experience provided an exemplary model all were destined to at least try to follow. The balance list of Britain's precocious achievements appeared remarkable and irrefutable:

- successive financial, agricultural, commercial, consumer, industrial, and transport revolutions that inaugurated capitalism
- the development of a vast global empire
- the invention of the individual and the nuclear family
- mass cities and an enlightened civil society
- a system of political representation and parliamentary government
- a modern, centralized, imperial state with an independent civil service

By any standard this was a formidable list, even if other nations like the Netherlands, France, Germany, and the United States could lay claim to some of these achievements and their own hallowed place in modernization theory. It was more remarkable because there was no seemingly good reason why all these phenomena should first occur in a small, dark, and wet island in a seemingly remote part of northern Europe. In modernization theory the question of *why* Britain became the first modern nation invariably resolved itself into explaining *how* it happened, to what effect and whether other nations could or should follow. There were, of course, many answers to these questions, but they shared an elevation of Britain's historical experience as singular and illuminating a path of development that all nations should proceed down (or avoid) to be successful moderns.[6]

The general view—first established in Britain during the mid-nineteenth century, consolidated with the academic invention of British history as a field, and celebrated a century later by modernization theorists on the other side of the Atlantic—was that Britain's modernity was exemplary because of its very uniqueness. Only Britain, the argument ran, was able to combine rapid economic liberalization and growth, imperial expansion, urbanization, and the growth of civil society with relative political stability. Unsurprisingly, given that this argument was the product of the triumph of liberalism in Britain and was subsequently reified in the United States during the Cold War (when the latter's colonial history appeared suitably distant in the rearview mirror), this was an inherently liberal view of modernization. It was premised on the understanding that Britain's historical evolution was spontaneous and organic. Britain's liberal modernity provided a blueprint for how national economies, societies, and cultures could be made anew without violent political upheaval. It held out a hopeful example of how other little countries could make it big and do so in a hurry.

Ironically, Britain's liberal and relatively stable transition to modernity was seen as unfolding rapidly, through changes so dramatic that they were understood as a series of revolutions. The Glorious Revolution of 1688 may have provided a constitutional settlement that allowed Britain to avoid subsequent political revolutions, but it experienced just about every other type of revolution—scientific, financial, agricultural, demographic, commercial, consumer, technological, industrial, in government and statecraft, Darwinian, to say nothing of the equally rapid processes of urbanization and imperial expansion. These revolutions were seen to be experienced in a profoundly interconnected fashion, and the entire process was rapid and irreversible. This was a big bang model of modernity.

Over the past thirty years these accounts of Britain's dramatic emergence as the first modern nation have been effectively demolished. Long before postcolonial theory, Anglo-Marxist social historians critiqued the way in which liberal modernization theory had celebrated Britain's supposedly peaceful transition to capitalism and democracy.[7] They insisted that there were no universal rules of historical development because the social determined locally specific responses to economic modernization and the politics they gave rise to. Their task became to explain the peculiarities of the British and why the working class had not risen like the sun at the appointed hour.[8] The process did not stop there. Within a generation the big bang model of Britain's modernization faced new revisionist challenges. These resulted in either a disavowal of Britain's very modernity or an emphasis on its deeply contested, gradual, and incomplete form.

Initially the revisionist challenge that emerged during the 1980s sought to refute arguments about British exceptionalism by locating its history in a broader European perspective.[9] Even as the comparative European dimension has receded, Britain is now seen less as the first modern nation than as an ancien régime. The Glorious Revolution of 1688, the argument runs, was no 1789, no 1848, no 1917. It was a revolution that reaffirmed royal authority and consolidated a form of aristocratic government that would prove remarkably durable—hence the increasing length of what became known as the long eighteenth century. The new game in town, to some extent apparent here in the chapters by Lawrence and Vincent, is explaining and dating the demise of the ancien régime, not the birth of a modern and imperial Britain.[10] Some point to the reform crisis of 1828–32; some, to the second wave of industrialization, rapid urbanization, and the Third Reform Act of the 1880s; others, to the strange death of liberal England and World War I; others, to World War II and the arrival of social democracy; others, to the political and cultural transformations of the 1960s; and still others, to the Thatcher government and the attack on corporate Britain in the 1980s.[11] Britain, the argument runs, never had a bourgeois revolution; it went straight from aristocratic government to a social democracy that remained deeply marked by a persistent paternalism. Britons, it is sometimes suggested, never stopped living in an old country and have never been modern.

Continuity then has become the new change. In place of an account of a rapid and revolutionary transition to modernity we have a new emphasis on the persistence of tradition and a *longue durée* that has become so gradual and spasmodic that it appears almost a stealth version of continuity.[12] Even where modern forms emerge—and no one seriously disputes that there were major economic, political, social, and cultural transformations—they do so under old structures and conditions. Those once considered the agents of modernization are now rebranded as aristocratic and gentlemanly—finance capitalists, factory owners, civil servants, public moralists, imperial administrators, Liberal Party leaders, even trade unionists and skilled laborers.[13] New wine perhaps but in decidedly old bottles.

Since the 1990s this revisionist debunking of Britain's modernity has accelerated as the imperial and postcolonial turns have made claims about Britain's role in the making of the modern world appear not just suspect but even an extension of an imperial project. Dispensing with the teleological and universal claims of modernization theory, many scholars now talk more neutrally of a modernity that has been pluralized into a proliferating number of alternative and regional forms across the world.[14] The rise of world or global history since the 1990s has also played its part, forcing historians to confront modernity as difference and divergence as well as integration and uniformity.[15] As Cooper has argued, all this has come at a certain cost, for it is no longer clear quite what the term *modernity* now denotes. Instead of seeing modernity as an analytical category that enables us to understand a process of transformation (with a logic however uneven) that was the product of European capitalism or the Enlightenment and the imperialisms they gave rise to, it is now regularly used to describe any context where the rhetoric of the modern is found. Simply put, modernity is now rarely understood as a historical condition but as a discourse, so that the burden of analytical work is to examine its varied uses and meanings and the politics that lay behind them.[16]

This has led to a further pluralization of modernity, with its hyphenated prefixes now extending beyond the geography of nation and region to cultural politics, subject positions, or spaces. Interwar Britain, for example, is now the home of a series of conservative, colonial, imperial, suburban, Sapphic, feminine, gendered, and metropolitan modernities.[17] Further afield one does not have to look far to discover books with titles in which modernities have been given attitude: they are dangerous, contested, embodied, hybrid, displaced, lost, refracted . . . the list continues. Insofar as there is coherence in the proliferation of modernity's prefixes it is that they focus on how a discourse of the modern is claimed and used to assert the interests of a specific subject, space, or politics. While this approach demonstrates a rising self-consciousness of living in a modern age it is unclear whether or how this changes over time and what is different about the various moments of modernity identified by scholars.

This volume takes a different approach. Our interest is in the conditions of modernity created by liberal visions of, and interventions on, the world. There is less concern here, or in the chapters that follow, with the meanings and multiple forms of modernity, with how the discourse of the modern was claimed and by whom. Yet not all the contributors remain convinced of the analytical utility of the term *modernity*, and some deploy differing understandings of its character as variously grounded in economic, social, political, or cultural conditions. Moreover, while a number of chapters concentrate on conditions that were specifically English or British, others emphasize how different conditions were always forged in relation to empire; the question of location or territory remains secondary to the historical process under investigation. For Crook the secret ballot was not an imperial formation, whereas for Epstein the division and representation of labor was, and Otter reminds us that the environmental forms of liberal modernity were transnational and decidedly extraimperial. Rather than insist on a single definition of modernity, the chapters provide different understandings of its character, location, and periodization that we hope will generate new ways of conceptualizing the peculiarities of Britain's historical development.

Liberalism is also a term with multiple associations. A key aim of this volume is to reopen dialogue between scholars who understand liberalism in divergent ways. In much of the existing scholarship those viewing liberalism from different perspectives often politely ignore one another's work, creating confusion and ambiguity over its meaning.[18] Yet before identifying potential points of convergence, we shall first outline what we consider the four main current approaches to understanding liberalism.

1. Intellectual historians focus on the development of a set of ideas that were primarily preoccupied with questions of political representation and the relationship between the individual and the state. After Locke the central purpose of these ideas in the British (but importantly not in the imperial) context was to maximize what was now considered the "natural" liberty of men as individuals. This was to be achieved by removing the obstacles that prevented its fulfillment—namely, aristocratic monopolies of power in the realms of politics (old corruption), religion (the established Anglican Church), and economics (mercantile monopolies and protective tariffs or wages). Care used to be taken to disentangle the British enlightenment and distinguish liberalism from varieties of

Whiggism, utilitarianism, natural rights theory, classical political economy, and feminism, which is why J. S. Mill was often taken to represent its classic articulation. Increasingly, however, the focus on a coherent and narrow set of political ideas has given way to an emphasis on a family of liberalisms and recognition of its broader social, cultural, and imperial roots deep in the eighteenth century and occasionally even the seventeenth.[19] Understanding the gendered nature of liberalism and its relationship to imperialism has been one important axis of this expansive view of liberalism.[20]

2. The varied genealogies of liberal political economy have also become a critical issue for intellectual historians.[21] Indeed, it is now impossible to consider liberalism as solely addressing the political. Economic liberalism—the belief that markets and trade generate the most wealth, prosperity, and social harmony when restored or left in their "natural" state, that is, open and free—was always a moral and political project integrally related to theories of liberal political freedom. We now recognize that the conflict between protagonists of a land-centered, mercantilist political economy and those with a more expansive protoliberal view of the wealth of nations as oriented to potentially limitless commerce and consumption informed the politics of revolution in 1688, the expansion and administration of empire, and the cleavages between Whigs and Tories throughout the eighteenth and early nineteenth century.[22] Less interested in economic liberalism as an ideology, political and economic historians have focused on the policies through which it was implemented and its effects. The politics of free trade are center stage in these accounts and serve to delineate the hegemony of economic liberalism from the repeal of the Corn Laws in 1846 to the eventual turn back to protection after 1931.[23]

3. Political historians give Liberalism a capital *L* and use it to describe the politics of the Liberal Party. That party finally emerged from Whig politics during the 1850s and became classically associated with the figure of William Gladstone. During the first decade of the twentieth century it reinvented itself as the vehicle of a "New Liberalism," which was nonetheless not enough to prevent its strange death in the era of the Great War.[24] Some of the clarity of this narrative has been lost in recent work that has emphasized continuities and connections between the politics of the Liberal Party and those of Whigs, Radicals, Unionists, and women's suffrage and

labor groups.[25] Yet the Liberal Party continues to be seen as the political expression of liberalism as a set of ideas, implementing this ideology as far as it was politically possible to do so.

4. Those historians influenced by Foucault and subsequent work on governmentality use the term *liberalism* to capture a new mentality and method of government that emerged in the late eighteenth and early nineteenth century. Far from being wedded to a particular set of ideas or the ideology of a political party, this mentality was the product of new forms of knowledge and expertise. In turn, they produced and justified new techniques of rule over those subjects deemed capable of self-government (the informed, industrious, healthy, and self-improving individual) as well as those others found incapable of it. Some have claimed that it is possible to identify eras of liberal government that stretch from the late eighteenth century through to the late twentieth.[26] As a political technology that extends far beyond the realm of politics and the work of the state, liberalism here is a diffuse rationality, generated by many actors from multiple sources and evident in a panoply of everyday practices and material environments. It is seemingly everywhere and nowhere.

Each of these ways of conceptualizing liberalism as a set of ideas, an economics and politics, and a technique of government has its limitations, but we want to dwell instead on what they have in common. All see liberalism as committed to maximizing what was described as the freedom of certain individuals—those Catherine Hall has termed "civilized subjects"—by ensuring their natural rights of religious, political, economic, and cultural expression and representation.[27] All agree that liberalism had its roots in the long eighteenth century but came of age during the nineteenth century and sought to "restore" what was projected as a natural condition of liberty and freedom through a series of reforms in each of these domains. Markets, civil society, and everyday life were all opened up to new liberal practices in ways that included new groups of people but continued to exclude many at home and across the empire. Indeed, animated by the work of feminist and postcolonial scholars, we now understand that liberalism was plagued by the tension between a universalizing impulse (which posited its principles as true and applicable across the globe) and a theorization of difference that marked out specific populations and territories as not quite ready for its freedoms. Some present this tension as inherent to structures of liberal thought and practice;

others insist it was a contingent product of the first half of the nineteenth century with the entrenchment of separate spheres for men and women, the delineation of the social and its problematic groups like the pauper, and the turn to empire and the codification of racial difference.[28] Either way, we are now aware of the limits of liberalism and how those excluded from its promises represented its constitutive outside. Liberalism was not just a matter of rights steadily extended to wider populations; its existence was premised on strategic forms of segregation and suppression. It was these contradictions that were first theorized and then politically exposed by those excluded from liberalism's promise of universality. Indeed, as George Dangerfield first suggested (in different terms), it was the return of the repressed—women, labor, and colonial subjects—that eventually accounted for liberalism's demise.[29]

Although superficially each of the four approaches to liberalism outlined above proclaims its autonomy, in practice they all often remain tacitly wedded to a social explanation of its emergence, viewing it as the expression of a rising bourgeoisie or at least the cultural values associated with that class: individualism, the nuclear family, and capitalism.[30] To a certain extent the thickening out of liberalism, the expansion of the term to incorporate various other intellectual traditions, political forms, and rationalities, has nuanced this social explanation. As with modernity, we must now acknowledge that there is no longer any change without continuity, that for all the novelty of the liberal project it remained marked by those ideological traditions, political formations, and governmentalities that it sought to displace.[31] While such an expansive view of liberalism appears to make periodizing its rise and fall in imperial Britain more difficult, there is in fact widespread agreement that the constitutive elements of liberalism emerge in the eighteenth century, crystallize in the nineteenth century, and unravel in the first half of the twentieth century. Despite the unevenness of this process across the economic, political, and social domains, we might also agree that it created new economic practices, governmental systems, and social formations that decisively shaped the modern history of Britain, its empire, and arguably much of the world.

Finally, we now need to ask in what ways Britain's liberal modernity was peculiar. This question returns us to the classic debate within British Marxism between E. P. Thompson and Perry Anderson centered on "The Peculiarities of the English," the title of Thompson's response to Perry Anderson's earlier critique of Britain as a "scelerosed, archaic society."[32] Anderson had argued that Britain's modernity was effectively smothered by gentlemanly capitalism and landed conservatism, whereas Thompson identified the "great arch of bourgeois culture" that constituted the peculiarities of English modernity.[33] Significantly, the terms *liberalism* and *modernity*, or even Britain, let alone the empire, did not figure explicitly in this debate. The nearest Anderson came to a discussion of liberalism was in his dismissal of utilitarianism as the "one authentic, articulated ideology" of the British bourgeoisie.[34] Although not deploying the term *liberal* or *modernity*, Thompson by contrast placed great emphasis on a number of attributes we might associate with it. First was the tradition of Protestant Dissent in Britain, seen as nurturing empiricism as an intellectual idiom and whose principal achievement was Darwinism. Second was political economy, that form of "economic protestantism" whose prime consequence was to install an idea of the free market as a force of nature. Third and finally, though much less elaborated by Thompson, was a "bourgeois democratic tradition" that contributed in turn to a popular "subpolitical consensus," which Thompson gestured toward rather than specified.[35] In this reading the Anderson-Thompson debate was an argument about the nature of Britain's liberal modernity and its arrested development viewed through a "history of classes."[36]

The debate about peculiarities has haunted historiography since the 1960s and not just in Britain.[37] It would be wrong, however, to assume that the ways in which peculiarity is understood have remained identical. The terms of debate have changed geopolitically and conceptually in interrelated ways. First, the debate about peculiarity was dependent on a wider comparative history or historical sociology, so that the peculiarities of the English became visible only in relation to other Western industrialized nation-states, notably Germany and France. These were the models that Thompson, borrowing from Dickens's Mr. Podsnap, lampooned as "Other Countries," but which were also taken as the natural comparators, whereas for Anderson France historically speaking remained the model of the liberal modern capitalist state. Second, the imperial dimension was not recognized as central to Britain's peculiarity or to the broader process of modernization.

Empire was acknowledged in this earlier encounter but mainly as "noises off"; center stage was occupied by the drama of class relations in Britain and more specifically the industrial heartlands of Lancashire and the West Riding. By contrast, the recent move to foreground Britain's colonial networks and her status as an imperial power has reversed the terms of the older debate. Now it is the comparative European dimension that has dissolved into the background. Attention has been redirected to relationships within and between colonies and metropole rather than to comparisons between different European imperial formations.[38] The thrust of much of this new historiography, therefore, is no longer to explain the stabilization of industrial class society but instead to illuminate the makings of modern multicultural Britain. In the process London has replaced Manchester as the focal point of the national-imperial story, represented as a global or cosmopolitan city disembedded from the nation-state. So we are left with a paradox: the analytically expansive turn to the imperial and transnational that rendered the more provincial Thompsonian view of peculiarities obsolete may actually reembed a reworked version of the island story.

We lament the loss of the comparative view apparent in the peculiarities debate and recognize this as a significant absence in the chapters that follow. We are certainly not suggesting that liberal modernity was unique to imperial Britain (France and the United States most obviously provided their own alternative republican models).[39] Indeed, we call for more comparative work that examines the ways in which specific historical processes were shared at similar moments by multiple countries. In Bayly's recent and influential account of the birth of the modern world all regions were present at the making of a liberal modernity—defined by new bureaucratic forms of statecraft, the growth of trade and consumption, and the emergence of civil society—once exclusively associated with the British historical experience. Going global in this way may allow us to see the West as a product of world historical processes, but as we have intimated, it also paradoxically runs the risk of collapsing complexity and difference and reifying a Western, and even specifically British, story of modernity. An emphasis on convergence should not displace comparison and the recognition of locally specific responses to shared historical processes. Liberal modernity was therefore not unique to imperial Britain, but its formation and character were peculiar as it emerged from and responded to a locally specific set of economic, social, political, and cultural conditions. Empire was only one important source of this peculiarity.

The peculiar nature of liberal modernity in imperial Britain did not stem solely from questions of geography and territory but also from the dynamics and temporality of its formation. Clearly, liberal modernity was not produced overnight by a series of revolutionary transformations. It was a gradual and uneven process that never achieved a hegemonic or ideal form—Smith and Mill did not describe the world as it was but the world they wished to inhabit—and always remained shaped and marked by its others. Nor is this simply a matter of there being no change without continuity, although that must be part of the story. Modernity had a dialogic character: tradition was invented as much as the traditional displaced; new religious missions and myriad forms of reenchantment proceeded alongside secularization; urbanization generated a valorization of the rural. In exploding the big bang model of modernity, we also want to challenge the view of it as a homogeneous process and singular condition. Modernity was multiform, not singular, produced from different processes that proceeded at uneven rates and according to different logics. Industrialization, imperialism, and democratization were classically seen to be marching in sequence and causal relationship with each other, but we might instead see them as unfolding according to their own separate if connecting rhythms and dynamics.[40] Viewed from this perspective the peculiarities of liberal modernity in imperial Britain were generated by the interaction of these distinctive processes, their complex imbrication, their differing temporalities, their territorially uneven application, and their unanticipated outcomes. Such an approach makes heavy demands of historical analysis, but it also allows us to talk once again of what made Britain modern without provincializing the history of the rest of the world as late or failed realizations of the exemplary British model of modernity.

There are dangers that in emphasizing the peculiarities of liberal modernity it becomes protean, apparent everywhere and nowhere, and lands us back in the very state of confusion about liberalism and modernity we have sought to escape. So what were its limits? First, in imperial Britain liberal modernity emerged out of, and adapted itself to, conditions that were local and specific. As Jon Lawrence's chapter in this volume reminds us, there was a persistent conservative tone to British political culture, leading him to talk of a hybrid "tory liberalism." However, many of these conditions were themselves the product of Britain's imperial and transnational relations and encounters. Britain's modern food system, as Chris Otter demonstrates, is unimaginable without these relationships: Britain's demand for cheap grain and beef was sustained and made possible by the agricultural development of the U.S. Midwest and Argentina. The limits of Britain's liberal modernity were less geographic than conceptual and experiential, that is, historical. Second, while we must acknowledge that liberal modernity had its constitutive outside, not all that was outside was constitutive; it could be just plain different. Historians of imperialism and colonialism, like James Epstein and Gavin Rand here, have rightly reminded us that much of imperial Britain's liberal modernity appeared distinctly unmodern and illiberal: the imposition of free trade, the use of unfree labor, the creation of traditional forms of authority and social systems, the suppression of civil rights, and the use of concentration camps, to name just a few of the more prominent examples of the violence of colonial rule.[41] We now tend to view these phenomena—in India, Africa, or, closer to home, in Ireland—not as exceptions to liberal rule but as a necessary component of it. They marked out the ordering of difference on which it rested, with one rule for those designated civilized subjects and another for those races, genders, and classes that constituted the rest. They also delineated the states of emergency that justified the suspension of the rule of law and the usual routines of liberal government.[42] However, the illiberalism of liberalism should not blind us to that which is not liberal. In nineteenth-century Europe alone there were many rival ways of being or becoming modern, with quite distinct economic, political, and social systems. Germany, France, Spain, and Italy provide obvious comparisons, as do the Russian and Ottoman empires on Europe's fringes and the various forms of fascism and socialism that emerged in the twentieth century. Modernity, in short, looks very different when viewed from London, Vienna, or Vladivostock.[43]

Third, the increasing attention paid to the rise and triumph of neoliberalism and postmodernity since the 1970s has raised fresh questions about periodization. If neoliberalism and/or postmodernity is now, when was liberal modernity, and what separated them? Neoliberalism can be understood as an attack on the forms of corporate political, social, and economic organization ("social democracy") that structured many international institutions and nation-states in the decades after World War II.[44] It arose as a response not only to the crisis of this order following the end of the long postwar boom in 1973 but also to new globalized systems of multinational capital (money markets, transnational corporations) and technology (information technology, military systems). Neoliberalism represented an ideological intervention that aimed to reorganize the political, social, and economic order through instruments such as the deregulation of financial markets and the imposition of an audit culture that sought to turn citizens into consumers of social services. Neoliberalism was therefore a response to a system that was no longer liberal in any meaningful sense.

So when did liberal modernity end in Britain? As we have already intimated, it is possible to see a convergence of decisive moments between the 1910s and the 1940s. These include the critique of liberalism as a political ideology by feminists, socialists, and colonial nationalists that led to the eclipse of the Liberal Party; the rise of the social as a key rationale of government in welfare regimes at home and development policies across the empire; and the collapse of economic liberalism with the displacement of free trade and the gold standard by protection, demand management, and the Sterling Area. Post-1945 social democracy in Britain remained marked by liberalism (not least in the ethos of the newly established welfare state), but it depended on a very different geopolitical framing in the context of the Cold War and decolonization. Likewise, when it took shape from the 1970s neoliberalism was a transnational process, and initially an Anglo-American one, as Mary Poovey's chapter concluding this volume indicates.[45] So imperial Britain's liberal modernity was preeminently a historical condition. It had its limits, its beginnings, and its end.

The chapters that follow investigate the conditions of liberal modernity in imperial Britain in broadly chronological fashion, from the late eighteenth century through to the early twenty-first century. In doing so, the question of definition—what was liberal modernity?—is inescapably linked to the questions of when and where it was to be found. The aim is for the chapters to ground the rather abstract nature of our discussion of liberal modernity so far in a series of concrete examples of its time, place, and nature. They frequently orient our attention to areas that have remained marginal to conventional discussions of liberalism and modernity, to labor and the environment, for instance, and locations such as Trinidad and the music hall.

Making the modern liberal was an inherently messy business, consisting of multiple historical processes that manifested themselves in geographically uneven ways and unraveled at different temporalities and according to distinctive logics. To be comprehensible and placed within a national framework, this messiness had to be condensed and given narrative form. Since the nineteenth century historical writing has been one of the most powerful ways in which the national experience of modernity has been understood and liberalism promulgated as a political ideology and a technology of rule. There is perhaps no greater ur-text of Britain's liberal modernity than Thomas Babington Macaulay's *History of England*, and we start with Catherine Hall's discussion of his famous third chapter. Published in 1848 as revolutions swept through the rest of Europe and the Chartist challenge in Britain largely evaporated, Macaulay's was a story celebrating how England—not Britain—had combined rapid economic and social transformation with the growth of civil society and the achievement of relative political stability. This was a decidedly English story; as Hall indicates, although he was no imperialist, Macaulay's project in his *History* was precisely to produce "civilized subjects," a condition itself premised on a stadial theory of race, nation, and empire that placed the white and male members of British civil society at its apex.

We then move backward and outward from Macaulay's island story as James Epstein explores the paradoxes and limits of liberal modernity as it emerged in imperial Britain in the late eighteenth and early nineteenth century. He does so by examining the operation of colonial rule in Trinidad, asking whether liberalism's promise of a free market for labor between the abolition of the slave trade in 1807 and the abolition of slavery in 1833 could be reconciled with the requirements of colonial production. Epstein reminds us of the experimental nature of colonial rule and the centrality of the emergent "liberal" state in propagating a range of failed emigration schemes for poor whites to perform free labor. Yet he also critically delineates the colonial fractures in the rule of freedom as Trinidad's plantations came to depend on unfree indentured Chinese labor. The next chapter, by John Seed, also tackles the question of labor under the conditions of the "free" market. It revisits Mayhew's description of the poverty of London's underemployed and Marx's searing analysis of the invisible forms of market regulation and discipline that they were subjected to in mid-Victorian London. Epstein's and Seed's chapters underline the place of discipline and coercion in the making of liberal markets and the positioning of diverse groups—from prostitutes and indentured Chinese laborers in Trinidad to London laborers—within a modern and imperial system of production.

Liberalism was fractured in other ways too. As Tom Crook argues, the conventional view that liberal modernity was characterized by increasing transparency of rule is historically flawed. Secrecy was integral and freshly embedded in Victorian England from the 1870s in practices as diverse as spying, masturbation, and voting. Thomas Osborne is more suspicious than many of the other contributors about using the term *liberal*, for he insists that it does not represent a substantive discourse or ideology that spreads virally through practices and institutions. Taking as his object the new forms of historical knowledge in Britain in the late nineteenth century, associated with the constitutional history of Stubbs and Maitland, Osborne suggests these can be best understood as a form of "liberal historicism," sharing an integral affinity with liberal modes of thought but in no sense expressive of liberalism as a political ideology. Tony Bennett likewise avoids any simple correlation between liberalism and historicism but still sees strong affinities grounded in the logics of nineteenth-century colonialism and evolutionism. Bennett's analysis of colonial policy related to Aboriginal groups in nineteenth-century Australia suggests a kind of inverse "manifest destiny" whereby an emphasis on will as capable of remolding habit, derived from J. S. Mill, was gradually replaced in later nineteenth-century anthropology by a view of habit as instinct, trapped in a cycle of repetition beyond the reach of either liberal subjecthood or history. Modernity here figures as a kind of foundational reference point around which judgments can be organized, hierarchies established, and histories written. What these chapters suggest, then, is that liberalism has acted as a "filament of thought," to use Osborne's phrase, which infused a variety of practices in modern imperial Britain that remained nonetheless not reducible to it.

The connection between liberalism and modernity (or its absence) is a theme that runs through the volume. Examining the world of late Victorian and Edwardian leisure, Peter Bailey suggests how the "liberal" and the "modern" can be seen to fit together. As an industry, entertainment was increasingly run on capitalist lines, bent on the production of "fun" in a manner that dispensed consumerized pleasure in carefully regulated doses and material spaces. It is this regime that Bailey, having his own fun and tongue only half in cheek, defines as "entertainmentality." Gavin Rand's chapter, which is equally attentive to the question of material form, echoes that of Epstein by questioning how far liberalism is helpful for understanding colonial rule. In British India, he suggests, it was the modernity of rule rather than its liberalism that is evident. The design and regulation of cities, such as Bombay and New Delhi, prompted interventions in the urban environment unimaginable in Britain itself.

The final four chapters in the volume roam across the nineteenth and twentieth centuries to identify the time, place, and nature of imperial Britain's liberal modernity. That Britain's liberal modernity has always been haunted by its past is the central theme of Jon Lawrence's chapter on the persistence of corporate and paternalist forms of government. The individualism of the "liberal subject" was held in check by the constraints of other, inherited forms of corporate belonging, whether to parish, trade union, or imperial nation. In this account it was not mass democracy, the end of empire, or even the "permissive moment" of the 1960s that dealt the death blow to this mode of governing so much as the populism of Thatcherism, with its assault on corporate Britain, from the BBC and professional groups to the trade unions. David Vincent likewise provides evidence of the longevity of a governmental culture of secrecy, upheld by the tradition of "honorable secrecy" among the political elite and persisting to the present despite the passing of the Freedom of Information Act in 2000. In the British case liberal democracy has been enacted in a modern political culture that was—and remains—deeply suspicious of popular sovereignty.

As the cases of Lawrence and Vincent suggest, this final group of chapters is concerned with those elements of liberal modernity assembled during the nineteenth century that continue to inform the history of the present. Chris Otter analyzes another shibboleth of nineteenth-century British liberalism, free trade, and discusses its transnational operations in relation to commodities such as coal and wheat. What is at issue here is the relationship between economic liberalism and the environment, understood in the context of commodity markets that were imperial and global in scope. Mary Poovey examines the career of a loose economic theory—the "efficient market hypothesis"—that sought to mathematically model Smith's understanding of the self-regulating market and underwrote the operations of global financial markets from the 1930s, only to be discredited in the 2008 financial crash. Her chapter encourages a consideration of markets as inseparable from the epistemologies by which they are understood and organized, and which are authorized and disseminated through specific institutional settings. It is a story that explores how the United States usurped the hegemony of imperial Britain in international financial markets following the abandonment of the gold standard in 1931 and reminds us of their continuing interplay through the deregulation of these markets in the Thatcher-Reagan era of the 1980s. In the chapters by Otter and Poovey, Britain's modern liberal economic development—that of the "first industrial society"—is seen as critical to, if not partly responsible for, our current global environmental and financial crises. Britain may have lost its empire, but the liberal modernity built on and around it continues to inform our contemporary understanding and experience of the world.

2. Macaulay: A Liberal Historian?

Catherine Hall

In December 1848 the first two volumes of Thomas Babington Macaulay's *History of England* were published to great acclaim. The enthusiasm for his history matched the excitement over Scott's *Waverley* decades earlier, and the books sold on the scale of Dickens's. The *History* was consumed by readers of every class, both men and women, and he received innumerable letters of thanks from all levels of society. Maria Edgeworth, by this time an elderly literary lady, called it "immortal" and was especially thrilled that she was mentioned and Scott was not. At another level of the social scale, an officer was committed to prison for a fortnight for knocking down a policeman; his French novels were taken away from him, but he was allowed to keep his Bible and Macaulay's *History*. And a gentleman in Lancashire "invited his poorer neighbours to attend every evening after their work was finished, and read the History aloud to them from beginning to end." At the end of the last meeting a member of the audience rose and moved a vote of thanks to Mr. Macaulay "for having written a history which working men can understand." The *History* was also a great success both on the continent and in the United States. Messr Harper of New York wrote to Macaulay, "No work of any kind has ever so completely taken our whole country by storm."[1] He was somewhat astonished, being well aware that his history had nothing cosmopolitan about it. Why did it have such appeal both at home and away—from the United States and Canada to Australia, New Zealand, and Japan? One answer was that the *History* told of the glories of a prosperous modern commercial nation, of the kind of society that some already enjoyed and that others could hope to emulate. Macaulay's *History* aimed to civilize its readers, to welcome them into the preeminent nation that was England as he told the story of "physical, of moral, and of intellectual improvement."[2]

Macaulay had a well-established position as a public man long before he finished the *History*.[3] Born in 1800, the first child of Selina Mills and Zachary Macaulay, who was already a leading opponent of the slave trade and associated with the Clapham Sect, he was destined for great things from his earliest years. A remarkably clever and bookish child, he astonished those who encountered him with his abilities. In 1803 the family moved to Clapham Common, and their modest house was a hub of discussion and debate during the dramatic years of the French wars. His adolescence was spent at a small private school and followed by his years at Trinity College Cambridge, a place that he deeply loved.

MACAULAY THE WHIG

By the time Tom left Cambridge the Toryism of his parents' circle had been displaced by a more questioning relation to politics. He was disturbed by Peterloo in 1819 and influenced particularly by the utilitarian thinking of his friend Charles Austin. By the mid-1820s his skills as an essayist were becoming apparent and his contributions to the *Edinburgh Review*, in particular his sparkling defense of Milton, made him an instant literary lion. Encouraged by Brougham, the leading advocate of a less hidebound Whiggism, he engaged in polemics with James Mill, challenging the democratic thrust of his arguments in the *Essay on Government*. He became associated with the Whigs—the party that had been out of power for decades but hoped for political change in the context of the struggles over Catholic Emancipation and reform.

In 1830 Macaulay entered the House of Commons for a pocket borough under the patronage of the Whig Lord Lansdowne and proceeded to make a reputation as a spectacular orator, defending the need for "reform in time" if revolution was to be prevented. He was widely recognized as having made a significant contribution to the success of the Whig cause: a limited franchise reform that secured aristocratic power while extending the vote to middle-class men. Adopted as one of the Whig candidates for Leeds in the aftermath of the Reform Act, he stood as a bright young Whig, one of the great hopes of the party, with a platform on reform, full civil and religious liberty, free trade, and the abolition of slavery. The election was fiercely contested, with Macaulay and his Whig counterpart, the local factory owner John Marshall, opposed by the Tory radical, Michael Sadler. Sadler made the struggle to limit factory hours central to the campaign. Macaulay admitted that a child's labor should be limited to fourteen or fifteen hours, but "if a man works over hours," he maintained, "it is because it is his own choice to do so. The law should not protect him, for he can protect himself."[4] He also refused to support household or universal suffrage, arguing, "If a householder has a vote, why not a servant? Why not a lodger? . . . [T]here is no such thing as a natural right in every householder to vote."[5]

His reward for his loyalty to the Whig cause was a seat on the government's Board of Control for India, quickly followed by his appointment as secretary to that board. A junior member of the Whig ministry of 1832, he played a major part in drafting the new Charter Act for India of 1833 and was then appointed to the new position of Law Member in the governor general's council. An opinionated, ambitious, and intellectually self-confident young man, he was never entirely comfortable with the vacillations of the Whig ministry. He longed, for example, for a more determined stance against the king's reluctance to appoint new peers in the face of the intransigence of the House of Lords on reform. Nor was he ever fully accepted in aristocratic Whig circles, for he was a parvenu, appreciated for his abilities but lacking the right kind of background and polish. He was not sorry to leave the Whig government behind him when he set out for Calcutta.

In India he followed the trials and tribulations of London politics with intense interest, finding them considerably more gripping than the daily diet of colonial administration. His distaste for what he saw as Anglo-Indian narrow-minded self-interest was matched only by his disdain for "the natives." A passionately metropolitan man, he longed for the end of exile. On his return to England, Macaulay had decided to devote himself to history writing, having secured a comfortable income from his Indian sojourn. History for him combined the pleasures of poetry and philosophy, of imagination and reason. It was the great classical historians, however, who combined statesmanship and history writing, who provided his model, and he retained his political ambitions, returning to government and the House of Commons in 1839. "I entered public life a Whig," he declared in his election speech, "and a Whig I am determined to remain." He used that word, he insisted, "in no narrow sense":

> I mean by a Whig, not one who subscribes implicitly to the contents of any book, though that book may have been written by Locke; not one who approves the conduct of any statesman, though that statesman may have been Fox; not one who adopts the opinions in fashion in any circle, though that circle may be composed of the finest and noblest spirits of the age. But it seems to me, that when I look back on our history, I can discern a great party which has, through many generations,

preserved its identity; a party often depressed, never extinguished; a party which, though often tainted with the faults of the age, has always been in advance of the age; a party which, though guilty of many errors and sometimes crimes, has the glory of having established our civil and religious liberty on a firm foundation; and of that party I am proud to be a member.[6]

Whiggism for him meant not being tied to doctrinaire positions. It was a style of politics that had evolved organically, its proudest claim in his view its leadership on issues of civil and religious liberty.

He was appointed secretary at war in Melbourne's government of 1839–41 but was not sorry to return to writing when the Tories came into power. He served again in the Whig government of 1846 as paymaster general. The Whigs of the 1830s and 1840s, as Peter Mandler and Ian Newbould have argued, had a distinctive style and political agenda, and they prevented the triumph of liberalism for two decades. They defended traditional aristocratic power with its paternalistic notions of rule *for* the people and followed a program of moderate reform of church and state to ensure the interests of property and prevent the spread of democracy. Confronted with poverty, disorder, and class antagonisms, they were preoccupied with national cohesion and concerned to demonstrate that the state identified with the nation. They did not believe that social and economic ills would regulate themselves: the state must intervene in certain areas and assume certain responsibilities. There were liberal aspects to their program, as in their support for the repeal of the Corn Laws, but Russell, a key figure in all Whig ministries, was never sympathetic to political economy. He aimed above all to ensure that the people were "cemented and bound up with the institutions and welfare of the country."[7]

Macaulay was part of this Whig political project. In 1846 his speech on the 10 Hour Bill, the speech he himself regarded as his best, marked his conversion to the need for the regulation of factory hours. As R. Q. Gray has argued, a regulated factory system came to be seen as a necessary part of the politics of social conciliation, complementing the repeal of the Corn Laws and ensuring that England did not go down a revolutionary path.[8] A secure nation depended not only on the inclusion of middle-class men into political citizenship, but also respectable working-class men into cultural if not full political belonging. This was a reconfigured national identity, one in which the moral and physical state of working people had a new significance. "Never will I believe," as Macaulay put it, "that what makes a population stronger, and healthier, and wiser, and better, can ultimately make it poorer. . . . If ever we are forced to yield the foremost place among commercial nations, we shall yield it, not to a race of degenerate dwarfs, but to some people pre-eminently vigorous in body and in mind."[9]

Progress was now linked to the "people pre-eminently vigorous in body and mind," not simply to the propertied. Macaulay was in the Whig cabinet in April 1848 when desperate plans were made to avert revolution. Those were dangerous days—but the danger was averted, and the Whigs were convinced that they were responsible for saving England from revolution, as on the continent, not only in 1832 but also in 1848.

MACAULAY THE HISTORIAN

Educated England now needed a new history of the nation. Macaulay's party belonging was unquestionably with the Whigs: he frequently thought in terms of who was "one of us." But what kind of historian was he? Many have argued that he was a Whig historian; others have suggested that his party alignment was abandoned in his history writing. In this chapter I raise questions as to whether this party alignment was loosened in his writing and replaced by a more liberal conception of his task, and whether this liberalism connects to the "imperial liberalism" constitutive of modernity that it is the project of this volume to illuminate.

Readings of Macaulay have augmented over time, marking the success of the *History* as a text associated with "the inescapable inheritance of Englishmen," part of the national story.[10] His *History* was not a celebration of the Whigs in the party political sense; indeed, he criticized Whig policies and people. For Leslie Stephen, "the Whiggism whose peculiarities Macaulay reflected so faithfully represents some of the most deeply-seated tendencies of the national character."[11] For John Clive, whose biography ends before the writing of the *History*, he was a loyal Whig—his task to contain democracy and counter Toryism.[12] For Joseph Hamburger, he was never really a Whig, rather a "classical trimmer," a pragmatist whose greatest concern was how to avoid civil war and achieve balance and stability.[13] For J. W. Burrow, he was a modern Whig, articulating an extended and inclusive form of Whiggism, requiring "only an acceptance of parliamentary government and a sense of the gravity of precedent."[14] For James Vernon, he aimed to revitalize a Whig politics with his argument that only a disinterested aristocratic government could prevent revolution.[15] For William Thomas, his *History* was above party, "politically speaking neutral," and it was vital to distinguish between the Whig party and the doctrine of progress associated with that tradition called "the whig interpretation of history."[16] That "whig interpretation" was defined by

Butterfield as "the tendency in many historians to write on the side of Protestants and Whigs, to praise revolutions provided they have been successful, to emphasise certain principles in the past and to produce a story which is the ratification if not the glorification of the present."[17] Most recently, for Robert E. Sullivan, the key to his history writing "was not abstract principle but the national interest."[18]

Macaulay was a Whig in party terms—not a Liberal as in the politics of the Liberal Party as it emerged in the 1850s. In the introduction to this volume Simon Gunn and James Vernon discuss three different approaches to liberalism: that of the political historians, that of the intellectual historians, and that of those influenced by Foucault. The political historians of the Liberal Party have not been concerned with Macaulay because his political career was over by the early 1850s. Intellectual historians such as J. W. Burrow and William Thomas have traced the distinctive elements of Scottish enlightenment, Whig, liberal, and utilitarian thinking in his writing.[19]

The existing historiography is central to any rereading of Macaulay. But it needs to engage with the debates over liberalism, race, and empire for his *History* provided some of the groundwork for the development of liberal and racial thought. Postcolonial and feminist perspectives have significantly shifted understandings of liberalism in pointing to the inadequacy of a conceptually singular definition whose framework is tied to a Western context.[20] Analysis of the place of colonialism in the liberal tradition has been very productive. Uday Singh Mehta's *Liberalism and Empire*, for example, argues that classical liberalism was built on a structural exclusion. The abstract universalism at the heart of liberal thought was erected on a Western intellectual tradition and set of experiences and rejected "the unfamiliar." It refused familiarity "with what was experientially familiar to others in the empire."[21] Macaulay, he suggests, can be read in this way. Jennifer Pitts, again a political theorist working primarily from a set of canonical texts, has shifted the grounds of Mehta's structural analysis, arguing for a contingent turn to exclusion among European intellectuals by the 1830s. The wide-scale skepticism about European expansion common in the eighteenth century was displaced by "an imperial liberalism [that] . . . provided some of the most insistent and well developed arguments in favour of the conquest of non-European peoples and territories."[22] Engaging with these arguments, Andrew Sartori suggests that the abstract universalism that is the focus of Mehta's analysis needs to be read alongside the "conservative contextualism," redolent of Burke, with its focus on the importance of historical specificity and a common national past, that is integral to much nineteenth-century liberalism.[23] For Macaulay, Burke was undoubtedly a key influence. From a South Asian perspective, Partha Chatterjee, building on the work of subaltern studies and drawing on Foucault, also explored the paradoxes of liberalism in the colonial context. His influential formulation of the "rule of colonial difference" resting on "the preservation of the alienness of the ruling group" offered a powerful interpretation of the creation of the colonial subject, a subject differentiated from the subject of the nation-state. [24]

Much of the discussion of liberalism and empire has focused on India, yet forms of liberalism were critical issues in the Caribbean and the colonies of white settlement too. Thomas W. Holt's study of the meanings of freedom across England and Jamaica in the early nineteenth century was one of the first texts to elaborate the different ways in which liberal freedom was articulated in metropole and colony, integrating intellectual, political, economic, and social approaches. Emancipation meant freedom from bondage for the enslaved. But emancipation was also intended to facilitate the development of waged labor, seen as a more productive system than that of slavery. Holt's analysis, drawing on Marxist traditions, demonstrates how any vision of full citizenship for black subjects was an impossibility in a society dominated by a white plantocracy determined to maintain its legal, political, and economic power. Struggles over the meanings of freedom were central to post-emancipation society, and the imperial government abandoned any belief in racial equality between the 1830s and the 1860s.[25] This was a shift that was to have profound consequences for imperial and racial thinking in the late nineteenth century, and Macaulay was typical of that post-abolition generation convinced that slavery was an evil but with little time for the African.

Patrick Joyce and Nikolas Rose, working with Foucauldian notions of liberalism, have focused on the technologies of governmentality. If freedom can be understood "as something that is ruled through, a way of exercising power, a technique of rule," then is it useful to think of forms of history writing as engaged in the practices of power, the making of free subjects? Can Macaulay be read as contributing to the ways in which liberalism becomes "deeply and widely diffused as a mentality of government" with the "active and inventive deployment of freedom as a way of governing or ruling people"?[26] Macaulay's *History* both created and educated the nation, gave each one of its readers a modern and civilized self to aspire to and identify with. His writing contributed to the making of a liberal subject, especially a white liberal subject. He constituted his readers as those cultivating a particular kind of self, a self that could value and practice freedom. His male readers were invited to identify with the values of education, industry, and independence, manly virtues, while his female readers could identify with familial, domesticated, polite forms of femininity. They were introduced to the history that had transformed them from rude and vulgar people, like those elsewhere in the world, whether in India, the Caribbean, or Europe in the dark ages, to the civilized subjects that they were or aspired to be.

Macaulay was no simple liberal imperialist. He was not actively interested in Britain's acquisition of new territories. One of the models of empire with which he worked derived from the American Revolution and was part of the Whig inheritance.[27] The demands of the American colonists in the 1770s, it was believed, had been badly dealt with by Lord North's government. A negotiated settlement should have been possible for the colonists were Englishmen. While Rockingham and Burke (one of Macaulay's heroes) had argued for recognition of the new nation and peace, Chatham could not bear "the dismemberment of the Empire" and pursued a war that was lost: the colonies became independent.[28] Colonies, Macaulay was convinced, were territories settled by white men and seen as offshoots of the mother country. They must be subject to imperial power. Yet when those colonies grew up, he argued, utilizing the familiar trope of the family, their independence might have to be recognized. During his years in politics, Australia, New Zealand, and Canada all claimed forms of responsible government. "During the feeble infancy of colonies," he believed,

> independence would be pernicious, or rather fatal, to them. Undoubtedly as they grow stronger and stronger, it will be wise in the home government to be more and more indulgent. No sensible parent deals with a son of twenty as with a son of ten. . . . Nevertheless, there cannot really be more than one supreme power in a society. If, therefore, a time comes at which the mother country finds it expedient altogether to abdicate her paramount authority over a colony, one of two courses ought to be taken. There ought to be complete incorporation, if such incorporation be possible. If not, there ought to be complete separation.[29]

In the case of Ireland, that troubled island divided as he saw it by both race and religion, only full incorporation was possible. Assimilation must be the solution to the "problem" of Ireland for Ireland was part of the "English" nation. The Irish must become English, just as in his view Scots had been successfully assimilated.[30] Ireland was complicated, for Irish Catholics were not easily assimilated, and in the hierarchies of whiteness constructed in nineteenth-century racial thinking, of which Macaulay's writing was a constitutive part, "aboriginal Irish" ranked low. Macaulay, like Mehta's liberals, sustained an abstract belief in civil and religious equality. Indeed, he was a strong supporter of Catholic Emancipation and stoutly defended the ending of discrimination against the Jews. In theory, all that was needed for "the infants" of nation and empire, whether the working classes or colonized subjects, to share in the fruits of citizenship was education and civilization. In his 1833 speech on the new Charter for India he famously looked forward to the day, undoubtedly long hence, when Indians might be "ruled by their own kings, but wearing our broadcloth, and working with our cutlery." "To trade with civilised men," he continued, "is infinitely more profitable than to govern savages."[31]

Until that day India's best hope was a form of benevolent despotism. India could not be free until it was civilized, and despotism was the only route to freedom. Imperial rule was justified on the grounds of the need for civilization, and only Europeans could civilize "the natives." The liberal principles associated with civilization—civil and religious equality, the rule of law, and the protection of property—were both universally valid and uniquely European.[32] England, meanwhile, was advanced enough to enjoy the benefits of representative government. Colonies of white settlement might look toward independence, but India was not a colony. Macaulay's vision in 1833 was more that of England as a great trading nation than England as a territorial empire. Yet his sojourn in India changed this. The empire was central to the nation's power, and any challenge to that authority must be crushed. White settlers were a tiny minority, and imperial power was maintained by the military. As he wrote in response to Gladstone's claim that India was ruled by "free stipulation," "It is by coercion, it is by the sword, and not by free stipulation with the governed, that England rules India."[33] India could not be an offshoot of England, an infant that would grow up as Australians and Canadians perhaps could. Its peoples were brown and black, locked in Hindu and Islamic superstitions, their ways of being equivalent to the dark ages. The adoption of English as the medium of instruction for an Indian elite, as recommended in Macaulay's Minute on Education, might be the first step in the civilizing process, but it also marked the distance it would be necessary to travel.[34] Macaulay's notions of the universal family were fractured by the racial hierarchies he constructed.[35] His was a liberal and reforming vision of nation and empire, mapped on to race, whether in terms of skin color or "absence" of culture—the two registers of racism. History belonged to the colonizers. As yet, India, Australia, Canada, and the Caribbean had no history: that day was to come.

MAKING SUBJECTS

Macaulay intended his *History* to be accessible to the nation. It should speak to common readers, those readers who had multiplied so exponentially in the early decades of the nineteenth century and who made successful authors rich men. He had learned from his experience with the *Edinburgh Review* that arguments should be presented as if they were plain common sense. The readers of this new, supremely successful, periodical were ordinary people—moderately educated middle-class men and women—and they needed a clear, simple style of writing. This was a liberal critical style, as Biancamaria Fontana has argued, that rejected "any ostentatious intellectualism" and adopted "the sensible, balanced viewpoint of the common reader."[36] The voice was that of the authoritative educated man writing on issues that a new generation of public men, risen through their own abilities, were engaged upon, issues of modern commercial society and the new problems that it posed. Edinburgh Reviewers believed in the traditional Whig values of liberty and the defense of the constitution, but they were never party men, and their major intellectual concerns were with the new times in which they lived. How to secure stability in a developing commercial society was a key question for them, just as it was for their most successful stepson, Macaulay. Their commitment to critical analysis, Macaulay's "noble science of politics," and to the importance of public opinion, epitomized by the success of their own periodical, resonated in Macaulay's concern with audience.

Their writing was eminently manly. Few women were allowed to grace the pages of the *ER*, and those who did wrote on "minor" matters, those deemed appropriate to female authors.[37] Macaulay, for his part, perfected an authoritative style and was celebrated by the critics for his manliness—the honesty, independence, and "good English values" that shone through his narrative. "A thoroughly manly writer," judged Leslie Stephen, is "straightforward, says what he thinks, [and is] combative but never base," with a spirit of justice and a strong moral compass, "proud of the healthy vigorous stock from which he springs."[38] "I open a school for men: I teach the causes of national prosperity and decay," Macaulay had written in response to one shocked father who felt that some of his detail was unsuitable reading matter for young girls. "I cannot admit that a book like mine is to be regarded as written for female boarding schools."[39] Yet the authoritative manly voice was not intended to detract from a female readership; rather it was part of the predominantly unconscious enterprise of demarcating male and female spheres. National histories were to be written by men who had the training and abilities to educate others in serious matters of politics. But female readers were essential. Macaulay was fully aware of the female market. As he had written to Macvey Napier, editor of the *Edinburgh Review,* in the early days of his work on the history, "The materials for an amusing narrative are immense. I shall not be satisfied unless I produce something which shall for a few days supersede the last fashionable novels on the tables of young ladies."[40] His "school for men" did not preclude women but rather situated male and female readers in different ways. Understanding "the causes of national prosperity and decay" might not be essential for women, but they too must know what was entailed in being a "civilized subject": one who was ready to engage fully in her proper place in the world. The *History* celebrated a range of masculine and feminine virtues associated with right living, critiqued the "wrong" kinds of men, those who were cruel, tyrannical, or lazy, and those women who were licentious, manipulative, or attempting to exercise "petticoat power." The high drama and romance of his tale made it eminently suited to reading aloud, whether in a family circle or the Mechanics Institute.

Macaulay was hailing, interpellating as Althusser has put it, new English subjects in his *History*—subjects of the nation, subjects of "the richest and the most highly civilized spot in the world."[41] While evincing very little interest in issues of labor and poverty, other than in terms of his fears of a disorderly mob, he was concerned to demonstrate that "progress" potentially brought with it improvements for all. A consistent enemy of democracy, he hoped that at some point in the future, all men might belong to the nation, rejoice as subjects in the enjoyment of their individual liberties and the security of their property. Those individual liberties included the freedom to worship, to speak, and to read, to participate in differentiated ways in the public world as citizens and subjects. Not all were fit to vote, yet all who were worthy, were "civilized," should benefit from England's prosperity. It was important to counter the pessimists who saw the advances of commerce and industry as destructive. Like the Edinburgh Reviewers he was convinced of the benefits of the new society and concerned to highlight the improvements that the expansion of trade and manufacture brought to all. "The labouring classes of this island," he acknowledged in his critique of Southey's conservatism in 1830, had grievances, produced both by themselves and by their rulers, yet they had enjoyed better conditions than their continental neighbors.[42] Huge improvements had taken place since the 1790s, despite war; population had increased and mortality diminished. Such changes heralded a better future.

By the time the first two volumes of the *History* were published, at the end of 1848, he hoped that this future had dawned. The collapse of the Chartist challenge in April that year had marked a watershed; while the continent had been riven with revolutionary struggles England had remained secure. "Remembered this day last year," he recorded in his journal on 10 April 1849, "the great turning point—the triumph of order over anarchy."[43] Part of the work of the *History* was to summon up the ordered nation, the modern nation, clearly demarcated from empire, in the process educating his readers to understand the benefits they enjoyed and welcoming them as fellow subjects. And as Hayden White has argued, nineteenth-century history writing, with its emphasis on continuity, wholeness, and closure, as against the chaos of a "natural" life, was supremely suited to the production of good citizens.[44] The majority of Macaulay's narrative was devoted to demonstrating the triumph of order politically. The year 1688 marked the establishment of a new balance of power between the crown and the parliament, with its limited monarchy, established rights of property, developing parties and ministerial government, the inauguration of some religious toleration, and an energetic free press.

Chapter 3, however, was markedly different. It was a disquisition on the transformation of English society between 1685 and the present—the culmination of the shift from barbarism to civilization. Here the history was charted through the emergence of a moralized social domain. Like the Scottish enlightenment theorists who so influenced him, Macaulay was convinced by notions of stadial development and saw the triumph of commercial society as bringing with it new forms of civilization. The stadial theories of his predecessors that involved four levels of development were in his writing, however, reduced to two: it was the binary of barbarism versus civilization that preoccupied him.[45] The *History* was predicated on the assumption that England was at the apex of this process, an assumption that perhaps Macaulay had to enunciate so clearly because of his own anxieties and uncertainties. Stability could never be assured, change happened in unexpected ways, and sons were not like their fathers. Macaulay never had a child, but his brainchild, his *History*, was his attempted bulwark against the enemies within and without who always threatened.

In chapter 3, rather than focus on the court, the camp, and the senate, which were seen as the proper interests of the national historian, he wrote of the social world of the seventeenth century, contrasting it with the 1840s. In his early writings on history he had celebrated the significance of the "noiseless revolutions," the social and economic shifts that underpinned political change, and his essays included much literary history. By the time he wrote his history of England, however, which he liked to compare to the great works of the ancient historians, especially Thucydides, he submitted to at least some of the limitations of the genre of national histories and devoted the majority of his many hundred pages to the doings of public men.[46] But chapter 3 addressed his readers directly, demarcating the extraordinary progress that England had enjoyed, "a change to which the history of the old world furnishes no parallel."[47] "Such a change in the state of the nation," he argued, "seems to be at least as well entitled to the notice of a historian as any change of the dynasty or of the ministry."[48] It demonstrated to his readers, and of course to himself, why they should marvel at the improvements that had been achieved in England in the present, celebrate the kindly and tolerant nation, and learn what kinds of men and women they should now aspire to be.

His evocation of the past was dramatic. In 1685 the north had been especially backward, and it had remained so well into the eighteenth century. Scottish marauders, bad weather, and poor soil had conspired to necessitate fortifications at night. Around the source of the Tyne "a race scarcely less savage than the Indians of California" were to be found. The women "half naked" and "chaunting a wild measure," the men "with brandished dirks" dancing "a war dance."[49] But England, unlike her neighbors, had been free from revolutions, insurrections, and "bloody and devastating wars": property had been protected, the law maintained, civil and religious freedom enjoyed.[50] This had made possible a transformation. Much of the country had once been "moor, forest and fen," and "many routes which now pass through an endless succession of orchards, hayfields and beanfields, then ran through nothing but health, swamp and warren." Wild animals roamed: foxes, red deer, and badgers shared the territory with wild cats, fen eagles, bustards, and "clouds of cranes."[51] "It seems highly probable," he maintained, that, thanks to enclosure, "a fourth part of England has been, in the course of little more than a century, turned from a wild into a garden." There was no trace here of the lost commons or the proletarianized laborers of his contemporary William Cobbett, a man whose writings he read voraciously despite the politics he execrated. A "hateful fellow," he commented in his journal, one whose style he greatly enjoyed but whose opinions left him disgusted.[52]

Changes in agriculture meant the transformation of rural society. The vulgar country squires of the seventeenth century had become country gentlemen, liberally educated in schools and universities, familiar with travel abroad, comfortable with London life and the delights of their country houses, their books and pictures. These were places that the urban middle class could now visit, observing patterns of living that they could emulate. "There is perhaps no class of dwellings so pleasing as the rural seats of the English gentry," Macaulay instructed his readers. "In the parks and pleasure grounds, nature, dressed yet not disguised by art, wears her most alluring form. In the buildings, good sense and good taste combine to produce a happy union of the comfortable and the graceful."[53]

How different this was from the past: prosperity had brought refinement. Once these country squires had mixed with the locals, their "chief pleasures derived from field sports and from an unrefined sensuality."[54] Their coarse talk in dialect, the enormous quantities of food and drink they consumed, their conduct at table, their ignorance of the great world beyond their land, and the childish notions they espoused all marked them as unpolished. The country squire of the seventeenth century, Macaulay opined, "hated Frenchman and Italians, Scotchmen and Irishmen, Papists and Presbyterians, Independents and Baptists, Quakers and Jews."[55]

In these days of religious toleration, by contrast, Englishmen could celebrate the civil liberties of dissenters, congratulate themselves on Catholic Emancipation, and even look forward to the ending of discrimination against the Jews. The old squires had dispensed rude patriarchal justice, possessed great family pride, were "accustomed to authority, to observance and to self-respect," but they were narrow-minded, usually Tories, critical of the city and commercial life, deeply associated with the established Church while neither knowing its doctrines nor maintaining its practices.

Meanwhile, their wives and daughters were in tastes and acquirements below a housekeeper or a stillroom maid of the present day. They stitched and spun, brewed gooseberry wine, cured marigolds, and made the crust for the venison pasty.[56] In those days the low level of women's education had been shameful. The "pure and graceful English which accomplished women now speak" was nowhere to be heard. In court circles licentiousness ruled, producing moral and intellectual degradation. "Extreme ignorance and frivolity were thought less unbecoming in a lady than the slightest tincture of pedantry." The qualities that made women into "companions, advisers and confidential friends" were nowhere valued.[57] This was a far cry from the politeness of contemporary commercial society, with the protected status of women marking the high level that civilization had reached.

If the country had been transformed so too had the towns and cities where wealth was created and accumulated. Once England had been barbarous—as India now was—but it had become a place of civilization. Manchester was now a "wonderful emporium," Liverpool a center of "gigantic trade," and Sheffield sent forth "its admirable knives, razors and lancets to the farthest ends of the world," but it was the rebuilding of London that exemplified the changes. In 1685 there had been no sign of the "immense line of warehouses and artificial lakes which now stretches from the Tower to Blackwall"; there was scarcely a stately building and none of the bridges "not inferior in magnificence and solidity to the noblest works of the Caesars." In place of this splendor appropriate to an imperial power, there had been "a single line of irregular arches, overhung by piles of mean and crazy houses, and garnished, after a fashion worthy of the naked barbarians of Dahomey, with scores of mouldering heads." Now city merchants recognized the charms of suburban domesticity and left their merchant houses in the evenings to retreat to their "long avenues of villas, embowered in lilacs and laburnams."

"We"—the imagined community of author and readers—would have been disgusted by the "squalid appearance" and poisoned by the "noisesome atmosphere" of even the fashionable parts of London in the past. In Covent Garden a "filthy and noisy market was held close to the dwellings of the great. Fruit women screamed, carters fought, cabbage stalks and rotten apples accumulated in heaps" at the doorways of the great. In Lincolns Inn Fields "the rabble congregated every evening" within yards of aristocratic establishments "to hear mountebanks harangue, to see bears dance, and to set dogs at oxen." Rubbish abounded; horses exercised; beggars importuned; crowds "hopped and crawled," persecuting any unfortunate grandee who appeared. Only in the mid-eighteenth century were railings and palisades set up and pleasant gardens laid out, marking clear boundaries between one class and another. St. James Square had been "the receptacle for all the offal and cinders, for all the dead dogs and dead cats of Westminster." It was very dangerous to walk in the city after dark: "The garret windows were opened, and pails were emptied, with little regard to those who were passing below. Falls, bruises, and broken bones were of constant occurrence."

Thieves, robbers, and dissolute young gentlemen swaggered by night about the town, "breaking windows, upsetting sedans, beating quiet men, and offering rude caresses to pretty women." With no machinery for keeping the peace, the "outcasts of society," "insolvents, knaves and libertines," ruled the roost alongside women "more abandoned than themselves." Cheats, false witnesses, forgers, highwaymen, "bullies with swords and cudgels and termagent hags with spits and broomsticks," all "relics of the barbarism of the darkest ages," terrorized the streets of London.[58]

All this was now changed. The city was safe, as 1848 had demonstrated. Parks were laid out, gardens had railings, the metropolitan police secured

order. In 1685 the gap between the country and the city had been unbridgeable. A Londoner "was a different being from a rustic Englishman," and
"a cockney , in a rural village, was stared at as much as if he had intruded
into a kraal of Hottentots." When "the lord of a Lincolnshire or Shropshire
manor appeared in Fleet Street," Macaulay recounted,

> he was as easily distinguished from the resident population as a Turk or
> a Lascar. His dress, his gait, his accent, the manner in which he stared
> at the shops, stumbled into the gutters, ran against the porters, and
> stood under the waterspouts, marked him out as an excellent subject
> for the operations of swindlers and banterers. Bullies jostled him. . . .
> Hackney coachmen splashed him from head to foot. Thieves explored
> with perfect serenity the huge pockets of his horseman's coat, while he
> stood entranced by the Lord Mayor's show. . . . Painted women . . .
> passed themselves on for countesses and maids of honour.[59]

If this rude bumpkin asked his way he was sent to the wrong place, if he
went into a shop he was "instantly discerned to be a fit purchaser of everything that nobody else would buy . . . secondhand embroidery, copper
rings, and watches that would not go." He would return to his country
mansion "enraged and mortified" by the "vexations and humiliations" he
had suffered. "There he once more felt himself a great man."[60]

The chief cause, Macaulay opined, preventing "the fusion of the different elements of society," had been the appalling state of the highways. The
"perils and disasters" encountered, from potholes to highwaymen, made
journeys comparable to those to the "frozen Ocean or to the desert of the
Sahara." Now all this was changed. "Reason" had "triumphed over" both
prejudice and cupidity: "our island is now crossed in every direction by
near thirty thousand miles of turnpike road."[61] "Those inventions which
abridge distance have done most for the civilisation of our species," wrote
Macaulay. They benefited mankind morally, materially, and intellectually,
removed "national and provincial antipathies," and made possible the binding together of "all the branches of the great human family."[62] The development of literacy and of the freedom of the press had also been crucial to
these civilizing processes. While once the only sources of knowledge in
the provinces had been newsletters, equivalent to those produced in India,
now the mail and the newspapers had together brought knowledge where
once ignorance had reigned. In the olden days meager information was
available on the state of the common people, a far cry from the Blue Books
of today. Historians "were too much occupied with courts and camps to
spare a line for the hut of the peasant or the garret of the mechanic."[63] And

a line or two was what these selfsame peasants and mechanics received in Macaulay's *History.*

The key to better days for Macaulay was not the material advances in themselves; rather, it was the new attitudes, the results of freedom. Capital and skill were not enough in themselves to effect "the long progress from barbarism to the highest degrees of opulence and civilisation."[64] People now thought differently; there was a more humane national character, less physical violence and cruelty, more awareness of responsibilities one to the other. Roads, railways, street lighting, markets, and the press had all effected changes in thought. Once society had looked "with profound indifference" on human misery. Now the state, "the legitimate protector of those who cannot protect themselves," had legislated on children's labor. In the course of ages the English had become "not only a wiser but a kinder people." In the past

> nowhere could be found that sensitive and restless compassion which has, in our time, extended a powerful protection to the factory child, to the Hindoo widow, to the negro slave, which pries into the stores and watercasks of every emigrant ship, which winces at every lash laid on the back of a drunken soldier, which will not suffer the thiefs in the hulks to be ill fed or overworked, and which has repeatedly endeavoured to save the life even of a murderer.[65]

Compassion must, he cautioned, be constrained by reason; otherwise it could produce some "ridiculous and some deplorable effects." Macaulay had no sympathy with what he saw as the excesses of the abolitionist movement and was in favor of capital punishment. But he rejoiced at the more merciful age, insisted that it was the "lower orders" that had benefited most from the "mollifying influence of civilisation on the national character." He warned against romanticizing the past and insisted that it was the discontents of the present that ensured continual improvements. In future times, he concluded, people might look back on the Victorian age as the time when "England was truly merry England, when all classes were bound together by brotherly sympathy, when the rich did not grind the faces of the poor, and when the poor did not envy the splendour of the rich."[66]

Macaulay's fantasy of the present was strongly willed and deliberately myopic. It was at odds with that of many of his contemporaries, from Dickens and Carlyle to Marx and Engels, and sits uncomfortably alongside the speeches and pamphlets of radicals, Chartists, and reformers of many ilks. He was engaged in ideological work: the work of making subjects. So is it helpful to think of this Whig politician as a liberal historian? Clearly his political life and his historical writing need to be considered together. Once he had fully committed himself to writing, a decision facilitated both by his great success and by health problems that impeded a more public life, he gradually withdrew from active political engagement. His writing was the most significant contribution he could make. Narrating a national story in popular form would, he believed, secure his legacy—as indeed it did. His conception of the nation and of English subjects was rooted in stadial theory, organized around the notion of a shift from barbarism to civilization. It was mapped temporally and spatially by constant reference to the rude nature of others—whether the English men and women of the past or the Indians, Turks, Lascars, Hottentots, negroes, and savages of many kinds—locked in dark ages and faraway lands, potentially capable, perhaps, of freedom. And there was always the enemy within to be contended with—the Chartists and socialists, the mob and the vermin that were not yet eradicated and threatened the stability so dear to him. Whig politics in the crisis of 1848 were not so different from the project of the *History*, structured as it was by fantasies of freedom, toleration, and prosperity for those who belonged to the nation. But his liberalism, and his "liberal subject," his belief in the enlightened rational individual, was strictly limited. His elaborate depiction of England's modernity, characterized by civil, religious, and economic freedom, was predicated on racial, ethnic, class, and gendered exclusions.

Perhaps William Williams, Macaulay's manservant, and his wife, Elizabeth, came close for him to representing his success in producing "civilized subjects." Together they served Macaulay, who liked to consider himself a good master, for many years, first in his chambers at the Albany, then at his imposing West London house, Holly Lodge. William was faithful, deferential, and voted Whig. For the most part he was suitably grateful, though deeply upset at being pensioned off in 1858. The couple settled in a house in Shepherds Bush, which they named Macaulay Villa. "Gave him the last edition of my history," Macaulay recorded when William visited him after his departure, "as he had asked me to do."[67]

3. Freedom Rules/Colonial Fractures

Bringing "Free" Labor to Trinidad
in the Age of Revolution

James Epstein

What does it tell us about nineteenth-century liberalism and the advent of modernity, if the mechanisms of liberal subjectivity cannot be projected outside the metropole or at least can only be realized in fractured or distorted terms? To what extent can liberalism prove indifferent to its own self-understanding; to what extent does the local truth of colonial power trouble the universal pretensions of freedom's rule? These are, of course, big questions and almost certainly not amenable to a single response. Scholars, especially those working on South Asia, have done much to elucidate liberal "strategies of exclusion" and the "rule of difference" through which colonial power sought ideological justification.[1] Yet the distinctions on which nineteenth-century liberalism's logic of exclusion rested and through which colonial dominance operated were occasionally troubled by their own inconsistencies and contradictions; they were never entirely secure, not least due to resistance from the subjects of colonial rule. The separation between "home" and "away" was not always easily maintained in liberal thinking or in liberal rationalities of rule.

Moreover, if we are concerned with the specific implications of liberal rule, a great deal turns on how we define *liberalism* and which thinkers we identify as situated within a liberal tradition. So Uday Metha and Jennifer Pitts can agree that Edmund Burke recognized the moral and political perils posed by British imperial expansion and credit him for speaking out forcefully against colonial injustice. However, despite the value that Burke placed on the prescriptive force of tradition, hierarchical social order, and the maintenance of established authority, Pitts argues for viewing Burke's imperial politics as "broadly liberal," based on its critique of arbitrary power and its commitment to "the moral equality of all human beings."[2] Time and place also come into play. Metha's core proposition, namely, that the abstract universalism of liberal theory contains an inherent propensity for exclusion and colonial dominance, tends to disregard historical change to which liberalism was itself subject. Thus eighteenth-century liberal suspicion of empire expressed in the works of Adam Smith, and others, was largely superseded in the nineteenth century by confidence in the project of liberal imperialism. By the mid-nineteenth century anxieties about democratization at "home" increased concern about how to draw the boundaries of political inclusion, which had significant consequences for liberal attitudes to empire and its subject peoples.[3] As for place, it would be mistaken to believe that universal principles of metropolitan liberalism were simply translated or imposed onto colonial sites. Intellectual history can take us only so far in understanding how imperial rule worked. As Kathleen Wilson observes, "In one sense, empire as a unit was a phantom of the metropole: all empire is local."[4] In his recent work on southern Africa, Richard Price shows how a culture of imperial rule and the formation of colonial knowledge emerged out of a process of encounter, exchange, and violence.[5] This is not to say that metropolitan ideas were not critically important but that they were mediated through a process of encounter. In what follows, I have tried to capture something of what Andrew Satori terms the embedded "conceptual structure of liberal thought in the socio-historical contexts of its articulation";[6] the chapter turns to a particular instance of "liberal" experimentation during the early period of British rule on the island of Trinidad.

In the late eighteenth and early nineteenth century, "free-born" English subjects declared themselves free from oppressive alien regimes, including that of slavery—thus those curious references to the Bey of Algiers to be found in plebeian radical rhetoric. As its counterpoint, British liberty was defined against slavery. Yet forms of customary service, forced enlistment in the armed forces, laws governing vagrancy, and the Masters and Servants Act all suggest the role coercion played within a broader Atlantic world for ensuring the performance of labor.[7] As the nineteenth century progressed, habits of industrial labor, including the internalization of time discipline, and the wage form itself became crucial to the cultivation of liberal self-governance among working people. Tellingly, recent studies by historians following Foucault's lead have paid scant regard to disciplinary regimes of labor in the formation of the modern liberal self, although labor discipline was a key mechanism through which Britons were daily ruled. Moreover, as Robert Steinfeld shows, the legal coercion of waged labor in the form of criminal sanctions (for contract breaches) "persisted well into the nineteenth century in the mature markets of the English metropolitan core for the simple reason that it served economic interests of employers."[8] The "modern myth of free labor" was, in fact, a product of nineteenth-century liberalism's project of self-understanding. From a broader global perspective, rather than postulate a binary relationship between free and unfree labor or see stages of management supplanting each other, we might consider strategies by which older norms and practices were changed, revitalized, reaccented, or discarded perhaps to be reinvented and thus remained lodged within reconfigured sets of capitalist social arrangements.

The abolition of slavery in 1833 became a hallmark of British national identity, a distinguishing act of liberal humanitarianism. For abolitionists, slavery represented a unique instance of "arbitrary and unlimited authority"; thus they drew a radical separation between slavery and other forms of coerced labor.[9] The four-year apprenticeship system reinstituted forced labor on West Indian plantations, but this was merely a stopgap measure. In one of those fine ironies of history, William Gladstone's father pioneered the transport of Asian indentured labor to work his sugar plantations in British Guiana. Doubting that black "apprentices" could be relied on, John Gladstone saw the need to find a source of labor that would make planters "independent of our negro population." In the late 1830s and early 1840s "Gladstone's coolies," as they became known, stirred anxious metropolitan debate about whether slavery was being reintroduced to the Caribbean.[10] As Madhavi Kale shows in her study of Indian indentured labor in the British Caribbean, for capitalists during the post-emancipation period, "free labor" simply meant mobile labor. The liberal narrative of progress from slave to free labor was disrupted by the reallocation of a hierarchical imperial regime of labor. Kale deconstructs the distinction between free and slave labor, arguing that "free labor" was "a plastic ideology based on emergent and historically contingent, gender-, class-, and race-inflected assumptions about the nature of freedom and labor alike."[11]

Rather than revisit the discourse of free labor in the age of liberal hegemony, I want to address an earlier period when the question of how colonialism in the Caribbean might be imagined without slaves was first posed. Initially the ability to identify a system of labor to replace that of slavery was central to advancing abolitionist credibility. Assessing practical alternatives to slave labor assumed greater urgency in 1807 with the abolition of the British slave trade.[12] This chapter explores the search for free labor on the eve of the slave trade's abolition, a signature moment in defining the rule of freedom; focusing on Trinidad, it relates a story about the unsettling of political rationalities of colonial governance and attempts (largely unsuccessful) to redefine the management of people and resources in the British West Indies.[13] While one might consider this a prehistory, or glimpse into the future of labor in the Caribbean, this is not my purpose here. In many respects later schemes to bring indentured Asian laborers to work on West Indian plantations and the constitution of the category "free labor" represent a discontinuity with the early nineteenth century. In an important sense it is the unevenness that needs to be stressed, the disjuncture in nineteenth-century liberal trajectories that commands attention. Certainly, the key terms of freedom and labor linked to speculation about what motivates or impels various groups of people to work for themselves or others recur, but their recurrence does not in itself necessarily suggest continuity but rather a reframing within an altered discursive and practical field, a "genealogical relationship."[14]

Different sites of empire present different possibilities at different historical moments. It is worth thinking about Trinidad in these terms, as a colony brought to a specific moment of possibility: a moment in which this locality offered an experimental theater with implications for British colonial development throughout the Caribbean and the world. As Lord Grenville told parliament, the government had always considered Trinidad as "a place for new plans of cultivation and colonial management." In 1797 Britain seized the island from Spain; it was ceded to Britain at the Peace of Amiens (1802). Trinidad's plantation economy and the large-scale importation of African slaves were very recent, connected primarily with newly arrived sugar planters who moved from neighboring French islands. Between 1784 and 1797 the slave population rose fourfold, from just under 2,500 to just over 10,000.[15] Previously a Spanish backwater, Trinidad overnight became an open frontier, attracting ambitious planters and a motley crew of casualties from other islands looking to revive their fortunes. It was precisely the colony's relative underdevelopment that made it crucial to colonial thinking.

Trinidad held a pivotal place in debates leading up to the abolition of the British slave trade in 1807; for abolitionists, who in the wake of the French and Haitian revolutions were in retreat, Trinidad—a large, fertile, and underdeveloped island—posed a critical test for preventing the spread of slavery. In 1802 George Canning calculated the scale of human misery were Trinidad's vast, fertile lands to be cleared and made ready for cultivation: one million new slaves, or nearly double that of the entire slave population of the British West Indies, would be poured "into the forests and morasses of Trinidad, to perish yearly, and yearly to be supplied by fresh importations." Canning appealed to the House of Commons to view

Trinidad "in a different light," offering a chance "for the establishment of a guiltless, bloodless colony." Instead of employing African slaves, he proposed an "experiment"; rather than make large grants or sales to "great capitalists," the government should look "among the class of men who will be induced to become residents in the island," requiring grants of land that would enable them to sustain themselves and their families "in a state of moderate independence." Such men might be found among soldiers serving in the West Indies, free persons of color and creoles from other islands, "peons" from the Spanish Main, native Indians, and others. In his response to Canning, Henry Addington, as chancellor of the Exchequer, announced that instead of selling crown lands in Trinidad the government had decided to appoint a three-person commission to survey the island and report its findings in order to formulate future policy.[16]

While the capacity to envisage a labor regime to replace slavery may have been a precondition for the abolition of slavery, finding an alternative was underwritten by more than humanitarian sentiment. British imperial expansion was driven by the need to finance and provision armies from local resources. However, as Christopher Bayly notes, the West Indies were exceptional in that the islands could never adequately provide for their own security. While whites were too few in number, the use of slaves and freed slaves could only be countenanced to a limited extent without subverting the region's whole economic system.[17] The Haitian revolution merely accented the problem of security. As the leading abolitionist James Stephen wrote in his *Crisis of the Sugar Colonies* (1802), with reference to the newly ceded island of Trinidad, "To found a new slave Colony . . . seems to me scarcely less irrational, than it would to build a town near the crater of Vesuvius."[18] Privately Canning solicited the support of William Windham, former secretary at war under Pitt. He rested his case against making Trinidad "a new sugar-growing, negro-driving colony," not on "the abolitionist, anti-negro-baiting, ground," but rather on the need "to lay the foundation of a new system of colonization for future military purposes."[19] The appointment of the Trinidad commission was linked to the British government's decision to arrest the colony's development as a slave colony. The commission was headed by Colonel William Fullarton, himself a product of the Scottish enlightenment and recognized as a reformer. The commission superseded the office of governor; the former governor, General Thomas Picton, was retained as second commissioner. In accordance with government policy, Lord Hobart, secretary for war and the colonies and the cabinet's only firm abolitionist, instructed the commissioners to investigate the best mode of developing Trinidad's resources.

He stressed "the advantages which might be expected to accrue from the introduction of an European yeomanry"; he noted the need to check speculation in land by keeping settlers "in the Class of Yeomen, Tradesmen, Artificers or Mechanics," and leaving "open to them such encouragement as may be requisite for giving a stimulus to their industry." He instructed the commissioners to consider, along with this new breed of yeoman farmer, the desirability of introducing implements to lighten field labor and strongly recommended "the superior advantages of the steam engine where it can be used."[20] Improvement and security were the bywords for future colonization.

As governor, Picton had set his sails against the changing winds of government policy. A staunch ally of the island's large-scale planters, he favored Trinidad's full development as a sugar colony. Indeed, his own speculations in land and slaves amounted to a small fortune. No doubt, his refusal to fall in line with new plans, along with his despotic rule of the island, contributed to his removal from the governorship. While there was general agreement that Europeans were unfit for field labor and the cultivation of sugar—less labor-intensive crops such as coffee, cocoa, and cotton were thought more suitable for white labor—Picton argued against all plans for "a colony of White settlers," citing the failure of such schemes on other islands. As Picton explained to Hobart, a European required three years of seasoning. With the best medical care, one-third of Europeans would perish in the first year, leaving their families as a burden on the community. A European attempting to support a family by his own agricultural labor "must lead a life of extraordinary fatigue and privation," driving him ultimately to rum and ruin. Moreover, given that "dislike of Labour" was what usually induced the European to leave his country, was it likely, he asked, "that he will become more inclined to it in a Country unfavourable to the production of enterprising Energies in a European?" Picton was no more encouraging about the prospects of other potential sources of labor. For example, Spanish peons were generally employed as jobbers used to fell woods and clear land for cultivation. However, they were deemed "incapable of any regular continued labour. Nothing but want can stimulate them to exertion and their activity never fails to disappear with the cause." Few native inhabitants of Trinidad had survived Spanish colonization; moreover, Picton reported that those who had survived, together with any Indians who might be induced to move from elsewhere, were utterly useless as workers. Picton condemned humanitarian improvers for misleading the country with their delusory and potentially costly schemes; slave labor was essential to sustaining production in the

West Indies. He roundly denounced "the representations of pretended phi-lanthropists" as to the condition of slaves, which was, "in point of comfort and care, at least equal to a great majority of the European peasantry."[21]

Suffice it to say, Picton's doubts did nothing to deter metropolitan visions for the colony's new future. The principal government scheme envisaged establishing a colony of five hundred Scottish Highland families on the island, elaborated in correspondence involving Father Alexander MacDonnell, chaplain to the First Glengary Fencibles, Charles Yorke, sec-retary at war, and Addington. This was a state-sponsored plan to redirect Catholic soldiers of disbanded Highland regiments from settlement in Canada to Trinidad and called for the government to provide transport, housing, tools, loans to hire labor to clear land, two chapels and two schools, salaries for a Catholic chaplain and an assistant who spoke both Gaelic and Spanish, and land granted forever to settlers in amounts based on military rank.[22] Trinidad was now proposed as an alternative to the Scottish Lowlands or Canada as a site of settlement and improvement for these warriors.

For over half a century, since the Jacobite rising of 1745, schemes to civilize the Scottish Highlands had abounded. The survey mapping of Scotland followed the suppression of the '45, a measure of military rule. In 1771 the Commissioners of the Forfeited Estates were charged to "Reclaim the Inhabitants of these Estates from their long habits of Sloth and inactiv-ity and reconcile them to the love of Labour, Industry, and Good Order."[23] The establishment of villages, construction of bridges and roads, encour-agement of new kinds of manufacture and employment, and attempts to improve agriculture had produced relatively small results, despite large state and private expenditure. The Highlands remained wild and remote, its inhabitants continued to live in what most commentators described as semifeudal dependence, poverty, and idleness. Thus the earl of Selkirk noted their lack of "habits of regular and steady industry," adding that the Highlander was accustomed to "independence and irregularity" approach-ing "to that of a savage."[24]

At the same time that the government was spinning plans to bring Highlanders to Trinidad, Lord Hobart received a report that had been solic-ited from Patrick Colquhoun; it detailed a lengthy proposal for transport-ing prostitutes from the metropolis to the colony. Colquhoun served as sti-pendiary magistrate at London's Worship Street police office; a prominent political economist, he wrote treatises on metropolitan crime, police, and indigence. As he explained in his *The State of Indigence and the Situation of the Casual Poor* (1799), "Labour is absolutely requisite to the existence of all Governments; and as it is from the Poor only that labour can be expected, so far from being an evil they become under proper regulations, an advantage to every Country, and highly deserve the fostering care of every Government." Thus "poverty" was not the "evil" to be targeted but "indigence," where the individual was unable to work or "knows not how to find employment when willing and able to work." As for those among the ranks of the unproductive vagrant or mendicant poor still found unwilling to work, "this part of the Community ought to be the peculiar objects of the National Police" charged with the responsibility of operating a new system of "houses of Industry."[25] However, as he was later to emphasize, "the great desideratum in political economy is to lead the poor, by gentle and practicable means, *into the way of helping themselves.*"[26] The resort to coercion only followed softer inducements to self-reform.[27]

The basic principles of moral persuasion and the "scientific" categorization and evaluation of social types figured prominently in the plan Colquhoun forwarded to the colonial office. Characteristically, he produced a list, enumerating the causes of prostitution in London and speculating on which categories of such women might be willing to abandon their shameful lives for a new start in Trinidad. The Magdalene hospital, lock hospitals, and workhouses of the metropolis offered potential recruits, women who otherwise had nowhere else to turn on their release but to the street. No women over thirty years old, or who had been on the town from an early age, or "who did not manifest certain marks of contrition," or who did not consider emigration an opportunity to better themselves and restore themselves to society should be recruited for Trinidad. For qualified recruits, the government would pay for passage, lend each woman £4 for apparel, and guarantee suitable employment until they either married or hired themselves into service. They would be "free settlers," free to choose their employment and their own partners. They were, however, to understand that they would face severe punishment for cohabiting outside of marriage or returning to prostitution. Any infraction or irregularity before leaving England would be punished by instant dismissal. "Acts of misbehaviour such as Intoxication or Instances of Lewdness" with seamen during the voyage "will subject the offender to the ignominy of being placed on the *degraded List*" and thus exclusion from the society of "well behaved women, and employed after arrival as servants to the well behaved, to perform such labor as shall be a meaner and more laborious kind." After arrival, free settlers found guilty of drunkenness, lewdness, or common prostitution forfeited all claims to protection and support and "shall be subject to imprisonment and hard Labour in the House of

Correction." Colquhoun thought there would be no problem meeting an annual target of four hundred to five hundred women for humanitarian resettlement.[28]

Colquhoun's suggestions reflected a broader metropolitan discourse within which older philanthropic perspectives were amalgamated with the more scientific views of political economists, aimed at promoting national moral regeneration and countering the rising tide of social and political disorder.[29] The disciplinary and moral logic associated with domestic reform was thus projected onto a site of colonial disorder in which the prostitute might be rehabilitated. Analogously, the Highlands represented a space for reclamation. The clearances instituted a forcible change in the system of ownership and usage of land whereby many landowners leased their estates to English sheep farmers, becoming capitalists as opposed to chiefs of armed clans. The pacification and clearance of the region were justified by a discourse of "improvement." Indeed, as Saree Makdisi writes, the clearances were also justified by a discourse of colonialism. The Highlands became "a site not only for the rehearsal of the multitudinous practices of 'improvement' . . . but a site for the rehearsal of Britain's larger colonial project: an imaginary zone in which the spatial processes of colonial penetration and development were practiced on a small scale."[30]

In the event, neither the scheme to settle Catholic Scottish Highlanders nor the scheme to reclaim metropolitan prostitutes in Trinidad came to anything. However, as exercises in experimental thinking, these sundry ideas shed light on how West Indian colonization free from slavery might be imagined. Such planning confirmed the British government's willingness to engage in ambitious projects of social engineering at the peripheries of empire, where social reconstruction involved marginalized groups, long-standing targets of domestic reform efforts. In effect, a set of social and geographic margins were to be reconfigured. Colonial solutions were offered for domestic social problems, just as Britain's social casualties were thought to supply the needs of colonial development.

The problems associated with these speculative ventures were also plainly in evidence. British fears of life in the Caribbean were long standing, exacerbated during the 1790s by the staggering death rate of European soldiers.[31] Critical to all thinking about labor schemes was the question of what beyond necessity would motivate settlers to engage in productive labor in the West Indies. Given the potential pool of recruits, how were habits inimical to industriousness to be overcome? Here, Colquhoun's reasoning revealed the difficulty of evaluating the springs of human motivation and the not too delicate balance to be struck between inducements to self-reform and coercion: the line between misfortune and criminality was thin. The "freedom" of retired Highland soldiers, many of whom had been compelled to join their regiments, was also at best severely limited.[32] Moreover, the very idea of reclaiming one's moral virtue in the West Indies would have struck contemporaries as richly ironic. The Caribbean was known as a site of moral loss, as a breeding ground for idleness, sexual license, and dissipation.

Hopes of establishing a white yeomanry in Trinidad went unrealized. However, among the various proposals submitted to Hobart in 1802 was an alternative for creating a bulwark against African slaves. Captain William Layman of the Royal Navy pressed the advantages to be gained from introducing an entirely different group of workers. After running through various categories of white settlers—including "industrious [Scottish] Protestants," former soldiers, and convicts looking to reduce their terms of transportation through good conduct—the author acknowledged that, in fact, improvement "could not be much advanced by the individual labour of Europeans or their unmixed descendants." Instead of relying on Europeans, he proposed turning to the Chinese, "whose disposition to migrate is known, whose Industry and Ingenuity are proverbial."[33] The formal proposals that laid the intellectual groundwork for establishing Chinese settlers as a "middle" group within Trinidad society reveal much about experiments in free labor, the construction of racial hierarchies, and the way in which a discourse of colonial development and governance was conceived across a series of linked imperial sites.[34] As with the other free labor schemes, the threat of slave insurrection, together with the abolition of the slave trade, formed the backdrop to this thinking.[35]

The full proposal that Layman put before the government set in motion plans that culminated with the arrival of Trinidad's first Chinese workers, coinciding with the abolition of the British slave trade.[36] He subsequently pulled together all the information that he had supplied to the government in the form of a pamphlet. The work's full title signals its ambitious scope: *Outline of a Plan for the Better Cultivation, Security, & Defence of the British West Indies: Being the Original Suggestion for Providing an Effective Substitute for the African Slave Trade, and Preventing the Dependence of those Colonies on America for Supplies* (1807). In effect, Layman outlined the transformation of the society and economy of the British Caribbean, not only substituting free labor for slavery, but also establishing a diversified system of cultivation based on "articles of eastern produce" (breadfruit, sago palm, melory tree, date tree, rice, etc.) in which Eastern husbandmen were skilled. Indeed, it was "scarcely possible, by any statement of political arithmetic," to estimate the total advantages to be gained from establishing "a skilful and industrious colony of agriculturalists and artisans of the east."[37]

Layman starts by inquiring whether it is in the interests of planters themselves to cultivate their estates "by the industrious hands of freemen." In the opinion of the "best writers upon political economy . . . no labour is so expensive as that performed by slaves." For, as Adam Smith explains, "a person who can acquire no property, can have no other interest but to eat as much, and labour as little, as possible. Whatever work he does beyond what is sufficient to purchase his maintenance, can be squeezed out of him by violence only." Layman acknowledges, however, that people with only the experience of the slave system could not be expected "to be able to form a comparative judgment between the advantage of employing freemen and slaves in the cultivation of the earth." Such men are "naturally prejudiced in favour of bondage, from habit and mistaken considerations of interest," and must therefore "be shown by *example* that the present system is *unprofitable*." Circumstances had temporarily allowed the colonies to flourish, serving "to hide the deformity, and cover the disadvantages, of this system," although current trends gave notice of impending decay and ruin.[38]

Given that false appearances and deep prejudices mask the true nature of the slave system, the benefits of free labor must be illustrated by example, as opposed to theory. Although sympathy for the condition of slaves appears at the edges of his text, Layman's formal reasoning is interest driven. His argument rests on the disinterested quality of his evidence, on the epistemological status of statistical reasoning—on the deep and complex logic of "the modern fact" as charted by Mary Poovey.[39] The disinterestedness and impartiality of the evidence guarantee the truth of the proposition that employing free workers rather than slaves favors the interests of planters. Furthermore, the pursuit of a policy motivated by self-interest most wonderfully produces a world where the interests of all concerned—planters, slaves, immigrant labor, and the imperial state—are harmonized. To this end, Layman compiles an elaborate set of calculations proving the unprofitability of slavery in the West Indies. Distilling the variables, the annual cost of a slave stands at £14—decrease in value equaling £5, interest on capital £4 16s, expenses of food, clothing, medical attendance, and contingencies coming to £4 4s. But this calculates only the cost of able-bodied workers in the field, not of all slaves on a given plantation or the expense of white overseers of forced labor, or the economic devastation caused by natural disasters.[40] In short, after detailing all cost variables and calculating the proceeds from the sale of sugar and rum, slavery is shown to make very poor economic sense.

Having established "the enormous and ruinous expenses" of the present system of cultivation, Layman proceeds to demonstrate the advantages of introducing "a system of cultivation by the hands of industrious freemen." Again, the force of example is paramount, as fictional calculations support the case. In the original documentation submitted to the government, Layman provided a table headed "Capital necessary to establish a Sugar Plantation and to cultivate the Island of Trinidad." On facing pages are detailed calculations "With Chinese" and "With Negroes" on corresponding 640-acre plantations. Extrapolating from these figures, Layman determines the cost of cultivating 1,360 square miles of cleared land with free Chinese workers as requiring "only £35,951,600—being £31,626,800 less than with Negroes."[41] In 1806 Joseph Barham, member of parliament and among the few West Indian planters sympathetic to gradual abolition, sought government assistance to move from fictional truths to practical exemplification. He proposed taking a Jamaican plantation in actual cultivation and substituting Chinese workers on long-term contracts for slaves. He maintained that "the results will immediately become apparent." Not only would "all motive, as well as all pretence," for continuing the slave trade immediately cease, but the Chinese would both "form a check on the Negroe [sic] population" and serve as "examples of domestic life & voluntary industry" by which "the moral & civil character of the Negroes cannot fail to be thereby improved."[42] The government eventually decided against sponsoring this experiment.

Crucial to all schemes, whether set in Trinidad or in Jamaica, was the estimate made of Chinese character, especially in contrast to that of Africans. Not only must settlers be inured to the tropical climate, but it was essential that they possessed the necessary "industrious habits" and "artificial" desires that Africans and native inhabitants so obviously lacked. Speaking in the Commons' debate on the abolition of the slave trade, Barham explained that a Negro could not be induced to work as a free laborer: "He has so few wants that nothing you can offer him in the way of money, will be regarded as an equivalent for his labour. . . . With him there is no privilege equal to that of being free from labour." Therefore, Barham believed, "the negroe should be made fond of free labour by degrees."[43] Layman concurred in this assessment, although he also understood freedom as a universal human desire; for this reason, the horrors of Saint Domingue threatened all the Caribbean. In 1802 Layman recommended to the government that "as the courage of the African is superior to his industry," West Indian regiments might usefully be sent to fight in South Asia.[44] Whether freed slaves could develop the sort of motivations, desires, and discipline essential for capitalist enterprise remained an open question.

In contrast to African workers, the Chinese were, Layman writes, "habitually industrious, sober, peaceful, and frugal, and eminently skilled in the culture and preparation of every article of tropical produce."[45] The Chinese were quintessentially a people driven by the prospect of gain. Layman drew on his own experience in the West and East Indies, as well as the writings of those who had traveled to East Asia. In their broadest terms assessments of the Chinese depended on forms of colonial knowledge about the Far East derived from Captain James Cook's voyages and Lord Macartney's failed mission in 1793 to open China to British trade in manufactured goods.[46] Robert Townsend Farquhar, lieutenant governor of Prince of Wales Island (Penang, Malaysia), also composed plans to introduce Asian free labor into the West Indies. According to Farquhar, "The leading opinion of a Chinaman consists in the belief that gain is positive good, loss positive evil, unembarrassed by those prejudices which influence the minds of weak and scrupulous people."[47] Unlike European settlers, the Chinese would work for wages on a contract basis and thus might directly substitute themselves for slaves. Moreover, as Layman maintained, the prospect of becoming small landowners after having fulfilled their labor contracts would provide an additional incentive "to industry, economy, and good conduct." In short, the Chinese were presented as the key to the improvement of the African creoles, the persuasion of the planter of the superiority of free labor over slave labor, and the gradual abolition of slavery.

> The Chinese husbandman, indeed, seems fitted by Providence to be the humble means of qualifying the hitherto ignorant and oppressed African for the enjoyment of rational liberty, by setting him a practical example of the blessings of to be derived from the application of free and honest industry, and by leading the West Indian planter, by the strongest human motives, *self interest*, to a full conviction of the policy of granting to his slave, at some future period, when thus fitted for the inestimable boon, that liberty for which God and nature designed him.[48]

Importantly, not only could the Chinese be motivated beyond the horizon of economic necessity, but under the right conditions they could be induced to embark on a long voyage to an unknown land of hard work and possibility. In late 1802 Sir George Thomas Staunton, who as a boy had accompanied his father on Macartney's embassy to China, wrote a long letter to the colonial office. Having recently returned from Canton where he served the East India Company, he reiterated the Chinese empire's strong dislike of foreigners and explained the difficulty of recruiting Chinese for emigration. However, while mainland China might remain closed to foreign intervention and direct recruitment, a large Chinese diaspora had spread through trade networks across the Malay and Indonesian archipelagos, including Batavia (Jakarta), Java, Malacca, and British-held Prince of Wales Island (Penang).[49] By late 1802 Hobart had initiated secret plans to bring Chinese husbandmen to Trinidad, plans requiring the cooperation of the East India Company and the governor general of India and mandating cautious handling so as not to incur the Chinese emperor's displeasure. The British government commissioned Kenneth MacQueen, an acknowledged expert on China with extensive recruiting experience in the Far East, for the task.[50] After considerable delay 143 Chinese were added at Prince of Wales Island, and another 53 were recruited at Calcutta from where they set sail for Trinidad. In October 1806, 192 Chinese arrived at Port of Spain to start their new lives.[51]

The scheme to introduce Chinese workers into Trinidad was driven from the metropolis. As with other such schemes for recruiting free labor to the West Indies, fantasy played a major role. In Trinidad officials scrambled to accommodate the new settlers. Soon after their arrival the governor issued a proclamation, explaining that the British government had found it desirable to introduce "a free race of cultivators, who from habit and feelings, will keep themselves distinct from the Negroes; and who, from interest, will be inseparably attached to the European proprietors."[52] Certain influential inhabitants welcomed the experiment. Archibald Gloster, Trinidad's attorney general and a large-scale planter, wrote to the London merchant Joseph Marryat, crediting Hobart for his "wisdom and forethought," as in his opinion "nothing will serve so much to secure these colonies, as a liberal introduction of these people." He noted that but for their dress "you would conclude them to be Mulattoes, or Mestees." Their intermediate position, between planters and slaves, but "attached" to European owners, was expressed in intersecting racial and social terms. Gloster maintained that substituting Chinese for "negro labour is out of the question" as the Chinese were unaccustomed to *the common business of a plantation* nor can we force them by the same methods." He saw the Chinese settlers aiding planters, attending their mills, working as "mechanics," gardening, and providing provisions for slaves.[53] The discourse promoting the introduction of East Asian labor into the West Indies emphasized the essential difference between independent Chinese and enslaved African workers. As Gloster understood, in the West Indies to do the work of slaves, planting and cutting cane, was to share a tainted equivalence with them. The notion of introducing a "free race of cultivators" who might substitute their labor for that of slaves was inherently contradictory given prevailing social and racial hierarchies and modes of production.

The scheme proved a disaster; many of the Chinese returned on the same vessel that had brought them. The failed Trinidad venture reinforced the growing disinclination of abolitionists to support experiments designed to test the economic superiority of free labor and coincided with leading abolitionists distancing themselves from the Sierra Leone project, just such an experiment.[54] Not surprisingly, Layman dismissed the idea that the dismal outcome at Trinidad invalidated his projections. He maintained that "the mistaken and ill-judged manner" of selecting settlers doomed the experiment from the start. Working through a Portuguese agent at Macao, MacQueen procured about two hundred "China men," "having nothing of Chinese about them but the name [and] . . . unaccustomed to the habits of their industrious countrymen." Moreover, having been gathered from different communities, they lacked the bonds of commonality necessary to successful emigration. Most fatally, MacQueen recruited no women.[55] Plenty of correspondence had, in fact, anticipated the problem of sexual relations and gender imbalance in light of the difficulties encountered in recruiting Chinese women.[56] Once the men arrived, Trinidad's governor, General Thomas Hislop, noted in a letter to the governor general of Bengal the necessity "for some time to come" of bringing women from India, "such as they [Chinese men] are accustomed to form connections with; as there is no class of females here who (in their present low condition) will intermarry with them, and consequently they find only among the Slaves opportunities of illicit amours."[57] Hierarchical social constructions based on work, gender, sexuality, and race militated against impoverished Asians dependent on nothing but their capacity to labor finding a comfortable "middle" ground in the West Indies.

Needless to say, Layman brings his expertise to bear on the subject of securing female companions for Chinese (male) workers. "Every man," he opines, "who has had much intercourse with China, or Cochin China, is aware of the ease with which, at least, the temporary services of females are purchased." Moreover, in China "females are invariably considered the property of parents, and are never parted with, even upon their marriage, but for pecuniary consideration." The reason that the existing system of emigration exclusively involves male workers is because the labor of women in agriculture is not required in Batavia or other islands and there is no lack of women for domestic service, junk owners and employers have no inducement to recruit women. All that is required to obtain Chinese women for emigration to the West Indies is "making it the interest of junk-owners to procure women."[58] In other words, a deal could be struck with the parents of young Chinese women for ready cash. As Barham explained in response to concerns raised by the Lord Commissioners in Trade, "The class of female we should then endeavor to procure, abounds all over the Indian Archipelago, & are sold by their parents & others to any purchaser." Since these women are not bought "for the purposes of Slavery, and are to be subject to no restriction but what Government may approve as beneficial to themselves, & equitable to the purchaser, this can in no degree be said to partake of the Nature of the Slave Trade." Barham reasoned, it is "rather the reverse, as it frees people from the condition of Slavery . . . placing them only in a state of modified restriction common even now to half the peasantry of Europe, & even in this state only for a time."[59]

The instability of the concept of freedom again emerges, here breaking along the lines of gender. How exactly did plans to barter for Chinese women to be brought to the West Indies independent of their own will, to serve as wives, paramours, or prostitutes, differ from slavery? The "freedom" of Chinese male immigrants was dependent on a denial of freedom to Chinese women, as necessary to producing a system of free labor and bringing an end to slavery. Barham's comparison of these women's condition to the "modified restriction" commonly placed on European peasantry echoes Picton's defense of slavery, equating the comfort and care of slaves to that of "a great majority of the European peasantry." Yet just as liberalism's universalizing ambition fell subject to the brutal realities of colonialism, we can recognize the utopian impulse driving the early-nineteenth-century search for free labor; a break in history seemed to open the possibility for a future quite different from the past. The complex rationalities of liberal governmentality, however, left unresolved the inherent contradictions of colonial rule in the West Indies.

In conclusion, we can venture several general observations. First, the degree of difference between liberal strategies of domestic and colonial governance was subject to considerable variability. We cannot separate metropolitan poverty debates about how to motivate the laboring poor to adopt habits of industry and independence from the labor question as presented in the Caribbean. Indeed, in important respects, the issue was not geographic but moral and ethical—what were the necessary conditions for producing the liberal subject whether in Trinidad or in London. On the other hand, Chinese immigrants, due to some mixture of cultural, ethnic, or racial attributes, appeared preternaturally industrious, beyond the need to discipline or punish; the mere inducement of material gain was enough to stimulate them to productive labor, thus resolving the very problem that liberal theorists and those in power posed for themselves. The Chinese possessed precisely those propensities to labor and desires for "artificial" wants that African slaves lacked. The element of sheer make-believe connected to such thinking should not be underestimated, nor the seriousness with which the colonial office treated the elaborate schemes of Layman, Barham, and Colquhoun. As Richard Price writes, "Empire was and is a utopian project. It rests on a series of assumptions that involve enormous leaps of faith, hope and sheer invention."[60] For this very reason, the imperial project proved itself not only exploitative and brutal but also often fragile and subject to failure; the distant realities at the colonial frontier frustrated the schemes and desires of metropolitan liberal imagination.

4. "Free Labour = Latent Pauperism"

Marx, Mayhew, and the "Reserve Army of Labour" in Mid-Nineteenth-Century London

John Seed

Modernity, liberal or otherwise, was not a term in Marx's vocabulary. The *Communist Manifesto*'s rhapsody about the revolutionary role of the bourgeoisie is often taken as an eloquent statement of the dynamic of modernity—innovation, constant change, radical uncertainty, the shock of the new.

> Constant revolutionising of production, uninterrupted disturbance of all social conditions, everlasting uncertainty and agitation distinguish the bourgeois epoch from all earlier ones. All fixed, fast-frozen relations, with their train of ancient and venerable prejudices and opinions, are swept away, all new-formed ones become antiquated before they can ossify. All that is solid melts into air, all that is holy is profaned, and man is at last compelled to face with sober senses his real conditions of life, and his relations with his kind.[1]

In one of the most influential readings of Marx as a voice of modernity, Marshall Berman describes this passage as "probably the definitive vision of the modern environment." Modernity as a rhetorical figure always seems to possess a powerful charge of energy, and Berman points to the "intense and extravagant images"—earthquakes, erupting volcanoes, abysses, and so on—that characterize Marx's writing, not just about the revolutionary moment of 1848, but also about the apparently solid and very unrevolutionary England of the 1850s.[2] What I am interested in here is not the Sturm und Drang dimensions of Marx's political rhetoric but the very different questions signaled in the final clause of this *Manifesto* passage: "compelled to face with sober senses his real conditions of life, and his relations with his kind." From one perspective modernity meant liberation from traditional restrictions, it meant new freedoms, the excitements and pleasures of new forms of art and of new and unconventional ways of living. The experience of several generations of working people in nineteenth-century Britain was less a matter of the exhilaration of modernity, however, and more about the complex forms of coercion concealed in the operations of "modernity"—the destruction of traditional patterns of work and community, deteriorating working and living conditions, economic insecurity, and forced migration. This is not, I want to stress, a matter of "exclusion," of the illiberal exterior of "liberal modernity," of its limits. On the contrary, these coercive effects radiate out from its very core. "Free labour = latent pauperism," in one succinct formulation in the *Grundrisse*. In the following pages I want to pursue this argument through a reading of Marx and in particular of his concept of "the reserve army of labour."[3]

In one of his articles for the *New York Tribune* in 1853 Marx reflected on the contrast between the very conspicuous forms of political reaction sweeping the continent in the aftermath of the revolutions of 1848 and the less obvious kinds of oppression experienced in England:

> On the Continent, hanging, shooting and transportation is the order of the day. But the executioners are themselves tangible and hangable beings, and their deeds are recorded in the conscience of the whole civilised world. At the same time there acts in England an invisible, intangible and silent despot, condemning individuals, in extreme cases, to the most cruel of deaths, and driving in its noiseless, every day working, whole races and whole classes of men from the soil of their forefathers, like the angel with the fiery sword who drove Adam from Paradise.[4]

The repression of despotic states with their very visible apparatuses of soldiers and public executions is easy to describe. Actions of executioners can be recorded and remembered. Countermeasures are possible too; they are not just tangible but also "hangable beings." By contrast, unemployment, hunger, forced migration have no very visible human agents. What kinds of rhetoric can represent, what kinds of history can remember, and what kinds of actions, political or otherwise, can oppose this "invisible, intangible and silent despot" that rules England (Britain)?

In the paragraph that follows Marx suddenly shifts focus to a particular case of starvation in London a few weeks earlier. Mary Ann Sandry, an Irish woman age forty-three, had been found dead.

> The deceased was lying on a small heap of straw without the slightest covering. The room was completely destitute of furniture, firing and food. Five young children were sitting on the bare flooring, crying from hunger and cold by the side of the mother's dead body.[5]

Marx makes no further comment. Here there are no executioners or soldiers or soldiers or despots, no drama of revolution and counterrevolution—just a woman dead of starvation in a cold back room. Marx gives no source for this story, but he probably read it in the pages of the *Morning Chronicle*, which documented how Mary Ann Sandry had arrived in London from Ireland with her husband and five children a few months before.[6] They had rented a single room in Shadwell, a slum area in the docks and one of the poorest districts of the metropolis. With their last five shillings the husband had bought some braces and was hawking them around the streets and pubs. But they struggled to survive on the pittance this earned, and the woman's health deteriorated. At her inquest another lodger in the house reported hearing her coughing all night and was alerted to her condition by the children. She died soon after, without any medical assistance, on a bed of straw without a blanket, in a room without furniture, fire, or food in the middle of a London winter. The husband told the coroner that they had not applied for relief because they feared being sent back to Ireland. There was some hand-wringing by the coroner's jury and the parish officers. The verdict was "natural death, accelerated by extreme want and destitution."

Marx's version of this story has its impact precisely because of its understatement and its lack of commentary. And, not least because of the association with the *Morning Chronicle*, it immediately calls to mind that great contemporary chronicler of the lives of the London poor, Henry Mayhew. It is astonishing that Marx never used the writings of Mayhew— whether the *Morning Chronicle* letters of 1849 and 1850, *London Labour and the London Poor*, published as a weekly during 1851 and then as a two-volume work, or the expanded four-volume version published in 1861 and 1862. Marx was hungry for information on labor conditions and devoured Blue Books and all kinds of official reports by factory inspectors, sanitary authorities, poor law commissioners, and so on, as well as other contemporary sources. So too did Mayhew, who called his own work "the first commission of enquiry into the state of the people undertaken by a private individual, and the first 'blue book' ever published in twopenny numbers."[7] In *Capital*, Marx utilized the *Morning Chronicle*'s reports on the condition of the agricultural laborers published in 1844 and 1845.[8] Why did he ignore the much more valuable materials produced by the *Chronicle*'s metropolitan commissioner in 1849 and 1850?

He could hardly have missed them. Mayhew's writing on the London working class appeared not just in the *Morning Chronicle* during 1850 but in the Chartist press as well. The *Northern Star*, the *Democratic Review*, and its successor, the *Red Republican,* each published substantial extracts by Mayhew during 1850 and 1851 and reported regularly on his activities. Marx and Engels not only read but also contributed to these papers.[9] Reflecting in 1859 on his move to London a decade earlier, Marx noted that it provided "a convenient vantage point for the observation of bourgeois society." His specific London vantage point from 1850 to 1856 was the crowded streets of Soho where he lived, often on a diet of bread and potatoes, cheek by jowl with the kinds of struggling artisans and street traders whose lives Mayhew was chronicling in such remarkable detail— and in publications that Marx regularly read and even contributed to on occasion. And yet never at any point did he refer to this well-known and unrivaled contemporary source of evidence on working-class wages and working conditions in the city in which he lived.

Perhaps the beginnings of an explanation can be found in Marx's editorial comments on an article on London tailoring by Georg Eccarius, published in the *Neue Rheinische Zeitung* in 1850.[10] Eccarius was a working tailor and a German Communist who had moved to London in 1846. Marx was enthusiastic about his unsentimental recognition that the day of the well-paid and skilled tailor in the small workshop was over. This was precisely one of the areas of London industry that Mayhew was investigating at this time, and he may have been silently subsumed alongside Weitling in Marx's comment: "The reader will note how here, instead of the sentimental, moral and psychological criticism employed against existing conditions by Weitling and other workers who engage in authorship, a purely materialist understanding and a freer one, unspoilt by sentimental whims, confronts bourgeois society and its movement."[11]

Marx was dismissive of what the *Communist Manifesto* called a "conservative or bourgeois socialism," which was "desirous of redressing social grievances, in order to secure the continued existence of bourgeois society." It was the predilection of "economists, philanthropists, improvers of the condition of the working class, organisers of charity, members of societies for the prevention of cruelty to animals, temperance fanatics, hole-and-corner reformers of every kind."[12] Mayhew could have fallen into most of these categories, with the decided exception of "temperance fanatic."

Marx was equally unimpressed by the political potential of the lowest strata of the urban population. They were, in the words of the *Communist Manifesto,* "the social scum, that passively rotting mass thrown off by the lowest layers of the old society." In the *Eighteenth Brumaire of Louis Bonaparte* (1852) Marx specifies in more detail, but with equal disdain, some of the constituents of the "lumpenproletariat" of Paris. They sound much like those who crowded the pages of Mayhew's *London Labour and the London Poor:*

> vagabonds, discharged soldiers, discharged jailbirds, escaped galley
> slaves, swindlers, mountebanks, lazzaroni, pickpockets, tricksters,
> gamblers, maquereaux, brothel keepers, porters, literati, organ
> grinders, ragpickers, knife grinders, tinkers, beggars—in short,
> the whole indefinite, disintegrated mass, thrown hither and thither,
> which the French call *la bohème.*[13]

Marx's account of the Parisian lumpenproletariat has been read in ways that converge to certain kinds of poststructuralist reconceptualizations of identity as performative, fluid, contingent, cosmopolitan, and, above all, discursive—and in pointed contrast to the kinds of abstract, unitary, essentialist, and reductionist notions of the working class that are sometimes found elsewhere in Marx.[14] This, in turn, converges to a much wider critique of Marx's failure to engage with the empirical realities of the working class—and more broadly of the political and the cultural—after the post-1848 defeats, drifting into the abstractions of political economy and/or Hegelian philosophy. This is, for instance, the main theme of E. P. Thompson's comments in *The Poverty of Theory*, according to which, in the course of his extended study of political economy, Marx was "turned" and became locked inside its conceptual horizons. For Thompson, any understanding of history and society must engage with relations and practices, to do with power and culture and sexuality and so on—in a word, with "experience"—for which political economy, and Marx, has no language.[15]

As Nicholas Thoburn has usefully argued, "lumpenproletariat" and "proletariat," elaborated in Marx's work of the late 1840s, are not straightforward empirically defined social groups or class subjects. Rather these categories are used to describe particular modes of political composition.[16] Marx was not interested in constructing an urban sociology. Instead he was concerned, for his own strategic purposes, to differentiate the proletariat as a disciplined and organized representative of the new social relations of industrialization from "the dangerous classes," the miserable and rootless poor of Europe's great cities, with their propensity for crime, violence, and riot. At the same time that Marx was marking out his political distance from the "dangerous classes," he was beginning to think in a different way about the formation of the working class and about the significance of its poorest strata. In 1845, in *The Condition of the Working Class in England*, Engels had already noted the existence, and the value to employers, of what he termed "an unemployed reserve army of workers."

His description of their social character corresponds closely to the social world described by Mayhew a few years later.

> This reserve army . . . is the 'surplus population' of England, which keeps body and soul together by begging, stealing, street-sweeping, collecting manure, pushing hand-carts, driving donkeys, peddling, or performing occasional small jobs. In every great town a multitude of such people may be found. It is astonishing in what devices this 'surplus population' takes refuge.[17]

Engels is evidently unhappy about the term *surplus population*.[18]

The Malthusian explanation of poverty, influential in shaping social policy in Britain at this time, was also a target of Marx's criticism. In lectures in Brussels in 1847 he argued that what was called overpopulation was not the result of the natural growth of population outstripping the means of subsistence. Bourgeois thinkers turned economic and social processes into laws of nature. On the contrary, declining wages, poverty, and vagrancy were the outcomes of complex forces driving the accumulation of capital and revolutionizing the means of production. Marx pointed to the key role of what he termed "a reserve army of unemployed workers" in fixing wage levels: "The wages of 1,000 workers of the same skill are determined not by the 950 in employment but by the 50 unemployed."[19] This argument was developed in *Wage Labour and Capital*, published in 1849. Capitalists, Marx says, "vie with one another as to who can discharge the greatest number of industrial soldiers."[20] Those who remained in employment were working harder and longer in a desperate attempt to resist falling wage rates. So, in an increasingly competitive labor market, wages fall and more and more workers find themselves out of work. At the same time, expansion on an ever-increasing scale leads to increases in "the industrial earthquakes" that, Marx says, "become more frequent and more violent." These crises in turn exacerbate falling wages, unemployment, and the economic insecurity of workers.[21]

Far from being a mere "indefinite, disintegrated mass," a parasitic counter-elite at the margins of the social order, as described in the *Communist Manifesto* and the *Eighteenth Brumaire*, the "reserve army" now began to occupy an altogether more significant place in Marx's analysis. It was nothing less than "a lever of capitalistic accumulation, nay, a condition of existence of the capitalist mode of production." In *Capital* the reserve army of labor is divided into three rough strata: the floating, the latent, and the stagnant. The first group, "the floating," fluctuates in numbers and membership. It consists of those who are temporarily unemployed during periods of economic crisis and who find work when trade revives. The second group, "the latent," consists of those not yet fully integrated into capitalist production—for example, parts of the rural population or women performing unpaid household labor. "The latent" thus form a reservoir of potential labor that drains into the floating stratum of the reserve army. The third group, "the stagnant," is more miscellaneous. It includes workers in "domestic industry," characterized, Marx says, by "extremely irregular employment": "Its conditions of life sink below the average normal level of the working-class; this makes it at once the broad basis of special branches of capitalist exploitation. It is characterised by maximum of working-time, and minimum of wages."[22] Then, finally, there is the "lowest sediment" of the working class, which is not really part of the reserve army at all. Here, quickly dismissed in passing as "vagabonds, criminals, prostitutes," there is the only mention of the "lumpenproletariat" in *Capital*. Marx pays more attention to those who inhabit "the sphere of pauperism":

> the demoralised and ragged, and those unable to work, chiefly people
> who succumb to their incapacity for adaptation, due to the division
> of labour; people who have passed the normal age of the labourer;
> the victims of industry, whose number increases with the increase of
> dangerous machinery, of mines, chemical works, &c., the mutilated,
> the sickly, the widows, &c. Pauperism is the hospital of the active
> labour-army and the dead weight of the industrial reserve army.[23]

For Marx, the reserve army is crucial to the reproduction of capitalism. "The industrial reserve army, during the periods of stagnation and average prosperity, weighs down the active labour-army; during the periods of over-production and paroxysm, it holds its pretensions in check."[24] Whatever the economic situation, then, the expansion and contraction of the reserve army restrains wages and disciplines labor. And, following from this, it enables the working day and the intensity of labor to be extended beyond human limits: "Capital asks no questions about the length of life of labour-power."[25] The reserve army provides a source of potential workers to replace those prematurely destroyed by inhuman working conditions.

There is a moment in *Capital*, in his account of the stagnant stratum (or strata) of the reserve army, when Marx seems close to underwriting the Malthusian notion of surplus population. These are by definition pretty much locked out of the labor market. And he notes their tendency toward larger families, so that this pool of surplus labor is "a self-reproducing and self-perpetuating element of the working-class."[26] But this is just one element of the "lowest sediment" of the reserve army. The crucial point about the reserve army of labor in Marx's account is that it is not some kind of stable "residuum" or "underclass" made up of particular types of people. Rather it is a volatile and continuously reproduced presence within the labor market.

Modern forms of production were constantly transforming not only the technical basis of production but also the division of labor, moving capital rapidly from one branch of production to another and requiring the mobility of labor not just between different kinds of work but also across geographic space. This, Marx says, "does away with all repose, all fixity and all security as far as the worker's life situation is concerned" and "constantly threatens . . . to snatch from his hands the means of subsistence."[27] In another section of the first volume of *Capital*, "The Nomad Population," Marx again underlines the contingency and insecurity of social experience for working people. These "nomads" are workers, generally drawn from the rural population, who are employed in short-term projects—as navvies on the railways, for instance, or as construction workers or brick makers. "They are the light infantry of capital, thrown by it, according to its needs, now to this point, now to that. When they are not on the march, they 'camp.'"[28]

Constant restructuring of production means a constant transformation of parts of the laboring population into casual labor or the unemployed. So the different positions within the reserve army are *temporarily* occupied by working people. An individual may pass through the floating, the latent, and the stagnant strata of the reserve army at different stages of life. She may, for instance, work around the home in her youth (latent), move into paid employment, experience spells of unemployment (floating), before ending her life as a sick pauper (stagnant). Here is a case, drawn from Mayhew's *London Labour and the London Poor*.[29] A "kindly-looking and hearty old man" of around sixty was one of eleven children of a prosperous farmer who sold up, lived on his capital, and left nothing to his surviving family.

> When father died, I thought as I should like to see London. I was a mere lad—about 20—and so I strolled up to town. I had 10s. with me, and that, with a bundle, was all that I possessed in the world.

Lodging in a public house, he could find no work, and after his 10 shillings were spent he found himself walking the streets. Eventually he began selling needles and then cutlery in the streets. He had made a good living at this for forty years, generally earning around one pound a week.

> I used to go round the country—to Margate, Brighton, Portsmouth— I mostly travelled by the coast, calling at all the sea-port towns, for I

> always did best among the sailors. I went away every Spring time, and
> came to London again at the fall of the year.

In the previous four years times had been hard. Slowly he and his wife had
spent their savings, which he needed to purchase new stock. Both of them
were in failing health and were now struggling to survive. Here, then, is
a man who had moved in and out of employment and the floating reserve
army of labor, who had tramped the roads of southern England as a nomad
during many a summer, and who was now heading into old age and a grim
future as a workhouse pauper.

Mayhew's *London Labour and the London Poor* is packed with hundreds of such narratives. In Marx, by contrast—or so the story goes—
there is little interest in the experience of individuals:

> here individuals are dealt with only in so far as they are the personi-
> fications of economic categories, embodiments of particular class-
> relations and class-interests. My standpoint, from which the evolution
> of the economic formation of society is viewed as a process of natural
> history, can less than any other make the individual responsible for
> relations whose creature he socially remains, however much he may
> subjectively raise himself above them.[30]

Marx's point is not, of course, that living, breathing, experiencing, thinking, suffering, real individuals are not important. The most cursory reading of the text of the first volume of *Capital* will find numerous detailed
accounts of the experiences of particular individuals, drawn from official
reports of all kinds and from newspapers.

> From the motley crowd of labourers of all callings, ages and sexes, who
> throng around us more urgently than did the souls of the slain around
> Ulysses, on whom we see at a glance the signs of over-work, without
> referring to the Blue Books under their arms, let us select two more
> figures, whose striking contrast proves that before capital all men are
> alike—a milliner and a blacksmith.[31]

And Marx goes on to document in detail the fate of Mary Anne Walkley,
twenty, whose death from overwork was reported in the London daily
papers in June 1863. (He has little to say about the blacksmith.)

It is tempting to pursue further Marx's reference to Ulysses speaking
with the dead—"the souls gathered, stirring out of Erebos." We will soon
come to another theme of the *Odyssey*—the nomad returning home disguised as a beggar: "Humped like a bundle of rags over his stick." But I want
to stay focused on the question of Marx and representation of working-
class experience. Concrete examples, drawn from numerous contempo-

rary sources, are plentiful in *Capital*. But note that "the motley crowd of labourers" whose experiences are so richly represented in official reports are, Marx says, "of all callings, ages, sexes." Different groups of workers— male or female, English, Irish, or Scottish, white or black, old or young—are vulnerable to different forms of coercion, but they are equally subjected to the coercion of capital. "The slave-owner buys his worker in the same way as he buys his horse," Marx says. "If he loses his slave, he loses a piece of capital, which he must replace by fresh expenditure on the slave-market."[32] The form is different but the principle is the same in the market for free labor: "For slave trade, read labour-market, for Kentucky and Virginia, Ireland and the agricultural districts of England, Scotland and Wales, for Africa, Germany."[33] In principle the labor market is truly liberal. As Marx never tired of repeating, capital will exploit the labor power of human beings irrespective of gender, race, age, or anything else. In practice there are sometimes contingent (never necessary) limits. Thus in England, as Marx and Engels commented on a number of occasions, cheap Irish labor was used to foment divisions within the working class. Similarly in the United States, slavery and the racist discourses that legitimized it served similar purposes: "In the United States of America, every independent workers movement was paralysed as long as slavery disfigured a part of the republic. Labour in a white skin cannot emancipate itself where it is branded in a black skin."[34]

The working people whom Mayhew talks to in London in 1849 and 1850 are not there in the streets through chance, or through the random fates experienced by individuals, or through some aberrant psychology or cultural failure of their own, or because of their gender or ethnicity. Questions of identity are pretty much irrelevant. However important the individual story, each is part of a much bigger story—the epic narrative of capital. Rather than counterpose the concrete in Mayhew to the abstract in Marx, I want to suggest that it is through the latter's conceptualization of the reserve army of labor that it is possible to make some kind of sense of the experience of the individuals who crowd the pages of *London Labour and the London Poor*. Whatever the peculiarities of their stories, they each experienced the pressures and the insecurities, the relentless overwork alternating with unemployment, of the liberal free market. It is in this sense that they are, in Marx's words, "the personifications of economic categories, embodiments of particular class-relations and class-interests," irrespective of other kinds of difference. They are subjected to forces greater than themselves but forces often invisible to themselves—or to Mayhew; or, for that matter, to any perspective that restricts itself to questions of experience, or culture, or identity.

One of the threads of the grand narrative of capital, invisible to public view, is the labor process: "the hidden abode of production, on whose threshold there hangs the notice 'No admittance except on business.'"[35] Analysis of the labor process constitutes the subject matter of substantial sections of the first volume of *Capital*. But it is the dynamic relation between what goes on in production and what goes on in the wider society that is pivotal to any understanding of the lives of the laboring majority. This relation Marx encapsulates in an antithesis: "anarchy in the social division of labour and despotism in the manufacturing division of labour." The latter is characterized by "a concentration of the means of production in the hands of one capitalist" and the "complete subjection" of the worker to his undisputed authority. But in the wider society anarchy takes the form of a "necessity imposed by nature, controlling the unregulated caprice of the producers, and perceptible in the fluctuations of the barometer of market prices." Labor thus experiences two forms of social authority: the despotism of the workplace and the arbitrary authority of competition imposed through the coercive laws of the market.[36]

Here is one example of how this dynamic works itself out on the streets of London. Many children, Marx says, "are from their earliest years riveted to the most simple manipulations, and exploited for years, without being taught a single kind of skill that would afterwards make them of use, even in the same factory."[37] He gives an example, drawn from what he describes as the "thoroughly conscientious investigations of the Children's Employment Commission." Formerly, apprentices in the letterpress printing trade had been taken through a course of training requiring the ability to read and write so that, after a period of several years, they became skilled printers. The introduction of the printing machine destroyed this work culture. Now boys from the age of eleven were employed in two very simple mechanical tasks, repeated for up to sixteen hours at a stretch. Most were discharged at the age of seventeen, illiterate, lacking any skills, and unfitted for other kinds of work. Thrown onto the streets, whatever their individual biographies, these displaced and unskilled lads were products of the restructuring of production and the labor market to fit the requirements of capital.

Most sections of the labor force in nineteenth-century London, and England, whether skilled or unskilled, experienced these two forms of authority: subjection in the workplace and anarchy and competition in the labor market. Most, then as now, knew insecurity of work, spells of unemployment, fluctuating wages, seasonal or casual labor, forced migration. General slackness of trade in London in July and August pushed significant numbers, including numbers of factory workers, out of employment. Many London workers tramped into the countryside to find harvest work, fruit-picking or hop-picking, brick making or navvying, in the summer months.[38] And many, as Marx indicated, through industrial accident, illness, or old age found themselves reduced to a state of permanent pauperism. There is no clear or stable boundary, then, between the regularly employed, the casual laborer, the reserve army of labor, and the pauper— or between those who were more or less fixed in one place and those who moved around. Working people moved between these situations, sometimes quite rapidly.

The vagrant is the human figure who embodies the negative freedom of the labor market. Tramping the roads, sleeping rough, begging a few pennies for a meal, applying to the workhouse or the casual ward was not some kind of cultural or psychological peculiarity of a minority of the population or some kind of marginal "underclass." It was the occasional resort of large numbers of working men and women, forced to look for work. Tramping on foot from place to place was a tough, dangerous, but rational response to an unstable labor market. The roads of nineteenth-century Britain were busy with these representatives of what economists call "labor mobility." Two examples. In the first four weeks of March 1848 the Board of Guardians at Alnwick, north of Newcastle-upon-Tyne on the great northern route from London to Edinburgh, recorded 721 "vagrants" (more than half of them Irish and almost a third Scottish) asking for relief at the workhouse as they passed through the town. These did not include Alnwick's settled poor. Nor did they include those who passed through and made no application. So a minimum of thirty people a day, every day, week after week, in all weathers—alone, in groups, or in families—tramped on foot through this small Northumberland market town.[39] And in the first quarter of 1848 in Preston, on the other main north-south route, the Board of Guardians relieved nearly 3,600 people tramping through the town— 40 or more every day. Preston's Casual Ward was, as a local newspaper reported, "the customary resting place at the end of the day's stage."[40]

This was one of the ways in which the population of nineteenth-century cities expanded. Of London's 1.4 million inhabitants in the census of 1851, nearly half were born outside of the metropolis. Historians have talked much of the growth of urban population through internal migration in the nineteenth century.[41] They have told us little about the human experience of migration. Most of London's new arrivals—between 30,000 and 50,000 people each year—arrived on foot, often with few possessions, looking for cheap temporary accommodation in a common lodging house, or, in more desperate cases, in the casual ward of the workhouse or at one of the charitable refuges that were opened for a few months each winter. Daniel O'Connell, in 1841, described the endless procession of newcomers, "tramping into London, by my door, without shoes, stockings, or shirts, with nothing on the head worthy of the name of hat, and with rags hardly sufficient to hide the nakedness of their bodies."[42] A letter in the *Morning Chronicle* in 1843 spoke of the numbers of starving people spending December nights in the streets and parks of London. Many of them were, the writer said, "honest and industrious work-people, who have left their homes owing to stagnation of trade in the manufacturing districts, or to a cessation of agricultural employment." He pointed to evidence from the Refuge for the Houseless Poor in Playhouse Yard: of nearly 9,000 homeless people relieved in 1842, only 582 belonged to London parishes.[43]

The unemployed working man or woman on the tramp looking for work was easily transformed into a vagrant—dropping out of the floating and into the stagnant stratum of the reserve army of labor. Newspapers of the 1840s and 1850s were full of reports of their misadventures. If they stayed too long on the roads their condition quickly deteriorated. Eating raw or bad food, they often suffered from debilitating stomach complaints such as dysentery. They were subject to malnutrition and thus vulnerable to infections and fevers. Within a fairly short time trampers became dirty and ragged and declined in strength and health. This made them unemployable. At this point they ran into increasing difficulties and found themselves criminalized as "rogues and vagabonds," in trouble with the police, pushed into a life at the margins with little chance of breaking free of it. Some resorted to strong drink as an anesthetic. Others tried petty crime to survive. An article in the *Ragged School Union Magazine* in 1850 noted the high incidence of summary conviction by magistrates for acts of vagrancy: "Some poor creature wandering about in a state of distress, is arrested by the police as a vagrant, or as 'a very suspicious character.'" He is then sent to prison for a month or six weeks, where he mixes with a variety of experienced criminals—"and by the time he leaves he has come to think that thieving is no such great crime after all."[44] Some came before the courts after a deliberate act of vandalism in order to get arrested and thus be provided with food and a bed. Richard Tronson, a man of twenty-four, put a stone through the window of the Anti-Mendicity Society's offices in Oxford in March 1848, an act of political irony that earned him a week's board and lodging in one of Her Majesty's jails.[45] Some died, on the roads, in barns and haylofts, in workhouses. Some committed suicide. A few hours' reading through the newspapers of the 1840s and 1850s will find numerous reports of the victims of labor mobility.[46]

The regime that sang the praises of the free market in labor and depended on it was bitterly hostile to the people forced to live with its brutal consequences. The pauper, the jobless migrant, the vagrant, the street beggar are variants of Agamben's *homo sacer*—the accursed man or woman, who is outside the law and has no right to live.[47] In Malthusian political economy, death was the sentence passed down to those who have, Marx said, "committed the crime of having ceased to be an object of exploitation yielding a profit to the bourgeoisie."[48] They were harassed by punitive legislation and by a Poor Law that both demanded labor mobility and penalized it. For a succession of Poor Law Commissioners and Select Committees, those applying for relief were not migrant laborers but professional vagrants. For instance, evidence that the number of applicants for relief in London was rising steeply after 1839 was ascribed to an order issued by the Poor Law Board in that year threatening any parish officer with dismissal if he refused to accept a destitute person into the workhouse. The 1846 Select Committee on District Asylums, a key document on policy toward vagrants in London, put considerable stress on this order as a *cause* of the increase. The "really destitute," it claimed, made up less than 10 percent of those who applied for relief at the casual wards of workhouses.[49] During the years 1839 to 1842 the economy plunged into a massive depression with huge unemployment. The situation began to improve from 1843, then plunged from financial crisis into depression again in 1847. The situation was exacerbated by the Irish famine and the flood of half-starved Irish families from 1846. But the Select Committee on District Asylums gives minimal attention to the fluctuations of the labor market in the capital. The Chartist Samuel Kydd noted at the end of 1848 that some recent figures put out by the Poor Law Guardians in London had focused on the increase of vagrancy in the early 1840s and again after 1847 but had omitted figures for the period 1844–46. Why? Because these latter were years when trade was brisk, employment increased, and applicants for relief fell. This proves, Kydd says, that "workmen were only idle vagrants when they had no means of being industrious citizens; and that they preferred work to want, and vagrancy rather than starvation, and its consequences—premature DEATH."[50]

The fluctuating number of paupers reflected the periodic changes of the industrial cycle, the seasonal demand for labor in and around London, and transformations of the labor process that were throwing thousands of working people onto the labor market and often onto the streets. Much contemporary discussion of the problem, official and unofficial, focused not on these economic pressures but on the vulnerability of public charity to exploitation by the idle pauper and the professional vagrant. The floating population of impoverished laborers, it was argued, was generated by the ease of access to workhouse casual wards. To justify such an implausible inversion of reality, there was resort to strange anthropologies—especially ideas of a race of migrants, unable to settle anywhere. The vast majority of those applying to the casual wards, according to an article in the *Daily News* in 1847, were full-time vagrants who chose this mode of life and who had a positive preference for "wandering misery to industrious and settled comfort": "It is strong in the Arab and Gypsy, and a bastard form of it makes the tramp." Such dubious anthropologies were commonplace in official discourse at this time, reinforced by moral arguments about a degenerate people who refused to work and who were parasitic on the labors of others—an ironic projection of their own comfortable but discomfited position, of course.

This is one important context of Mayhew's investigations (and Marx's critique of political economy). If we turn back to *London Labour and the London Poor*, we find precisely this failure to understand the realities of the labor market for vast numbers of working people and the same resort to crude anthropologies and tired liberal nostrums. It is useful to remember the sheer scale of Mayhew's project. He initially produced for the *Morning Chronicle* between October 1849 and December 1850 some 82 articles, perhaps a million words of writing. He then produced an additional 63 weekly parts of *London Labour and the London Poor* in 1851 and 1852. Almost all these weekly parts and about a third of the *Morning Chronicle* letters were included in the volumes of *London Labour and the London Poor* that appeared in 1861, augmented by new material, some of it written by others, in a fourth volume published in 1862. No wonder, then, that this huge set of writings, initially drafted at such speed and reedited up to a decade later, is profoundly incoherent if taken as a single body of work. But this, for historians, is counterbalanced by its remarkable richness of ethnographic detail and its documenting of the minutiae of working-class London.

After Mayhew's break from the *Morning Chronicle*, however, there is a shift away from the social and economic structures of the London trades and difficult questions about the causes of low wages, overwork, and bad housing—and toward "cultural" explanations. Many passages in *London Labour* repeat the familiar litany of the failings of the laboring poor: lack of family discipline, lack of education, the negative influences of the urban environment, and so on. Mayhew is one more weary master of the house, sighing about the inadequacies of servants. He is also "a traveller in the undiscovered country of the poor," investigating a distinctive "race" separate from the rest of English society—indicating the symmetries of colonial rule inside as well as outside the imperial metropolis.[51] The first volume of *London Labour* begins with a discussion of "the wandering tribes," among whom there is "a greater development of the animal than of the intellectual or moral nature of man," even possessing their own physiological characteristics: "high cheek-bones and protruding jaws." They assume a familiar form in contemporary London: "paupers, beggars, and outcasts, possessing nothing but what they acquire by depredation from the industrious, provident, and civilized portion of the community."[52] Mayhew goes on to list as characteristic of this "race" the usual catalog of vices ascribed to the laboring man (though as likely to be found among the scions of the propertied classes): improvidence, a deep dislike for hard work, inability to identify consequences from present actions, a taste for drugs and alcohol, a love of gambling.

In his *Morning Chronicle* letters and in the pages of *London Labour and the London Poor,* Henry Mayhew dignified laboring people with a voice and with a capacity to make sense of their own lives and the world they lived in. He listened to them and, questioning some of his own presuppositions, was educated by them. There are many marvelous passages of writing in Mayhew that take us into the streets and backyards and workshops of London around 1850 in a way that no other contemporary source does. Ultimately, however, Mayhew's investigations were profoundly ambiguous and sometimes vitiated by his own incomprehension—and by his repetition of standard ideological devices to legitimate that incomprehension. Marx's genius was, through a long critical engagement with political economy, to develop concepts that provided some kind of *political* explanation of why there was unemployment, casual labor, economic insecurity, crowds of people struggling to survive on the streets of London. It was not because of their own inadequacies, their moral failings, their taste for strong drink, or the peculiarities of their own biographies, much less their belonging to a different migratory race. Their stories illustrate in numerous forms the forces that Marx identified and named. Or to put it another way, Marx provides ways of making sense of some of the stories in *London Labour* that Mayhew himself, overwhelmed by his material, could not.

In an important section of the *Grundrisse*, reflecting on the relationship between the abstract and the concrete, Marx asks, how do we begin to consider a given country "politico-economically"? "It seems to be correct to begin with the real and the concrete, with the real precondition, thus to begin, in economics, with e.g. the population, which is the foundation and the subject of the entire social act of production."[53] If we examine this proposition more closely, he says, we find that it is false. To start with the population is to start with an empty abstraction if we do not think further—about how the population is divided into social classes, for instance. These classes, in turn, remain nothing but empty terms unless there is some understanding of wage labor and capital in that country, which in turns requires some grasp of the division of labor, of exchange and prices, and so on. As the starting place for any understanding of a particular country, the population, as such, would be "a chaotic conception," Marx says, leading "from the imagined concrete towards ever thinner abstractions until I had arrived at the simplest determinations." This is how early political economy proceeded, concluding with "a small number of determinant, abstract, general relations such as division of labour, money, value, etc." But it is possible to move from simple abstractions—labor, division of labor, exchange, and so on—back by a reverse journey to the concrete, through detailed research and through critical use of concepts, "until I had finally arrived at the population again, but this time not as the chaotic conception of a whole, but as a rich totality of many determinations and relations." So the concrete is not the same as the empirical object—the given country for which he wants to provide a "politico-economic" account. "The concrete is concrete because it is the concentration of many determinations," Marx says.[54] It is both the point of departure and the point of arrival of the analysis—but the journey between requires critical thinking and a continuous dialogue between concepts and empirical materials. As Marx commented in the preface to *Capital:* "in the analysis of economic forms neither microscopes nor chemical reagents are of assistance. The power of abstraction must replace both."[55] In other words, we must abstract in thought the various determinations—conceptual, ideological, empirical—that are concentrated in the concrete object of analysis, since we cannot isolate them experimentally in a way that a chemist could. The "power of abstraction" is the capacity to work critically with these determinations and their relations—to think critically about the limitations of a concept or of particular empirical data.

In certain respects, I would suggest, Marx's conceptual journey away from the street sellers and casual laborers he passed every day in the streets of London brought him closer to "the concrete" as "the concentration of many determinations"—and to the dead Irishwoman Mary Ann

Sandry and to the dead needle maker Henry Morgan, tramping the roads looking for work—than did Mayhew's seductive hermeneutics. In this way, in *Capital* and in other writings of the 1850s and 1860s too easily dismissed as "economic," Marx inaugurated a language and a political subject in uncompromising opposition to that "invisible, intangible and silent despot, condemning individuals, in extreme cases, to the most cruel of deaths, and driving in its noiseless, every day working, whole races and whole classes of men from the soil of their forefathers."

5. Secrecy and Liberal Modernity in Victorian and Edwardian England

Tom Crook

One distinguishing feature of modernity is the existence of surveillance technologies and myriad inspection and accounting practices dedicated to making people and things visible. Michel Foucault, of course, remains the preeminent theorist of this aspect of modernity. Although more than thirty years have passed since its original publication, *Discipline and Punish*, with its much-quoted analysis of Jeremy Bentham's panopticon, is still the key work.[1] In recent years, however, scholars of modern Britain have contested and complicated Foucault's account of disciplinary power. This complication has moved in two complementary directions. On the one hand, historians have examined practices of surveillance and inspection in relation to liberalism, understood in the third sense outlined in the introduction to this volume. Thanks to the work of Chris Otter and others we now know that inspection in Victorian and Edwardian England was always a fraught and frustrated process, conditioned and restrained by at least two liberal demands: economy and taxpayer thrift, which made for meager resources and insufficient staffing levels; and public accountability, which meant that inspectors were open to legal challenge and public questioning.[2] If inspection is a key facet of governmental modernity, then in liberal modernity it is a decidedly messy, politicized affair, far removed from the slick machinations of disciplinary power evoked by Foucault.

On the other hand, historians and literary scholars have questioned the utility of Foucault's disciplinary model of power in the context of England's peculiar path to modernity. Lauren Goodlad's *Victorian Literature and the Victorian State* is exemplary in this respect.[3] In her opening chapter, "Beyond the Panopticon: The Critical Challenge of a Liberal Society," she suggests that England's "idiosyncratic" culture of governance was, if anything, pastoral and patrician rather than disciplinary and bureaucratic.

Indeed, in England the kind of bureaucratic ethos necessary for the enactment of disciplinary power—objectifying, centralizing, standardizing—was fiercely resisted throughout the nineteenth century. While not entirely absent, it was held in check by a variety of political impulses, derived from a rich repertoire of traditions (including, among others, evangelicalism, civic humanism, and Anglo-Saxon constitutionalism), which meant that England developed in a decidedly different fashion from her continental neighbors, France and Germany. Here Goodlad points to a number of distinctive features: the persistence of a gentlemanly ethos of administration, the resort to pastoral relations between classes rather than disciplinary modes of surveillance, and the ongoing attachment to the principle of local autonomy. In short, for Goodlad, Foucault's model of disciplinary power simply does not square with the empirical peculiarities of English modernity.

Recent work, then, has provided a twofold complication, at once political (in terms of liberalism) and national (in terms of the peculiarities of England), of the account of power put forward in Foucault's *Discipline and Punish*. My aim in this chapter is to argue for still greater complexity and to do so by focusing on secrecy and the intentional concealment of certain activities in Victorian and Edwardian England. In particular, I examine three practices: spying, masturbating, and voting.[4] Secrecy, of course, adds an extra element of empirical complexity. Evidently liberal modernity not only involves making people and things visible; it also involves covering them up. However, my argument is more than empirical. It also seeks to offer a new way of thinking about the history of secrecy and liberal modernity. In brief, the guiding assumption is this: secrecy protects practices and people whose place within a given system (legal, political, etc.) is undecidable and ambiguous—and thus in excess of the system to the extent they cannot be wholly accounted for by the system—but which nonetheless form part of the system and play a role within it. Put another way, secrecy covers over practices and people whose status is paradoxical: they exist and are necessary, yet they also call into question the rationality and morality of the systems that they otherwise make possible and inhabit.

In this way the chapter argues against thinking in terms of more or less: of a given society becoming more or less transparent over time as disciplinary power gradually displaces earlier forms of power. As has been noted, scholars such as Otter and Goodlad have greatly complicated our understanding of disciplinary power and the way it is embedded in, and resisted by, peculiar cultures of liberal governance. However, they remain

wedded to the Foucauldian idea that modernity involves the gradual, if by
no means total, displacement of secrecy by governmental tactics of visibility and publicity. There is, in short, still a tendency to think in terms
of more or less. By contrast, I argue that secrecy is necessarily implicated
in the enactment of liberal modernity; that it is possible to think in terms
of both more secrecy and more transparency. To properly move "beyond
the panopticon," as Goodlad puts it, requires that we think secrecy and
visibility, ambiguity and clarity, *together.*

Thinking secrecy and transparency together also amounts to acknowledging their necessary entanglement, the way they are always implicated
in—or folded into—one another. The logic of this implication can be
illustrated with reference to two recent critiques of the work of Foucault.
Both demonstrate how secrecy relates to the problem of rationality and,
especially, the *limits* of rationality. Otherwise put, they show how the
necessary entanglement of secrecy and transparency derives from an
epistemological limit. Here they exemplify what is a common, albeit variously expressed, thematic within "poststructuralist" thought: namely,
how any attempt to provide a total account of the origins and functioning
of a given system always falters, foundering on elements of contradiction
and paradox. In short, there are always elements within a system that
cannot be integrated or rationalized by the system itself; and it is precisely
these elements that, as the work explored below demonstrates, are made
secret.

One of these critiques has been provided by Stefanos Geroulanos, who
focuses on the relations of vision and power that underpin Foucault's
theorization of a disciplinary society. For Geroulanos, Foucault's model
of disciplinary power ultimately rests on the invocation of a gaze that
is all-seeing but that itself is unseen, and that—contra Foucault's analysis—thus recalls a theological model of power. The best example of this is
Foucault's reading of the panopticon. The basic design of Bentham's panopticon is well known. It is an annular building, at the center of which is a
tower. The tower commands a complete view of the regimented, uniform
cells, stacked like boxes, that make up the inner periphery of the building.
There is no escape from the gaze of the inspection tower. All is transparent. However, the gaze emanating from the tower is, as Foucault himself
puts it, "unverifiable." No one knows whether they are being looked at
or not, and so everyone assumes that they are always being watched.
Ultimately, because the gaze is unverifiable, the inmates internalize the
gaze themselves, which is what makes panoptic power so supremely efficient. It is this essential blind spot—this fundamental aspect of secrecy—

that Geroulanos exploits to suggest that Foucault's account of panoptic power turns on "a structural analogy of modern power and the divine."

> Lacking evidence of the presence of a supervisor, the subject turns a visual unavailability into an epistemological one. He assumes a spectatorial presence that is at once empirical and transcendental: empirical, because of the very real threat of punishment; transcendental, because of its omnipotence and near-divine force. And what acquires divine status (in a very real sense) is not the person in the tower but the very possibility of a person looking from the tower—in other words, the very centre of the structure. The architecturalized omnipotent gaze formalizes the all-seeing God, at once present and absent, and reinscribes him as a Great Observer: whether it is the whole of society or nobody that is watching, the Great Observer reappears, served by the precarious yet unconfirmed absence of any real gaze. The epistemological unavailability, the absence of a divine observer, confirms his existence.[5]

For Geroulanos, what is divine is not the person in the tower or the gaze as such but the fact that the person or gaze cannot be verified, the fact that the gaze cannot be accounted for and so assumes the status of an indefinite possibility that cannot be resolved. Put another way, the gaze cannot be known; it is "unverifiable." Yet its undecidable status—is someone really looking from the tower or not? the question cannot be resolved one way or the other—is also what enables the panopticon to work as it does, and it is this that means it recalls a form of power that, for Geroulanos, is divine and sacred. Hence the paradox of the panopticon: the panoptic gaze exceeds the principle of transparency on which Bentham's panopticon is based; yet the unaccountable nature of this gaze is also that which enables the panopticon to work as it does. Secrecy grounds the functioning of the panopticon while also remaining distinct from it, in excess of its morality and rationality. In this way it relies on a gaze that is neither inside nor outside the panopticon, neither present nor absent. Thus amid what appears to be the total triumph of transparency, secrecy in fact remains, as a necessary, indeed central, element of the system that cannot be accounted for by the system itself. In fact, the whole panopticon pivots on this epistemological limit, this obscure threshold between inside and outside, as manifested in the unaccountable gaze.

The panopticon no doubt represents an extreme instance of the problematic at stake: it is, after all, as Foucault notes, a kind of utopia of power. Yet, as Giorgio Agamben's *Homo Sacer* demonstrates, the same problematic (the entanglement of secrecy and transparency) is also evident in the

domain of constitutional law and the legal formulation of modern sovereignty.[6] In contrast to Geroulanos, Agamben critiques Foucault's model
of biopower. While Foucault distinguishes between sovereign law and
violence, on the one hand, and biopolitical power, on the other, Agamben
demonstrates that they are necessarily implicated in one another. Here
Agamben points to a foundational point of obscurity that at once grounds
the law and ties the law to the fate and security of the human body. For
Agamben, this necessary relationship between sovereign law and the body
is manifest in all those activities of the modern state shrouded in secrecy:
state-sponsored murder, torture, summary detention, and espionage. In
Homo Sacer, he dwells on the example of Nazi concentration camps. In
the sequel to this work, *States of Exception*, however, he provides a fuller
repertoire of historical examples. Here he points to the existence of constitutional measures that, since the time of the French Revolution, have
allowed for the proclamation of "states of emergency" and allied scenarios
in which legal norms can be suspended. Among other examples, he points
to the 1914 Defence of the Realm Act in Britain and Article 48 of the 1919
Weimar Constitution.[7]

As Agamben argues, these are not ad hoc, incidental provisions. Rather,
they express a necessary relationship between law, violence, and the body
at the heart of all modern constitutions. The key question that underpins
Agamben's analysis is this: what founds the law, what grounds sovereign
juridical power? For Agamben, it is violence and force, and normal circumstances, in which legal norms work alongside biopolitical strategies, always
bear a relation to this foundational violence. Crucially, for Agamben, this
violence is neither legal nor illegal, neither outside nor inside the normal
order of legal rationality. The logical reasoning behind his analysis might
be briefly summarized as follows. The law cannot found itself. A decision
must found the law: a decision must be made as to where, to what, and to
whom the law may be applied. Yet this decision, since it establishes the law
and its field of application *in the first place*, can be neither legal nor illegal.
From the point of view of the law it is undecidable. How, then, is law established? For Agamben, it can only be established through violence: through
an act, backed by force, that declares, in a summary fashion, that this is the
law and this is what it applies to. Legal rationality is thus limited: the legal
order, that is, cannot account for itself and its genesis in its own terms.

It is on this basis that Agamben isolates the central paradox of modern
constitutions: namely, their inclusion of provisions that empower certain
persons in certain circumstances to suspend the application of the law so
as to ensure the law's perpetuation. It is these provisions that recall, and

keep in play, the foundational violence necessary to establish legal order in the first place. Paradoxically, to ensure that the law is always upheld and applied, the law must also contain provisions that allow for its suspension in certain circumstances, that is, those circumstances that are judged to threaten the normal order of things in which the legal/illegal binary distinction holds. These judgments and the actions they sanction are "pure," as Agamben puts it, since they are neither legal nor illegal. They appeal to necessity, to special and exceptional circumstances, and in so doing affirm that the law depends on decisions of an extralegal nature (but note: not illegal decisions, since the very existence of the law itself is held to be at stake). In short, modern law exists in excess of itself. It bears a necessary relationship to decisions and actions that are at once inside and outside the rational functioning of the law. From the point of view of the legal system, they are undecidable, neither legal nor illegal; and it is precisely these decisions and the actions they enable (espionage, torture, etc.) that are made secret by the modern state.

The two critiques of Foucault outlined above are analogous. They trace a similar structure of ambiguity, and of relations of inclusion and exclusion. If Foucault equated modern power with visibility and accountability, then they point to irreducible elements of secrecy: of that which is set apart and made secret, but which remains folded into that which is transparent. To be clear: it is not that secrecy and transparency are the same. Nor is it that they support one another only by way of negation and difference, what would amount to a simplistic relation of otherness. Rather, the secret is that which inhabits the transparent in a relation of both inclusion and exclusion. Indeed, the secret is precisely that which disturbs simple relations of identity and difference because it remains as a necessary, yet ambiguous, element within transparent configurations of meaning, order, and rationality. In short, the secret—that which is intentionally covered up—is that which is contained within a given system without being accountable to it in terms of its own particular rationality or morality.

In terms of rethinking the history of secrecy and liberal modernity, the critiques outlined above suggest two very general points of guidance. First, they suggest that we should abandon speaking in terms of more or less: of a society or state becoming more or less transparent over time, or more or less secretive. They suggest in fact that transparency and secrecy, visibility and obscurity, might grow together, or indeed decline together. Second, they suggest that what is made secret bears a confused relation to that which is otherwise openly acknowledged, even celebrated. Put another way, they suggest that the historian should attempt to discern the epistemological problems that, in any given domain or system of thought and practice, make the entanglement of secrecy and transparency necessary.

Of course, in the case of Victorian and Edwardian England, it is certainly possible to speak of the gradual diffusion of a "light of publicity," to use a term employed by Patrick Joyce.[8] Much theorized in the eighteenth century (especially in France), accountability to public opinion became a recognizable political principle in the 1820s and went on to become a defining feature of the Whig-liberal ethos that dominated British politics up until the 1880s. The great profusion of Blue Books from midcentury, together with the marked expansion of the press, meant that the period 1830–1914 was characterized by hitherto unprecedented scrutiny of government and society. Other developments might be noted: the growth of professional inspectorates, the expansion of domestic visiting societies, and the rebuilding of city spaces so as to allow for the open circulation of people and goods.

These new practices can all be viewed in terms of the establishment of a liberal society committed to rational debate, economic competition, open government, respectable morals, and independent citizenship. However, this same society also indulged in myriad secret activities that brought into question these liberal values, activities such as spying, masturbating, and voting, discussed below. That some account needs to be given of the epistemological problems posed by secret activities has already been mentioned. Yet it is also clear, in light of the work of Goodlad and others, that some account must be given of the peculiar way in which these secret activities were managed and talked about in the context of England's distinctive culture of governance. Some account, in short, must be given of English idiosyncrasies and the circumstances in which they were formed, including logistical considerations of order and discipline.

There is, however, a further consideration, one prompted by the very fact that it is possible to write a history of secret activities at all; which is to say, the very fact that it is possible to determine the anxieties they generated and the ways they were governed. Here it is necessary to confront a pronounced political peculiarity, one that persists today: simply that in liberal societies, in marked contrast to absolutist and authoritarian societies, things that go on in secret are public issues. Of course, in liberal societies the publicity accorded secret activities is most apparent in the case of voting, where election results are subject to prolonged public discussion, but it is also the case with spying and masturbating. The latter two activities maintain a public presence, even if they are not talked about with the same intensity as voting. In this way secrecy obtains a measure of transparency and publicity. Liberal citizens know what they do not know and recognize limits regarding what they can and cannot know; and this is possible only because of the existence of a public sphere in which secrecy and secret activities are discussed. Indeed, in the case of Victorian and Edwardian England, spying, masturbating, and voting gave rise to abundant discourse.

The complication this introduces is at least twofold. On the one hand, publicity ensures that activities carried out in secret are not entirely repressed or ignored. It enables the secret to be talked about. It enables the secret to be placed under revision and to be exposed to ongoing ethical and political claims regarding its validity, even its very existence. On the other hand, publicity ensures that what is secret can still function. Since it can be talked about and acknowledged as such (as secret), what goes on in secret can also prosper and even become more rigorously practiced and entrenched. In general, then, the publicity accorded secrecy serves a regulative function but one that is nonetheless unstable. It is what enables the secret to exist in a dynamic fashion, whereby what is secret is alternately repressed and refined, discussed and denied.

What follows is an attempt to incorporate these various considerations into a brief account of spying, masturbating, and voting. In so doing, it deals with three systems: respectively, legal, sexual, and political. Of course, spying, masturbating, and voting constitute very different activities. From an epistemological point of view, however, they are similar: each represents an element contained within a system that cannot be rationalized by the system itself. They are at once inside and outside a given system. In this respect, they are also paradoxical and signal the impossibility of total system.

Spying.   Liberal governance maintains an uneasy relationship with spying, just as it does with other secret activities that while acknowledged to be contrary to the normal laws of civil society are practiced nonetheless (torture, for instance); and this uneasy relationship is very much apparent today. To return to Agamben's analysis outlined above, liberal governance empowers certain individuals in certain circumstances to suspend the law in order to allow for the security of the law and its field of application. In so doing, it touches on an epistemological limit, for it involves recourse to a mode of reasoning whose grounds are ambiguous—neither legal nor illegal—but that is nonetheless included in the legal system and the constitution that defines it. A mode of reasoning, in other words, that is intrinsic to legal order and its maintenance but is also difficult to speak of and whose articulation is necessarily brief if it is articulated at all. Yet at the same time spying is not entirely secret. Liberal subjects know it goes on. Occasionally there are embarrassing disclosures and subsequent inquiries. The extent of spying is never disclosed in its fullness, but liberal subjects can glimpse something of its existence.

The Mazzini espionage affair, which erupted in June 1844, can be read with these considerations in mind. Although there were no front bench resignations, the matter was debated in Parliament and covered extensively in the press. The affair was prompted by the accusation that the Tory Home Secretary, Sir James Graham, had ordered the opening of mail addressed to the Italian radical, who was then resident in England. The government agreed to an inquiry. Significantly, however, it agreed only to a secret inquiry conducted by committees representing the Lords and the Commons. This was not without precedent: secret inquiries had been commissioned in the 1810s regarding the suspension of habeas corpus and the governance of "dangerous meetings and combinations" involving radicals.[9] The two committees responded swiftly, publishing their reports in August. They confirmed that Mazzini's letters had been opened and that information had been passed to foreign powers.

The affair was roundly condemned in the press and in terms that reflected a strong attachment to classical values: secrecy, that is, was equated with meanness; openness was equated with honor and magnanimity. It was common to invoke the peculiar "nobility" of English morals and the nation's instinctive respect for individual liberties. It was also argued that the affair represented an insult to England's traditional status as a safe haven for political refugees. An article in the *North British Review* asked rhetorically, "Was it not a gross and base deception to open letters which would never have been written had not the honour of the English been relied upon?" "It is mean to open letters," it added, but "meaner still" to betray the trust of émigrés like Mazzini.[10] Others declared that the affair was "subversive of the English constitution."

The two committee reports provided the same defense. Both argued that there were certain circumstances in which espionage was necessary, namely, circumstances in which there was a threat to national interests. Unlike the Lords' report, which was silent on the matter, the Commons inquiry elaborated—though at no great length—on why Mazzini's letters had been opened, stating that, according to "high sources," he was involved in a plot that might "disturb the peace of Europe."[11] Both reports were also keen to stress that the power to open letters had always been exercised with restraint. The Lords' report suggested that it had been used only "sparingly" during the past twenty years, and that when it had, the Home Secretaries in question had been directed "by an earnest and faithful desire to adopt that course which appeared to be necessary, either to promote the end of justice or to prevent a disturbance of the public tranquillity or otherwise to promote the best interests of the country."[12]

The use of secret powers was thus justified, but it was by no means clarified: neither report dwelled on the notion of national interest and its relation to law. Indeed, the Commons' report, though much more elaborate than that of the Lords, explicitly refrained from inquiring into matters of legal principle. Here it performed two maneuvers. First, it appealed to precedent, in particular, a statute law passed in 1711, under the reign of Queen Anne, which had empowered secretaries of state to open letters in times of emergency. The constitutional status of present practices was thus reduced to that of past law. Second, it then refused to inquire into the legality of past law.

> In preference to discussing the purely legal question, how far the Statute of Anne, in recognizing the practice, on the part of the Secretaries of State, of issuing Warrants to open letters, engendered it lawful for the Secretaries of State to issue such Warrants, Your Committee propose, so far as they have materials for that purpose, to give the history of this practice, prior to and subsequent to the passing of that Statute.[13]

The report went on to detail, at great length, all the occasions, since the sixteenth century, when such powers had been exercised. In short, the question of legal principle was fudged, and it was simply asserted that spying was an unfortunate necessity and had always been practiced. Espionage was thus judged constitutional.

The Mazzini affair resulted in the termination of certain offices and practices, including the abolition of the Secret Department of the Post Office. Yet as David Vincent argues, both in his contribution to this volume and elsewhere, the affair marked the beginning of a *new* culture of secrecy, one that was more organized and entrenched than its predecessor.[14] The Mazzini affair, of course, was a signal reminder of public aversion to state secrecy. However, as Vincent stresses, the state also faced a growing logistical problem: the expanding mass of official correspondence, which in some departments of state, such as the Home Office, Foreign Office, and Board of Trade, had grown threefold or more during the second quarter of the century. It was becoming increasingly impossible for departmental heads to deal with every single piece of correspondence. Potentially sensitive state information was becoming more and more vulnerable to leakage at a time of increased demands for public accountability.

Two facets of the culture of secrecy that emerged out of this logistical problematic might be mentioned. One represents a decidedly English innovation: the figure of the reformed civil servant that emerged in the wake of the Northcote-Trevelyan report of 1854. Notwithstanding the rhetoric of efficiency, the primary concern of civil service reform was to secure a class of gentlemen administrators distinguished by their moral character and capacity for corporate self-sacrifice and quiet reserve. While they were to be better educated than their predecessors, reform was emphatically not about securing a Benthamite technocracy or a new breed of experts. On the contrary, it was about reaffirming the links between the English state, liberal pedagogy, and traditional institutions of elite education, in particular, Oxbridge and the leading public schools. In brief, reform was about securing English gentlemen who by virtue of their breeding could be trusted to keep silent on important matters of state—to know what should not be made known to the public and to act with according discretion.

In time, this distinctly English tradition of "honorable secrecy" was supplemented by a second, and altogether less subtle, means of ensuring control over government information: the Official Secrets Acts of 1889 and 1911. These acts targeted not those who occupied the upper echelons of the state but the expanding corps of lower-grade administrators—precisely those hired to deal with the growing informational complexity of governance, all of whom, it was thought, were more susceptible to financial inducements. Referring to purposes that might be antithetical to "the interests of the state," the acts criminalized the unauthorized disclosure of "official information." Secrecy was thus made into a statutory part of the British constitution, and in the case of both acts there was remarkably little in the way of parliamentary debate or legal elaboration: the acts contained only a dozen or so carefully worded sections.

Masturbating.   The problem of masturbation is hardly unique to liberal societies. Yet its precise status as a problem has varied considerably. Today it is regarded as a normal part of one's sexual development. The Victorians, by contrast, denounced it as an "evil." Morally it was judged an "abomination," while physically it was linked with disturbances of every conceivable anatomical structure and physiological system. Not everyone, of course, shared the evangelical assumption that it might lead to eternal damnation, not least the many medical writers on the subject. Furthermore, various tactics were pursued, most commonly "talks to boys" and the dissemination of pamphlet literature; only rarely was there resort to the use of preventive technologies appended to the body. Even so, it is abundantly clear that during the nineteenth century what was often referred to as the "secret vice" constituted a peculiarly intense site of governmental anxiety.

The work of Thomas Laqueur suggests that the intensity of this anxiety bore a profound relation to the liberal values of Victorian society.[15] In brief, his argument is that masturbation represented both an affirmation and a negation of the logic of enlightened individualism. "It was a vice of paradox," to quote Laqueur.[16] On the one hand, masturbation combined three forms of pleasure that were otherwise thought to play a constructive role in the order of society and the cultivation of a liberal self: the pleasures of the imagination, viewed as central to the functioning of a literate reading public; the pleasures of domestic and personal privacy, seen as an antidote to the public worlds of work and government; and finally pleasure itself, viewed in utilitarian terms as an important spur to private gain and collective wealth creation, as well as procreation and population growth.

In this respect masturbation was the perfect embodiment of liberal subjectivity and the various pleasures thought to sustain it. Indeed, these same pleasures were also at work in making masturbation such a difficult problem to contend with in the first place. Though hardly a Victorian invention, print-based pornography witnessed a significant expansion of its market during this period, and there was also the emergence of notorious districts specializing in the sale of illicit literature, such as Holywell Street in London. We might also instance the population growth that took place, which made for increasingly chaotic city centers characterized, so the social investigations of the time suggested, by unprecedented levels of sensual indulgence, including drinking and prostitution. In short, masturbation crystallized and connected with various pleasures and problems intrinsic to liberal society. To this extent masturbation could be rationalized and understood.

Yet masturbation also represented a radical negation of the very society whose pleasures and problems it otherwise exemplified in a consummate fashion. It was, of course, entirely antisocial. It was also an act of nonexchange, which had no other end than the pleasure it generated. Unlike male-female sexual relations, which generated progeny as well as pleasure, masturbation had no compensatory virtue, no other goal that might provide some kind of meaning. Nor was it dependent on the supply of women or pornography. Pornography and prostitution, though considered problems, were at least dependent on some kind of marketplace, and it was on this basis that both were subject to statutory regulation during the

Victorian period: respectively, the Obscene Publications Act (1857) and the Contagious Diseases Acts (1864–86). By contrast, masturbation required only the imagination, whose workings were limitless.

In this way, as Laqueur's analysis suggests, it amounted to a form of freedom that ultimately could not be rationalized within the framework furnished by liberal society and its various values, including the providential reasoning used by some to make sense of greed and prostitution. And yet, at the same time, it bound together pleasures that were otherwise deemed necessary and entirely natural. In other words, masturbation amounted to an excessive amalgam of body and mind that was neither natural nor unnatural. It was neither fully present within nor wholly absent from the overall design of society and nature as manifested in human sexuality. As Jean-Jacques Rousseau termed it, in a phrase that Jacques Derrida has exploited, masturbation was a "dangerous supplement": a negation of nature contained within nature, whose natural status was thus undecidable.[17]

The great panic that engulfed masturbation was not restricted to England; it was a pan-European phenomenon. Nor was it of nineteenth-century origin; it initially developed in the early eighteenth century. But in England, as Alan Hunt has argued, the panic reached its peak during the late Victorian and Edwardian periods and was focused on a specific segment of the population: public school boys.[18] At least two factors shaped this English peculiarity. One relates to the more general rationale for public schools, namely, the concern to secure a future caste of gentlemanly leaders equipped with good moral character and robust physical health. This concern had been evident since at least the 1850s, but it became especially pronounced during the late nineteenth and early twentieth century, amid fears of physical degeneration and the erosion of Britain's military and imperial might.

The other factor is the logistical problem that arose as part of the distinctive culture of public schooling and the use of dormitory accommodation. In particular, there was no consensus on the precise spatial arrangement of the dormitories, for reasons of both moral and physical health. Some hygienists recommended the use of partitioned cubicles containing beds and washbasins, partly by way of securing privacy and partly by way of mitigating the spread of infections.[19] Others, however, argued quite the opposite. "I must regard cubicles as the worst invention ever planned for schools," stated Clement Dukes, an authority on school hygiene. "For evils are possible in cubicles and small rooms which are unlikely, or almost impossible, in large open dormitories." Indeed, cubicles did more than just facilitate masturbation; they incited it: "Cubicles, in my opinion, are a direct invitation to a boy to practise and teach secret acts, which he dare not commit before a whole room."[20] For Dukes, cubicles threatened to encourage an "evil" that, unchecked, might corrupt an entire school.

The panic surrounding masturbation gradually diminished during the first half of the twentieth century, and by the 1970s the sexological-psychological approach, initially formulated by Havelock Ellis and Sigmund Freud, had become mainstream. The idea that masturbation might play a positive role in the sexual development of the self remains dominant today. Whether or not, during the Victorian and Edwardian periods, the mass of literature surrounding masturbation served to prevent or incite the practice is unclear; the practice itself was never described, only its consequences. What is clear, however, is that the postwar literature on the subject served to refine and intensify its practice, beginning in the 1970s, when feminists first claimed that masturbation was a source of liberation. A similar dynamic of discussion and refinement thrives today via the mediation of the internet. Even so, guilt and pathology remain, and it hardly constitutes a public act. Although now considered normal, it is still linked to desires that open on to excessive fantasies and it continues to signify profound social and sexual shortcomings. As Laqueur concludes, "It remains poised between self-discovery and self-absorption, desire and excess, privacy and loneliness, innocence and guilt as does no other sexuality in our era."[21]

Voting.   In England, the use of a secret ballot for parliamentary elections dates back to 1872, some forty years after it had first been debated in the House of Commons. Before 1872 elections had been conducted openly, as large-scale public assemblies, in which electors were required to record their votes in a poll book. As is well known, open voting was accompanied by violence, intimidation, and bribery, much of which was organized and ritualized, including the participation of nonelectors. To this extent, electoral corruption was systematic. After 1872, with the passage of the Secret Ballot Act, voters were able to anonymously mark a ballot paper and then deposit it in a sealed box. In other respects, however, the post-1872 regime involved greater clarity and public transparency: nonelectors were excluded from the polling place, the count was formally regulated and open to the scrutiny of party agents, and all ballots were uniform and printed at public expense. The vote constituted a single—and indeed secure—point of obscurity within a system that was otherwise designed to be more efficient, disciplined, and publicly accountable.

Today voting by secret ballot is regarded as an essential constituent of liberal freedom and we are accustomed to thinking of it as a universal human right. The rationale is that the secret ballot helps to protect voters from corruption. It is certainly true that just such a rationale informed the passage of the 1872 act. However, not everyone thought that the secret ballot would enhance the practice of citizenship. Far from it in fact, and there was widespread ambivalence regarding its moral and political credentials. It is this ambivalence that points toward the epistemological problem posed by the act of voting in liberal societies. In this case it concerns the political domain and its relation to other domains of governance. More precisely, it concerns the political domain, conceived as a realm of collective representation and equality, and its relation to other domains of governance, most notably the economic, where private interests and material inequalities are considered legitimate.

In modern liberal societies, as Pierre Manent has recently argued, the political domain, composed as it is of competing political parties, functions as a zone of mediation for issues that are nonpolitical in character and reflect a society composed of diverse sectional interests and profound inequalities (of wealth, health, and education, for example). The political domain, in short, is the space where nonpolitical issues are discussed and resolved in a collective fashion through the agency of popularly elected parties. Yet these issues, to the extent that they assume a society composed of various interests, identities, and inequalities, also run counter to the logic of the political domain. Rather than assume that society is heterogeneous, the political domain assumes that society is homogeneous and composed of equal citizens, all with the same rights, entitlements, and capacities, including the right to vote.[22]

In this way the act of voting embodies a paradox. It is an act that affirms membership in a society composed of equal citizens while also allowing for the expression of sectional and financial interests that affirm and enable profound differences and inequalities. Otherwise put, voting embodies a political morality committed to equal citizenship; everyone has the vote, and voting displays membership in a society where all, regardless of class, culture, and status, can participate in collective decision making. At the same time voting runs counter to this morality since it allows for the assertion of personal interests, including financial interests, that relate to a society conceived entirely otherwise—a society of multiple interests, affiliations, and inequalities. Voting thus occupies a space that is at once political and nonpolitical: it unites society while it divides society. It is an act that, from the perspective of the political system and its morality, is undecidable, neither wholly political nor wholly nonpolitical. Here, as in other domains, secrecy covers over an act whose status is paradoxical. Democratic elections are of course much discussed. Before, during, and after election day they are accompanied by an outpouring of discourse. Yet the very point where democratic power is enacted—the point of voting—remains entirely unaccountable. Lucid discussion hovers over a void: ultimately, no one knows precisely how people voted.

For the likes of Manent and others, this peculiar relationship within liberal society between the political and the nonpolitical dates back to the nineteenth century and can be seen in the tension that emerged between classical and modern political ideals—between "ancient liberty" and "modern liberty."[23] Of course, this tension was explored at the time (most notably perhaps by Alexis de Tocqueville and J. S. Mill), and it is also true that classical and modern values mixed in rich and diverse ways (as in something like Whiggism). Crudely, however, this tension might be formulated as follows. On the one hand, values inherited from the ancient world affirmed a conception of citizenship based on openness, a concern for the public good, and, above all perhaps, the possession of "independence," which was all about the ability to *exclude* from politics economic considerations and narrow sectional interests. On the other hand, modern ideals, inherited from the Enlightenment, asserted the naturalness and political legitimacy of individual interests. They also equated citizenship with the exercise of equal rights concerning, among other things, freedom of thought, association, and economic acquisition.[24]

Precisely this tension informed the debate regarding the secret ballot. J. S. Mill provided the most robust articulation of classical values. In *Considerations on Representative Government* (1861), Mill argued that the vote was a "public trust" and that the voter was "under an absolute moral obligation to consider the interest of the public, not his private advantage."[25] Open voting encouraged the voter to reflect properly on the public good. It was a valuable reminder to the voter of his duties to the wider community, and the possibility that the voter might be challenged at the polls meant that he went forth having formed robust opinions as to his choices. Secret voting, by contrast, encouraged selfishness and endorsed the idea that a vote might be cast in the name, as Mill put it, of either "personal" or "class interests."

Mill's argument was returned to time and again during the 1860s and early 1870s, and many Tories and Whigs made precisely the same point: the vote was a public trust, not a right, and still less a means of asserting sectional interests. Mill refrained from talking in terms of Englishness, but not so the majority of the secret ballot's opponents. Open voting was manly and noble and entirely in keeping with the country's proud tradition of electoral independence. Ultimately, voting in secret bore "the badge of slavery" and represented the very antithesis of political citizenship.[26] As the case of Mill demonstrates, not all radicals were adherents of the secret ballot. Nonetheless, only radicals emphatically asserted the argument—incorporating the modern premise noted above—that the vote was a legitimate means of defending one's private interests. The best example is a pamphlet published in 1868 by the prominent secularist George Jacob Holyoake, in which he declared, quite simply, "It is no affair of my neighbour how I vote, or for whom I vote, or why I vote—since I exercise no power or freedom which he does not equally possess, and which I do not equally concede to him." Holyoake concluded, "For guarding my personal interests in the state the Ballot is all this to me."[27]

Comparatively speaking, Britain was not the first state to adopt a properly secure method of voting. Earlier, in 1856, the Australian states of Victoria, South Australia, and Tasmania had adopted the secret ballot. Indeed, the "Australian ballot," as it was known, provided the model for British reform. But neither was Britain an international laggard. Belgium, the United States, Italy, Germany, and France—all these states followed Britain's (and Australia's) lead.[28] Even so, echoes of the English debate could be found elsewhere, and it was by no means wholly peculiar. In both France and the United States, for example, open voting was defended on the grounds that it was honorable and manly. Similarly, French and American advocates of secret voting pointed to the enhanced security it afforded. Yet the tenor of debate was much different, and in England it was especially polarized and fraught. In France and the United States it had been common practice since the late eighteenth century to employ a ballot paper on which the voter inscribed his choices before depositing it in a box. While the vote was still cast in the midst of a public assembly—which meant that it was not entirely secure—the voter nonetheless enjoyed a degree of privacy not granted to the English parliamentary elector, who was obliged to declare his choices openly and have them inscribed in a poll book. Thus, in England by the 1860s the choice (at the parliamentary level) was between a wholly open system and a wholly secret system. Accordingly, the political stakes were comparatively greater than elsewhere, and the act of voting was subject to more intense reflection on matters of principle.

In the event, however, the adoption of the secret ballot in 1872 turned on more than matters of principle. Coming only a few years after the franchise extension of 1867, which almost doubled the electorate, logistical considerations of order also played a part. As the Select Committee convened in 1869 to review parliamentary electioneering affirmed, electoral violence was endemic and there was a growing need to speed up the invariably protracted process of public voting in the context of a bigger electorate. Many of those who backed the secret ballot in 1872, including then–Prime Minister William Gladstone, regarded it as a mixed blessing and did so only reluctantly. To be sure, the Ballot Act was designed to afford the voter more protection at the polls, and in this respect it was an immediate success. Yet for so many at the time it also enshrined a wholly corrupt conception of citizenship, based on the idea that the vote could be wielded in the name of personal interest rather than the public good. The debate thus brings into sharp relief the ambiguities surrounding the exercise of the vote in liberal societies, committed as they are to both political equality and the free play of diverse interests, identities, and inequalities. These days we seem to have forgotten its contested genesis, though the act itself still remains current: the provisions passed in 1872 continue to provide the main source of statutory guidance today. In Britain, as elsewhere, liberal democracy, otherwise esteemed for its transparency and openness, maintains a fundamental relation to secrecy.

The aim of this chapter has been to provide a sketch of how the history of secrecy and liberal modernity might be rethought in the context of Victorian and Edwardian England. It has been guided by the assumption that secrecy protects people and practices whose place is ambiguous and undecidable: ambiguous and undecidable, because, though they inhabit and enable areas of governance, they also call into question the morality and rationality of these same areas. The general argument has been that we should not necessarily equate liberal modernity with the growth of transparency and governmental practices of surveillance. In addition, we should attend to the growth of secrecy and trace the ways in which transparency and obscurity, rationality and secrecy, are entangled. To do so, it has been suggested that we need to embrace a number of different layers of analysis. In the above, some attempt has been made to attend to three: considerations of logic and epistemology, logistical considerations of order and discipline, and finally considerations of political and cultural peculiarity.

Much more work remains to be done on the subject of modernity, liberal governance, and secrecy, and it might be that the argument advanced here requires modification, perhaps substantial modification. But if valid, it suggests that we might think again about the limitations—the blind spots—of what scholars, after Foucault, term "liberal rationality" and develop a richer, more complex sense of what it encompasses and what it does not. It is not the case, it should be emphasized, that secrecy points to hitherto overlooked zones of irrationality within liberal society, or, for that matter, illegality or immorality—indeed, liberal societies, past and present, quite happily bring before the light of publicity subjects and practices deemed immoral, irrational, and illegal—rather, secrecy brings to light precisely those zones where binary thinking breaks down: those practices and people that liberal rationality cannot quite account for in its own terms; those people and practices that elude precise articulation, explication, or rationalization but that remain nonetheless as a necessary part of society.

In this way secrecy is also a reminder of the necessarily incomplete nature of the project of modernity and of that which thwarts definitive rationalization. Perhaps, then, the panopticon might still serve as a key icon of modernity. But not the panopticon as Bentham or Foucault understood it. Rather, the panopticon in which, to recall the opening of this chapter, secrecy still shines through to disturb, but also make possible, the transparent functioning of power.

6.   Was There a Liberal Historicism?

Thomas Osborne

What follows is concerned with the relations between liberalism as a political rationality and the writing of history. I shall argue that the idea of linking liberalism with certain kinds of modern history writing—above all, with the discourse of constitutional history—is intriguing, and not without rewards, but necessarily limited. The argument, though, is not really just about history. The point of the exercise is also to say something more generally about the specificities and necessary limits of Foucauldian understandings of liberalism itself.

The use of the term *liberalism*—as it has been deployed in studies inspired by Michel Foucault—can be criticized for being rather overgeneralized. The notion of liberalism seems to be just about everywhere in Foucauldian work. Mention governmentality, and liberalism is inevitably invoked. Some Foucauldian authors have written of liberal "modes of government" as if liberalism, for Foucault, had been a kind of expressive epoch rather than a particular rationality of government coexisting with other rationalities. Recognizing the implicit problems with the Foucauldian concept of liberalism, others have defended the terminology on grounds, in effect, of pragmatism. Whatever its limitations, the term is useful for opening up a space of research that is both historically sensitive and theoretically self-conscious; for instance, to take one example, an understanding of liberalism as a formula of rule in the nineteenth century oriented to the "rule of freedom," mapping the varied ways in which liberalism was a material technology of government, articulating space, water, blood, publicity, and the very streets of the Victorian city.[1]

THE LIBERAL ARCHIVE

But what about the specific links between history writing itself and liberalism?[2] Can we talk about a specifically liberal kind of history writing emerging as an aspect of the "rule of freedom,"—that is, a form of history writing that is liberal in the Foucauldian sense, not as a component of an ideology of *political* or normative liberalism, but as an aspect of a liberal political technology of government?

The question itself begs the question as to what a liberal political technology actually *is*. We could begin with quite a wide view. In the Foucauldian literature liberalism is often rather mechanically contrasted with the political technology of "police" on the one hand and with neoliberalism on the other.[3] Foucault himself contrasted liberalism at one point in his lectures with "raison d'état" and with the cosmo-theologies of communism and totalitarianism.[4] Used in this way, it is easy to see how liberalism could be understood as being just about coextensive with the emergence of something like an "open society." Under such broad definitions almost any history that was not state history or what Jacques le Goff calls "royal history" of one sort or another would qualify as liberal.[5]

We might take the late 1830s and 1840s in England as an example of thinking about liberalism and history in this rather broad manner. What we have here might be characterized as the separation of the historical archive from the exigencies of immediate state power.[6] The point about the archive in this sense is that it is putatively "open" and thus at a remove from the contingencies of power.[7] Albeit largely financed by the state itself, the archive goes public. The symbol of this moment is the opening of the Public Record Office in 1838, making documents available to the public at lower fees than previously and allowing for the better preservation of records and the publication of calendars, indexes, and manuscript editions of state papers.[8]

The point about this moment is that the liberal state took on the task of making available the facts that it had historically recorded about itself. This event might profitably be related to what Ian Hacking, in his archaeological investigations of statistical reason, once termed the "avalanche of printed numbers" that occurred in the same period.[9] What was important here was precisely that the numbers were printed and thus publicly available for discussion. History writing is somewhat different. Here the notion of a primary source typically indicates that the basic forms of evidence are such because they were *not* originally published, and the role of the historian became identified not least with the scholarly labors of preparing primary sources for publication—hence, for instance, the import of the Rolls series for the establishment of the norms of the English historical profession.[10] In any case, as with statistics then so with history; the archive takes on a public character.

It is certainly the case that without a sense of a more or less openly available public past recorded in material traces there can be no liberal sense of history. What emerges here is something like history for its own sake, or at least history putatively represented *in itself*, entailing a distinction between primary and secondary sources that some—notably R. G. Collingwood—have regarded as being integral to the very idea of modern history writing.[11] In Foucauldian terms, it could be argued that this distinction establishes the task of history writing along lines broadly analogous to those of early political economy, that is, analogous to the economy as a field that is prior to and ancillary to government, such that the past becomes a field recorded in traces that is in principle available to a public—albeit mediated by forms of historical expertise—and not just usable for the immediate ends of government itself.[12]

On the other hand, there are some limitations with this rather broad way of looking at things. First, although the establishment of modern archival institutions is no doubt a condition of liberal history writing, it is quite obviously not the whole story. After all, such developments can be understood in terms of much broader, more general, categories— which are not reducible to liberalism—such as modernization or professionalization.[13] Moreover, the turn to the archives and to the "facts in themselves" was not least a Rankean idea, a German phenomenon, and one that is, again, not obviously reducible to liberalism. English history writing was, in any case, generally backward in these terms, as its foremost practitioners were apt to acknowledge, and it was only in the 1880s—with, notably, the founding of the *English Historical Review*— that anything like an independent historical "profession" could be said to have emerged.[14]

Second, such developments can just as easily be understood not in terms of liberalism but in terms of transformations in cultural understandings of time. It has been well recognized, by Koselleck and others, that the "acceleration of time" that occurred during the industrial revolution led to a fundamental transformation in the relation of society to its past.[15] The demands of culture may, then, be more causally relevant than those of government reason in this context.

LIBERAL GOVERNMENT

So if liberalism—at least in any wide sense—is not the whole story it may be worth limiting our ambitions somewhat. Perhaps we can do this not least by providing a clearer definition of what liberal governmentality—as opposed to liberalism as a political ideology or sociological epoch—actually entails in this context. While acknowledging that liberalism was a fast-evolving not to say inconsistent category in Foucault's thought, let us say that it has two basic components when understood not as a form of avowed, normative political ideology (not a concern for Foucault in the least) but as a form of political technology or governmental rationality.[16]

There is the principle of the *immanence* of the domain to be governed. Liberalism, on Foucault's conception, implicates a "natural" domain around which technologies of government situate themselves. In Foucault's writings this is usually associated with the emergence of the idea of population and with the idea of the economy. Political economy is the epitome of a discipline that emerges to formulate knowledge relating to these natural domains, in this case the economy as an autonomous field. Later governmentality literature adds the idea of society, or "the social."[17] After political economy we have criminology, statistics, sociology, and kindred disciplines.[18] Foucault's notion of security is closely tied to this idea of the government of natural domains; government exists to preserve the natural integrity or security of the population, the economy, society. In this sense, liberal government is immanent to these domains, or rather such government insofar as it *is* liberal has to respect this immanence. All transcendent, exterior, sovereign-type forms of intervention—whether in terms of the coup d'état or the top-down incursions of law—will be problematic for liberal government.

Actually, liberalism is not opposed to the principles of law, but it is, so to speak, operationally suspicious of forms of sovereignty in general and legal sovereignty in particular. The law has technological effect rather than ideological transcendence: "Regulation has not been sought in the law because of the supposedly natural legalism of liberalism, but because the law defines forms of general intervention excluding particular, individual, and exceptional measures, and because participation of the governed in drawing up the law in a parliamentary system is the most effective system of governmental economy."[19]

For Foucault, liberalism is not least a critique of sovereign forms of reason, whether royal, legal, or state reason. Liberalism in this sense is also reflexive; it is inherently critical of the exercise of government and such critique is *part* of the proper exercise of government. Indeed, Foucault draws the parallel between the idea of the critique of state internal to liberalism and that of the Kantian philosophy of the critique of reason.

Then there is the principle of *freedom*. Liberalism posits the subjects of population, economy, and society as putative subjects of freedom, endowed with capacities for self-directing, self-governing activity. Freedom here is less a normative, ideological, or political value (as one finds for instance in J.S. Mill) than it is a principle and a means of government. It is a component, in short, of a governmental technology. As such the principle of freedom is only the correlative of the naturalistic principle of immanence. In the *Security, Territory, Population* lectures, where Foucault first—very briefly—broaches the notion, liberalism is associated with, above all, technologies of security that respect the immanent nature of things in the name of freedom itself: "The game of liberalism—not interfering, allowing free movement, letting things follow their course; *laisser faire, passer et aller*—basically and fundamentally means acting so that reality develops, goes its way, and follows its own course according to the laws, principles, and mechanisms of reality itself."[20]

The principles of immanence and freedom, then, might be our yardsticks of liberal technologies of government. Can aspects of the emergence of modern history writing be considered an instance of such liberalism? Was there, in this particular sense, a *liberal historicism?*

CONSTITUTIONAL HISTORY

It needs to be stressed and restressed that it should not be assumed that we might be looking for a liberal historicism in the work of those who were avowedly liberal in *political* or ideological orientation; nor should we expect to find any historical work that is straightforwardly the epistemological *expression* of political liberalism. Rather, the best we can do is to attempt to locate a fit—a conjunctural affinity perhaps—between one or other thought style within historical reasoning and our twin demands of liberal government in the principles of immanence and freedom.

One candidate for this is the field of constitutional history, which emerged in the later decades of the nineteenth century but which had its origins in the earlier work of Hallam, as famously critiqued by Macaulay.[21] Truncating this heritage somewhat, the main focus here in these brief remarks is on the work of the doyen of the constitutional history thought collective, William Stubbs.

To what sort of historicism—understood in a general sense as any means that seeks to ground the present on the basis of history—did Stubbs give his signature? What was the field of constitutional history as Stubbs saw it? It was certainly a history that took as its object an integrally immanent field of phenomena. In the preface to the first volume of his *Constitutional History*, Stubbs declared that this sort of history is the history, above all, of social, political, and cultural institutions, in contrast to those sorts of history that focused on the glories of war or the struggle for fame.[22] History, for Stubbs, was, one might say, more about the government of men than the luster of power.

In this sense, his history writing was to be decidedly *not* about sovereignty and hence—as Stubbs liked to insist—very *un-Roman*. By way of contrast, it is difficult to resist quoting at this point what Foucault said about the "Roman model" of history writing.

> The traditional function of history, from the first Roman annalists until the late Middle Ages, and perhaps the seventeenth century or even later, was to speak the right of power and to intensify the lustre of power. It had two roles. The point of recounting history, the history of kings, the might of sovereigns and their victories (and, if need be, their temporary defeats) was to use the continuity of the law to establish a juridical link between those men and power, because power and its workings were a demonstration of the continuity of the law itself. History's other role was to use the almost unbearable intensity of the glory of power, its examples and its exploits, to fascinate men.[23]

Stubbs's history is certainly not about the glories or infamies of power in this sense. Instead of the political transcendental of sovereignty, institutional history posits something like a natural domain of human affairs. F. W. Maitland, a historian admittedly rather more divergent in orientation from Stubbs than is sometimes acknowledged, defined constitutional history in a way that here at least complements Stubbs's approach: "Constitutional history should . . . be a history, not of parties, but of institutions, not of struggles, but of results; the struggles are evanescent, the results are permanent."[24] History in other words is a homogeneous field of continuities, not a divided field of battles and sovereignties; and even where fissures appear, beneath lie continuity, immanence, consistency.

Constitutional history is posed quite specifically against forms of historicism that are tied exclusively to questions of sovereignty and, above all, legitimation through law. History must be seen in terms of the immanence of its own forms, and this not least explains Stubbs's hostility to the philosophy of history, which attempts to impose its own deductive logic on the past.[25] But nor, for Stubbs, is constitutional history simply the history of law. The historical study of law is not the same thing as the legal study of history any more than it is the reduction of law to "theoretic principles."[26] It is well known that Stubbs and other constitutional historians such as Freeman were in some ways hostile to the legal profession and to history understood simply as the history of law.[27] Constitutional history—contra authorities such as A. V. Dicey—was not to be just a history of legal powers but also a history of institutions—including, understandably enough, legal institutions—in their natural contexts, that is, naturalized fields of government in which laws were embedded.[28] Law is thus seen as the effect of institutions more widely and is not simply the object of analysis sui generis. Constitutional history is not just about law; here the constitution is not really a legal framework at all but something more like an assemblage of forms of government, emphasizing above all the freedom engendered in local forms of organization and their continuities over time.

Even Maitland, who was far closer to being something of a bona fide legal historian than Stubbs, insists that law has to be understood in contrast to general jurisprudence, as a living, evolving product of consciousness.[29] Law, for him, has a naturalistic aspect; its very image of itself evolves—even Anglo-Saxon law—and is not the fixed thing misconstrued by jurists and legal historians.[30] This attitude of Stubbs and Maitland is less actually a matter of a resistance to law and lawyers than it is a question of a difference in the image of law that one adopts. Take, for instance, Stubbs's well-known dislike of the Romans and what he saw as the legalism of the empire. For Stubbs, English history is the naturalized history of law and government in their given contexts and not the story of the descent of codified law from the Roman model. In a nutshell, it is about Germans, not Romans. And it is quintessentially the history of freedom. For Stubbs, the object of this history was to be integrally European and thus post-Roman: the history of the "new" nations—France, Germany, England—following the collapse of Rome. But freedom itself is understood as Teutonic, not Greek or Roman; and in some ways—as the whole project of the *Constitutional History* aimed to show—the best Germans, that is, the most Teutonically minded, actually remained the English.[31]

The focus of the history of freedom in constitutional history was not simply to be founded in a "sovereign" institution such as the state. Of course, the state is important; but history shows that government is about more than just the government of the state. The government of men—through law and (especially important for Stubbs) through religion—is naturally best conducted closest to the generative sources of freedom, which is to say at a localized level; hence the historian must himself know this level intimately—and this is not least why his labors must properly belong to the department of history and not to the departments of law or politics.[32] This attitude to state, law, and history entailed an interesting twist on the well-worn idea of the Norman Yoke and its relation to the history of English law.[33] The proponents of those forms of political historicism that bemoaned the Norman presence had argued that the Normans had imposed a foreign despotism on the existing legal institutions of the Anglo-Saxons, thus coding the Normans in terms of illegality and the Saxons in terms of legality. The seventeenth-century debates over these matters unsurprisingly turned on questions of the interpretation of law that was to be applied here. Coke versus Bacon, and so on.

The constitutional historians, however, took a different view from either alternative, one that is quite consonant with—if hardly reducible in an expressive or functionalist sense to—a liberal perspective on government. Stubbs for instance held that the Anglo-Saxons had a naturalized system of law, one indigenous to the culture, if Teutonic in its essence, but that the Normans, by integrating the polity, ironically enough enabled this system to persist, albeit in more centralized and disciplined form. The Normans, in other words, completed what the Anglo-Saxons began. Nor is there much trace of the forms of "race war" of political historicism in the rather special sense of that term deployed by Foucault in the *Society Must Be Defended* lectures. If Freeman was a racist this seems to have been directed at contemporary Turks rather than medieval Normans, while Stubbs's constitutional history was more or less indifferent to the "racial" origins of the protagonists other than to make the point that, in effect, insofar as we are free we are *all* Germans.[34] The nation transcended race, or at least it transcended the race *war*. For after all, if we are all Germans we are also all Normans too, the Normans having supposedly added the virtue of self-restraint to the Anglo-Saxon virtues of freedom and self-reliance.[35]

Stubbs's distinction between medieval and modern history is also of interest here. Modern history, he claims, is the story of ideas and powers, whereas medieval history is the story of law and rights, that is, law as a limitation of power as well as a guarantor of it.[36] Thus medieval history takes as its object not the history of sovereignty or of ideas but the history of freedom organized in the context of the government of men. If there is a seemingly Whiggish twist to the overall picture it is that increasingly such arrangements have focused on questions of land rather than rights and obligations, that the government of men has become increasingly territorial in focus. But for all that this may indeed seem like a Whiggish perspective, it can also be construed as being at least consonant with a liberal one insofar as the function of liberal government is to critique the forms of the government of men in the name of a freedom that applies to populations rather than the sovereignty of territorial accumulation. Constitutional history is not least a critique of the overterritorialization of the concerns of law at the expense of freedom; it is a critique in the name of freedom. And without being a reflection on freedom, what uses would there be for the pursuit of history?[37]

Certainly, a critical perspective is very much part of the liberal coloring of Stubbs's project. He regarded the activity of historical research as a critically reflexive project in a way that, again, bears some contrast with then-prevalent understandings of legal expertise. The function of history, for Stubbs, is ethical more than just legal: "at once the process of acquisition of stocks of facts ... and ... an educational discipline directed at the cultivation of powers for whose development, as it seems to me, no other training is efficacious."[38] The legal expert merely applies the letter of the law; the historian cultivates understanding. This means that history is better preparation for the arts of government than is law—a view that, of course, in Stubbs's case at least, has to be taken in the context of the struggles over law and history that led up to the separation of the Oxford history faculty from that of law in 1871.[39]

To sum up, constitutional history concerns itself with the history of freedom under the immanent conditions of government. It is not a form of political or, still less, ideological historicism any more than it is "Roman history," the royal or state history of sovereignty, or the history of law. Although it may not simply be an expression of a liberal mentality of government, it is not necessarily in contradiction to it, and perhaps—at most—there is a sort of integral affinity between certain kinds of constitutional history and liberalism understood as a technology of government.

LIMITATIONS

At the beginning of these reflections I suggested that there were necessarily to be limitations to any argument linking certain forms of history—in this case constitutional history—to the phenomenon of liberalism. As I have emphasized, it is not a question of saying that an outlook such as that of Stubbs is *inherently* liberal in a political or overtly ideological sense. For one thing, there are other, rival ways to think about it. John Burrow has stressed what he sees as its conservative, Burkean provenance in political terms.[40] Actually this does not seem quite right. For Burke, continuity and tradition were paramount. Revolutions, dramatic change—these interrupted the continuities. For Stubbs, there is continuity, but there is also conflict. Continuity is what lies beneath conflict, beneath the revolutions and conquests—which were themselves seemingly facts of life, facts of history, not necessarily to be regretted.

But in any case Stubbs's approach to history is certainly not the adjunct of a political or ideologically declared liberalism, though it can be claimed to be something in itself like a liberal historicism—perhaps, as has been suggested here, to be contrasted with the political historicism described by Foucault in the *Society Must Be Defended* lectures. Whereas political historicism—equally opposed to the "Roman model" of history—focused on the historical injustices pertaining between races and classes, liberal historicism was concerned with the historicism of freedom understood not as an absolute value but as a means of governing men in the "natural" state of society. Of course, the focus on the Anglo-Saxon and medieval past was in this sense a projection, the Anglo-Saxons here providing a sort of critical image of the possibilities and limitations of the government of freedom itself. But there is nothing especially surprising or unusual, historiographically speaking, in projection of this sort. Nor was it, needless to say, a question of projecting Anglo-Saxon England *as* a liberal society, only the privileged source for a reflection within a concern for freedom that characterized a later one.

Liberal historicism should not be seen, anyway, as an *expression* of the ideas of political or ideological liberalism. What is at stake is not whether or not Stubbs, or Maitland or whoever, was or was not a political or ideological liberal. If we were just looking for liberals, we might more profitably have focused on Gardiner or Bryce, two historians who were passed over for the Cambridge Regius chair largely because of their political liberalism.[41] Or even Macaulay. But liberal historicism is not the same thing as political liberalism. Indeed, when understood in terms of its relation to government, a liberal historicism could *not* be ideologically or party-specific at all since it would thereby fail to project itself as inherently separate from immediate political concerns and thereby fail in its liberalism itself. In this sense, paradoxically enough, liberal historicism in our sense of the term can *never* be ideologically or politically liberal. Just as, for liberal government, the economy has to be projected as a domain separable from government itself, so does history, for liberalism, have to exist objectively and outside ideological partisanship—in that sense, the very idea of a *liberal* history, unlike, say, a socialist history, would actually be a misnomer if not a contradiction in terms.

But, more than this, it is probably a mistake ever to think of particular schools or thought-styles within disciplines such as history as being *constitutively* liberal or not liberal in any case. Similar thematics can serve divergent ends, as would be clear were there space to discuss here the contrasts between the English version of constitutional history as compared to, say, its German version, the latter being obviously far less amenable to any kind of analysis based on liberal governmental reason. In any case, we need more nuanced ways to think about this sort of problem. According to the way that Foucault seems to have thought about it, liberalism is not a dye that colors everything it contacts; it is rather more like a filament of thought that comes into opposition with and gets sometimes refracted, sometimes reinforced, sometimes deflected by other existing lines of thought. Liberalism or other forms of discursive practice are never simply embedded in history as if so-called modes of government were akin to modes of production. Rather they run through institutions and practices with their own logic but one that is separable from the history of those institutions themselves. We cannot really speak of eras of liberal government, neoliberal government, and so on. At least not in a Foucauldian sense. To invoke liberalism in Foucault's conceptual usage of that term is always to make an abstraction from particular classes, groups, institutions, or persons, an abstraction, indeed, from history—and especially social history—as usually understood.[42] In any case, the conceptual history of forms of liberal governmentality and the social history of actually existing liberalism itself remain—and must remain—necessarily in some tension.

7. Habit, Instinct, Survivals: Repetition, History, Biopower

Tony Bennett

In 1844 Lord Stanley, secretary of state of the Colonial Office, wrote to Sir George Gipps, colonial governor of New South Wales, regarding a report that Gipps had forwarded to him from Captain G. Gray. Drawing on his experience as the commander of an expedition into the interior of Australia, Gray had dwelled on the lackluster results of all the attempts that had so far been made to civilize the Aborigines. Stanley acknowledged that it seemed "impossible any longer to deny" that such attempts "have been unavailing; that no real progress has yet been effected, and that there is not reasonable ground to expect from them greater success in the future."[1] Yet he was reluctant to accept the conclusion that followed from this. Noting that he could not admit "that with respect to them alone the doctrines of Christianity must be inoperative, and the advantages of civilisation incommunicable," he declined to believe that Aborigines "[are] incapable of improvement, and that their extinction before the advance of the white settler is a necessity which it is impossible to control."[2]

Kay Anderson argues that Stanley's equivocations over this matter were symptomatic of a moment when Australian colonial discourses were poised between two options. On the one hand, both Christian salvationist discourses and the secular progressivism of Enlightenment stadial theory allowed—indeed, urged—that the Australian Aborigine might be improved. Set against these views, increasingly influential somatic conceptions of race rooted racial divisions ineradicably in the body and, thereby, removed Aborigines from both the Christian time of salvation and the progressive time of civilization, placing them instead in the dead-end time of extinction as the inevitable losers in the struggle for existence with a superior race. This somatization of race initially took the form of polygenetic accounts of racial divisions that called into question both Christian and Enlightenment accounts of human unity. While Darwin's account of evolution opened up a space in which Aborigines might be enfolded within civilizing programs by denying that racial differences were innate or constituted unbridgeable gaps, Anderson suggests that subsequent developments in anthropology placed Aborigines beyond the reach of such programs by consigning them to the newly historicized twilight zone between nature and culture represented by the category of prehistory. As survivals of the past in the present, Aborigines presented the difficulty not of being innately different but of being too far away in time. Still on the cusp of the journey from nature into culture, they had simply too far to travel across the eons of evolutionary time separating them from the properly historical time of their colonizers before the imperatives of racial competition resulted in their elimination.

I have no quarrels with this account; far from it.[3] However, part of my purpose in this chapter is to argue that the distinctive dynamics that connected a belief in the "unimprovability" of Aborigines and the doctrine of survivals in the late nineteenth and early twentieth century depended on the ways in which the relationships between habit and instinct were reconfigured in the context of post-Darwinian social, political, and anthropological thought. For this pluralized and historicized the concept of innateness in ways that reordered its relations to race. This argument also serves as a vehicle for a broader purpose: to shade and qualify the role that has been attributed to habit within liberal forms of government in the post-Foucauldian literature on governmentality. This has largely been concerned with habit as a mechanism distinguishing where the assumption that individuals are to be governed through their capacities for freedom should apply and where, instead, more coercive forms of rule should be brought into play.[4] Where behavior has become so habituated through frequent repetition that it trespasses on the capacity for the will, guided by reflexive judgment, to be freely exercised, the shutters have been drawn on liberal strategies of rule in favor of reinforcing the mechanisms of habit as an automated form of self-rule. This argument has proved of considerable value in highlighting the wide range of exclusions—of race, class, age, and gender—through which liberal government has been constituted. Its chief limitation is that it fails to take account of the different places that habit has occupied within the architectures of the person associated with different discourses and strategies for organizing "the conduct of conduct." By "architectures of the person," I have in mind what Nikolas Rose characterizes as a historically mutable set of "spaces, cavities, relations, divisions" that are produced by the infolding of diverse ways of partitioning the self and working on its varied parts that are proposed by different authorities.[5] I develop this argument by examining how post-Darwinian social, political, and anthropological thought shifted the place that habit occupied within the architecture of the person that had been proposed by classical liberalism by refashioning its relationship to custom on the one hand and instinct on the other. The consequence of this, I argue, was a distinctive habit-instinct nexus that inscribed the governance of "unimprovable" Aborigines in a specific form of biopower.

First, though, to provide a contrapuntal historical backdrop to these concerns, I look at the role played by the concept of habit in earlier moments in the development of English liberal political thought.

HABIT, CUSTOM, AND THE WILL: A VIRTUOUS CYCLE

Patrick Joyce's account of the anxieties that clustered around the role of habit in mid-nineteenth-century British conceptions of liberal government provides a good point of departure for these concerns. Joyce attributes these anxieties to the position that habit occupied within an architecture of the person wherein, by mediating the relations between desire and compulsion, it problematized the subject as the locus of both stasis and change: "habits are ingrained in nature, but can none the less be broken by the power of the will."[6] If both personal and social development required that the force of habit be broken, this could only be with a view to installing another set of habits in its place. "Habit," as Joyce puts it, "must counter habit."[7] The exercise of the will must both pit itself against habit and instill a new set of routines through which conduct is regulated if the ideal of a constantly self-renovating personhood that is capable of both transforming and stabilizing itself is to be realized so that society might continue to progress through the free activity of its subjects. The case Joyce has most in mind is that of John Stuart Mill's account of the logic of the moral sciences—first published in 1843—which reconciles freedom and necessity by attributing to the will the capacity to remake habits and, by thus reshaping the self and asserting mastery over habitual forms of conduct, to exercise a capacity for moral freedom.[8] In Mill's account, as Melanie White glosses it, "the presence of the 'will' and an established foundation of good habits generate the dispositions necessary for the responsible exercise of freedom," while it is the role of character to judge which habits further and which impede its own moral dynamic and thence to begin "a slow process of developing counter-habits and routines in order to reinforce the will, and also to reflect changes in the moral expression of one's character."[9]

Yet it is notable that at no point does Mill's discussion of habit go beyond the dialectic of will and habit to open up questions concerning the relations between habit and instinct, understood as either a natural foundation for habitual dispositions or a hereditary mechanism for their transmission across generations. In this respect, his account echoes Locke's assessment that education, fashion, and custom prevail over innate dispositions in accounting for habitual regularities of conduct. Mill's view of the part played by reflexive judgment in reviewing the hold of custom similarly echoes Locke's account of the role played by moments of "uneasiness" in opening up to inspection the customs that, through repetition, have come to be installed as the habits that constitute a particular "relish of the mind."[10] Here, then, in Locke's account, habit operates as a vital mechanism in a virtuous cycle through which conduct is endlessly shaped and reshaped.

This stands in contrast to Kant, for whom habit, understood as instinct, stood in a vertiginous opposition to the will, which, in accordance with the Kantian project of purifying subjectivity to free it from all material contingencies, had little habitual about it. In *Anthropology from a Pragmatic Point of View*, Kant distinguishes physical anthropology's concern with "what nature makes of the human being" from a pragmatic orientation toward anthropology concerned with "the investigation of what he as a free acting being makes of himself, or can and should make of himself."[11] As such, he attributes habit wholly to natural or quasi-natural forms of conduct that, since they are driven by necessity, are devoid of moral significance. Since it "is a physical inner necessitation to proceed in the same manner that one has proceeded until now," Kant argues, habit "deprives even good actions of their moral worth because it impairs the freedom of the mind."[12] For Kant, this association of habit with instinct aligns it with nature. Habit arouses disgust because "here one is led *instinctively* by the rule of habituation, exactly like another (non-human) nature, and so runs the risk of falling into one and the same class with the beast."[13] The only exception that is admitted to the rule that "all habits are reprehensible"[14] is where they testify to the power of intentionality versus nature, as in the adoption of mechanical culinary habits to offset the effects of old age. Here, then, far from being inscribed as a mechanism in a virtuous circle of conduct formation, habit is clasped together with instinct as a couplet through which the power of nature as necessity works and to which the power of culture—understood as the capacity for free self-shaping—stands opposed. "The animal creature he sets up as a foil to the human being," Sankar Muthu argues of Kant, 'is instinctively driven. The movement from animality to humanity is one toward freedom and culture."[15]

It is this aspect of Kant's work that informs Mill's later essay *On Liberty* (1859). Unlike his earlier discussion that focused on the relations between habit and the will, Mill's discussion here is organized in terms of the contrast between custom and character: "A person whose desires and impulses are his own—are the expression of his own nature, as it has been developed and modified by his own culture—is said to have a character. One whose desires and impulses are not his own, has no character, no more than a steam-engine has a character."[16]

Where character is an inoperative force, however, this is because conduct is subject to the despotism of custom rather than the grip of habit. Although there are often areas of overlap between them, the two concepts are not identical. Custom, as Colin Campbell notes, may, as in the case of sutteeism, consist of singular rather than frequently repeated acts, just as the reasons for taking part in such acts may rest on conscious volition rather than—as the stock definition of habit—mechanical, unthinking repetition.[17] In Mill's case, the despotism of custom is sometimes attributed to such a mechanism. He attributes conformity to custom among some peoples to their lack of any faculty except that of "the ape-like one of imitation."[18] This is not, however, the organizing core of Mill's account. If the spirits of liberty, progress, and improvement are the attributes of character that stand opposed to custom, these can only flourish where they are supported by the political conditions of democracy, which—through the mechanism of discussion—allows individual variation to become an active force in social life. "I have said," Mill writes, "that it is important to give the freest scope possible to uncustomary things, in order that it may in time appear which of these are fit to be converted into customs."[19] Conversely, the despotism of custom prevails wherever the mechanisms of discussion are underdeveloped or held in check. It is this aspect of the character/custom opposition that serves as the basis for Mill's account of the distinction between societies with and without history in the sense that Koselleck gives to this term: that is, the expectation that the future will be different from both the present and the past as a result of the changes initiated by self-conscious subjects acting within developmental time.[20] Here again, then, where character serves as a principle that can call custom to account, habit, custom, and the will interact as parts of a virtuous cycle of character formation but one that develops along a progressive historical trajectory.

However, if history is impossible where these conditions do not apply, this is because, for different reasons in different historical circumstances, character and custom have locked in on one another in vicious, self-enclosing cycles of immobility. Mill thus interprets Asiatic societies as societies that while once historically dynamic have since exited from history through the enforcement of custom associated with "Oriental despotism." By contrast, he construes primitive societies as ones that have never entered history, either because they are societies in which "the race itself may be considered as in its nonage"[21]or because they are "anterior to the time when mankind have become capable of being improved by free and equal discussion."[22]

These, then, are some of the ways in which the concept of habit informed the early development of modern liberal political thought. Its role in this regard, however, varied depending on the place it occupied in relation to adjacent concepts within different architectures of the person that laid out different relations of internal action of the self on self (will:habit/culture:instinct/character:custom) as one of the mechanisms through which liberal government operates. It is against this background that I look next at how the place of character within the architecture of the person mutated in relation to what Stefan Collini calls the "historicisation of character," which played a key role in the last quarter of the nineteenth century in the transition from the earlier laissez-faire orientation of classical liberalism to the formulations of the new liberalism that envisaged a more interventionist role for the state, in particular, in aiding the development of character.[23] This was, however, no longer a character system organized in terms of either an opposition or a virtuous cycle between will and habit, culture and instinct, or character and custom. Rather it laid out the person as a series of historicized, developmental gradations between custom, habit, and instinct—that is, more in the form of a slope than an opposition—and interpreted instinct not as a pure nature opposed to culture but as an accumulating stock of conscious actions passed on into the automated forms of instinct via the mediatory roles of habit and inheritance.

The main intellectual development prompting this revision of the earlier character system of classical liberalism was Darwin's *Origin*. Published in the same year as Mill's *On Liberty*, this prompted a succession of attempts—on the part of Walter Bagehot,[24] Henry Maudsley,[25] and Lloyd Morgan,[26] for example—to account for how the forms of conduct acquired by habit in one generation could be passed on to the next as a set of inherited instincts by being deposited in the nervous system or some equivalent quasi-physical mechanism. This was, of course, very much a case of "creative treason," which, as Laura Otis notes, owed less to Darwin, who by and large resisted the view that characteristics acquired by one generation could be inherited by the next, than it did to Baptiste Lamarck's account of the inheritance of acquired characteristics and, later, to Ernst Haeckel's biogenetic "law" that ontogeny recapitulates phylogeny.[27] More fundamentally, perhaps, the view that living beings are shaped by their interactions with their environment depends on a Lamarckian conception of the relations between the organism and its milieu, in contrast to the emphasis Darwin placed on the struggle between different forms of life as the chief mechanism of variation.[28] Nonetheless, the result was a decisive refashioning of the architecture of the person that, as Otis summarizes it, introduced a new element into this architecture—that of "organic memory," which "placed the past *in* the individual, *in* the body, *in* the nervous system"[29]—while also laying out the person as a part of developmental sequence in which conscious and unconscious processes, the social environment and nature, interacted in new ways. It was an architecture within which "memory and heredity, habit and instinct" operated "as points on a continuum" leading to a "steady accumulation" of competencies across generations, and which meant that the body could be read as "a record, a palimpsest, perhaps, of its interaction with its environment, in its own lifetime, in its grandparents' lifetimes, and in the lifetimes of its distant ancestors."[30]

It is the place accorded habit within such historicist revisions of character by the late-nineteenth-century generation of social, sociobiological, and anthropological theorists that especially concerns me here. My interest centers on the role they played in fashioning one of the more peculiar forms of liberal modernity associated with imperial Britain in the new terms of intelligibility they proposed for the "unimprovability" of Aborigines and their consequences for the development of new forms of biopolitical administration.

FROM HABIT TO INSTINCT: SOMATIC ACCUMULATION, EVOLUTION, HISTORY

In her preface to the English translation of Félix Ravaisson's *Of Habit*,[31] Catherine Malabou locates its concerns at the junction of two philosophical traditions. The first, following a line from Aristotle through Hegel to Bergson, treats habit as a constitutive aspect of human existence: that is, as a permanent disposition and a virtue in stabilizing conduct. The second, operating in terms of the mind-body dualisms that run from Descartes to Kant, interprets habit as pure negativity: "the disease of repetition that threatens the freshness of thought and stifles the voice . . . of the categorical imperative."[32] Malabou argues that Raivaisson's text mediates the relations between these two traditions by interpreting the stabilities produced by the repetitive mechanisms of habit as the precondition for the acquisition of an aptitude for change through which living beings are able to take part in the production of an open-ended future.

A key aspect of Ravaisson's argument here concerns his account of the relations between habit and instinct. In contrast to Kant, who places both of these on the side of nature in opposition to culture and the will, Ravaisson places habit between the will and instinct, interpreting it as the mechanism that translates actions initiated by the will into a "second order" set of instincts through which "primitive instinct" is transformed into an accumulating set of competencies. "Habit," as Ravaisson puts it, "transforms voluntary movements into instinctive movements."[33] This posits an architecture of the person in which "habit is the dividing line, or the middle term, between will and nature; but it is a moving middle term, a dividing line that is always moving, and which advances by an imperceptible progress from one extremity to the other."[34] It is not, however, only the dispositions of the individual that are affected in this way. It is through the linking mechanism of habit that nature itself is gradually transformed. "In descending gradually from the clearest regions of consciousness," Ravaisson argues, "habit carries with it light from those regions into the depths and dark night of nature."[35] The result is an ascending slope, without any abrupt transitions or dualistic oppositions of a Kantian type, through which all forms of life—from the will or motive activity to the simplest forms of life—are connected via the mechanism of habit.

Ravaisson's work was informed by contemporary developments in physiology and had a continuing influence on the subsequent deployment of the life sciences, where it provided a materially grounded alternative to the antinomies of Kantian philosophy. This was true of the development of the relations between biological and social evolutionism in Britain. In *The Principles of Psychology*, for example, Herbert Spencer accounts for the differentiation of reason and the will from the instincts not as a set of constitutively different faculties but as the outcome of evolutionary processes of differentiation in which habit and—as an addition to Ravaisson's formulations—memory mediate the relations between reason, will, and instinct. The individual organism, Spencer argues, responds to changes in its environment that it experiences as external shocks; frequent recurrence of the same shocks produces corresponding changes in the internal structure and dispositions of the organism; such repeated changes in dispositional behavior lead to progressively more complex divisions in the organization of the nervous system. If Spencer attributes the development of reflexes and instincts, and the higher faculties of will and reason, to this same general process, his subscription to a Lamarckian conception of the relations between milieu and organism allows for the transgenerational accumulation of competencies as a set of hereditable instincts.

The relations between "conscious memory" and "organic memory" (Otis borrows the term from Spencer) are central to this process. Conscious memory comes into play when the connections between a particular set of psychic states induced by changes in the milieu are no longer coordinated through the automatic mechanism of habit; and it passes away when such coordination once again becomes automatic by being passed on as part of an accumulated instinctual inheritance that is transmitted to the next generation via organic memory. Here Spencer remains faithful to the assumptions of Locke's empirical psychology while simultaneously recasting them. True, there are no innate faculties or ideas prior to experience, but this does not rule out the possibility of there being historical forms of innateness that are the somatic accumulation of the successive experiences of past generations that have come to be coded into the body as a set of compound instincts. And it is only this accumulating legacy of past experience that opens up the space and the time within which the higher faculties of reason and the will might emerge and be exercised. There is no break here between habit and the will, just a seamless transition: "And this [sic], the cessation of automatic action and the dawn of volition, are one and the same thing."[36]

Henry Maudsley, whose writing on habit and the will played a significant role in late-nineteenth- and early-twentieth-century liberal thought,[37] similarly stresses that there is "no break or pause in the ascent from monad to man."[38] Simple reflex actions depend on "a nervous machinery formed and fitted through remote ages now to act automatically,"[39] whereas acquired reflex actions are subject to gradual formation through repeated practice, eventually becoming automatic. The exercise of the latter is an art the individual learns for himself, whereas the performance of the former is "a function which has been learnt for him in a dateless past and he now inherits ready-made."[40] The will is merely "the present culmination of organic evolution,"[41] and, as such, it is the result of "the same process at work now by virtue of which in the remote past the habits of prehistoric ancestors have become the instinctive and reflex faculties of today."[42] But this is true only for some races as Maudsley goes on to differentiate races in terms of the depths of their inheritance of the somatic accumulation of the experience of earlier generations: the deeper the inheritance, the further the race has progressed. This leads him to suggest that habit might serve as a mechanism that will eventually "perfect a rational and moral nature of the human species" by bringing the habits of less-developed races under the influence of more civilized ones. However, he immediately closes the door on this prospect, protesting "how puerile and pernicious a practice it is to attempt to force the habits of one level of civilisation on people who are on a lower level, especially on those who are on a level of barbarism."[43] The problem here, given an architecture of the person laid out as a set of dispositions linearly connected to one another along an evolutionary trajectory, is one of sequence. How can the habits of those with fully developed somatic inheritances be grafted onto those for whom inheritance remains at a prehistoric level? It was in response to this problem—a problem produced by the doctrine of survivals developed during the interval that separates Maudsley's and Spencer's texts—that new, biopolitical terms of reference were brought to bear on the question of the Aborigine's capacity for improvement.

EXITING HISTORY: SOMATIC AND CULTURAL "FLAT-LINING" AND THE LOGIC OF BIOPOWER

Let me recap. My purpose so far has been to consider the different roles that have been accorded habit depending how it has been distinguished from or aligned with other aspects of conduct in the architectures of personhood associated with different tendencies in British liberal social and political thought. However, these are not always so clearly distinguishable in practice. To the contrary, elements of different traditions were quite frequently in play in debates concerning the relations between habit and the regulation of conduct. Their implications for the "unimprovability" of Aborigines were consequently framed in different ways at different points in time, even by the same person. This was true of Baldwin Spencer, who initially construed the conservatism he attributed to the Arunta[44] of Central Australia in the terms proposed by Mill's account of the opposition between the despotism of custom and the democratic principle of discussion as the chief mechanism through which variation is introduced into a polity.

> As among all savage tribes the Australian native is bound hand and foot by custom. What his fathers did before him he must do. If during the performance of a ceremony his ancestors painted a white line across the forehead, that line he must paint. Any infringement of custom, within certain limitations, is visited with sure and often severe punishment. At the same time, rigidly conservative as the native is, it is yet possible for change to be introduced.[45]

To account for how such limited kinds of change might come about, Spencer invokes the principle of discussion. However, he does so in a way that explains how change can occur (it is prompted by the discussions that take place when different local groups meet) but at the same time be constrained within definite limits (these discussions are not free discussions between equals of a kind necessary to promote variation but are dominated by the authority of male elders with the result that change is possible only within the conservative limits endorsed by those elders).

There is nothing surprising in this. As the son of a Manchester nonconformist liberal family, Spencer—a prominent academic and museum administrator—was well schooled in classical liberalism. He was, as a natural historian by training and an ethnographer by vocation, equally well schooled in Darwinian thought and its application to the fields of anthropology and archaeology. While never eschewing his earlier position, his later explanations of the "unimprovability" of Aborigines drew more on the terms of a racialization that inscribed backwardness in the body by interpreting the Aborigine as the product of a bloodline that had failed to respond to the dynamics of competition.[46] The problem here, to recall Anderson's account, was that of being too far away in time to be susceptible to the influence of civilizing programs. However, this comprised less a shift from innatist conceptions of race than a historicization of the basis on which innatist racial distinctions were drawn. In contrast to polygenetic accounts of innateness, Spencer and his contemporaries drew on the post-Darwinian traditions, discussed above, in which innateness had been historicized. Different races were the bearers of the different "innatenesses" that they inherited as a consequence of the ways in which the dynamics of the relations between will, reason, habit, and instinct had been played out in earlier generations.

It is in this respect that the doctrine of survivals—the keystone, according to George Stocking,[47] of late Victorian imperial anthropology—played such a crucial role in both the conception and administration of race in colonial contexts. Initially elaborated by Edward Tylor,[48] it organized what Patrick Wolfe calls the "spatiotemporal triad" of imperial modernity, a triad consisting in "'our' (i.e. Europeans') savage past, 'their' (i.e. colonised natives') ethnographic present, and 'our' civilised present."[49] The aspect of this doctrine that is most relevant to my concerns here consists in the role it accorded rituals as part of a distinctive technique for deciphering the relations between past and present. Wolfe attributes this partly to anthropology's need for an object of analysis and a technique of decipherment that would legitimate its claims to disciplinary autonomy by distinguishing its objects and methods from those of geology and philology, which provided the master discourses for interpreting the remote past by means of the material and/or textual forms it had left behind. He finds the model for Tylor's move, however, in Max Müller's "disease of language" theory. Initially propounded in 1861, this argued that linguistic forms continued to circulate after their original meanings had been lost or had withered. Tylor latched on to the role Müller attributed to empty, mechanical repetition in accounting for the persistence of such withered forms of language use. For it suggested that rituals, too, might be construed as practices that had persisted through time in a similar "withered" form and might therefore serve as extant carriers of their original meanings.

This, then, provided imperial anthropology with its distinctive disciplinary maneuver through which the analysis of current ritual practices could also serve as the means for reconstructing a prehistoric culture that still survived in the present. It was this disciplinary maneuver that presented the "unimprovability" of Aborigines in a new light in their constitution as a site of both somatic and cultural "flat-lining": that is, of persisting, like an electrical time-sequence measurement that shows no activity, constantly on the same level. This was not, however, because the persistence of rituals meant that the role of habit per se was too strong among "primitive" peoples. The problem was rather that, in the case of "the primitive," the dynamic set of relations posited by Ravaission and, later, in a more evolutionary framework, by Herbert Spencer through which responses to a changed environment are worked through from conscious action via habit into instinct so as to build up a progressively accumulating set of instincts is blocked, locked in on itself, through the endless repetition of an original habit-into-instinct cycle. The consequence of this for Aborigines, paradoxically, was that they were depicted as having *too thin* a stock of instincts to be civilizable. Still on the cusp of the transition from nature to culture, Aboriginal conduct is interpreted as being guided by an original set of instincts—by, in Ravaisson's terms, a primitive rather than a secondary nature. To the degree that these have been repeated over the intervening millennia as survivals of an incomplete transition from nature to culture, so their power is increased by dint of the force of repetition, with the consequence that they now exercise a more or less ironlike grip on conduct. This logic is clearly discernible in Henry Pitt Rivers's account of the reasoning underlying his anthropological collection in which he adapts Tylor's account of survivals to interpret the tools and weapons of "primitive" peoples as similarly survivals of earlier forms. Drawing on both Spencer's *Principles of Psychology* and Tylor's *Primitive Culture*, as well as John Lubbock's equally influential *Prehistoric Times*,[50] and presenting his argument as an evolutionary confirmation and extension of Locke's critique of innate ideas, Pitt Rivers construes the relations between habit and instinct in both animals and humans as being governed by essentially the same principles.[51] Just as the habits acquired by animals via either domestication or their reasoning on experience become instinctive and are passed on as such to their offspring, so similar processes are involved in the relations between the roles played by the "intellectual mind" and the "automaton mind" in regulating human conduct.

> We are conscious of an intellectual mind capable of reasoning upon unfamiliar occurrences, and of an automaton mind capable of acting intuitively in certain matters without effort of the will or consciousness. And we know that habits acquired by the exercise of conscious reason, by constant habit, become automatic, and then they no longer require the exercise of conscious reason to direct the actions, as they did at first.[52]

The conclusion Pitt Rivers draws from this is that "every action which is now performed by instinct, has at some former period in the history of the species been the result of conscious experience."[53] This conception forms part of a mechanism of development according to which the more that simple ideas derived from experience are passed on into the automated forms of instinct, the freer the person is to respond to new and more complex ideas. The key hinge in this mechanism is habit, which Pitt Rivers interprets as a form of conscious learning involving the intellectual mind but which then becomes routinized via repetition. It is through habit that the lessons of experience are passed on into instinct in accordance with an accumulative logic in which the completion of one habit-to-instinct cycle frees up the space for another such cycle, leading to an ever-growing set of instinctual responses constituting the automated mind.

The colonial sting in the tail of this argument comes when Pitt Rivers argues that "the tendency to automatic action upon any given set of ideas will be in proportion to the length of time during which the ancestors of the individual have exercised their minds in those particular ideas."[54] This is why lower animals, whose instincts have not been modified to the same degree as those of higher animals, are more predisposed toward automatic forms of action: they have practiced the same set of automated responses for longer, with a consequent increase in their hold on behavior. The position of the Aborigine is broadly similar. Poised forever on the cusp of the nature/culture divide, the Aborigine never moves beyond simply imitating natural forms and adapting these for certain purposes (Pitt

Rivers accounts for the development of stone-age tools in these terms), which are then performed repeatedly across generations. The consequence is that "in proportion to the length of time during which this association of ideas continued to exist in the minds of successive generations of the creatures which we may now begin to call men," then so "would be the tendency on the part of the offspring to continue to select and use these particular forms, more or less instinctively—not, indeed, with that unvarying instinct which in animals arises from the perfect adaptation of their internal organism to the external condition, but with that modified instinct which assumes the form of a *persistent conservatism*."[55] For the savage and especially, as Pitt Rivers's paradigm of savagery, the Aborigine, the problem is that the mechanism of habit has not worked with sufficient vigor to build up an accumulated stock of "modified instincts" but only a thin layer of these, which, due their endless repetition over millennia, have acquired an unusually binding grip on conduct. Pitt Rivers does not cite him, but Bagehot's formulations point in the same direction. When he asks what the difference is between prehistoric man and "modern-day savages," Bagehot answers that the former were "savages without the fixed habits of savages."[56] In all other respects identical, prehistoric man "differed in this from our present savages, that he had not had time to ingrain his nature so deeply with bad habits, and to impress bad beliefs so unalterably on his mind as they have. They have had age to fix the stain on themselves, but primitive man was younger and had no such time."[57]

As an armchair anthropologist, Pitt Rivers wrote at a distance from the immediacies of colonial rule—as did Tylor, Bagehot, and Maudsley. Nonetheless, their formulations contributed to the organization of the discursive ground that mediated the relations between the "settler" and the Aboriginal populations in late-nineteenth- and twentieth-century Australia. Baldwin Spencer's role was pivotal in this regard. Having worked alongside Henry Balfour in arranging Pitt Rivers's collection for display at Oxford before he moved to Melbourne, he was also acquainted with Tylor, in a period of imperial science when Australia's scientific institutions were still, to a considerable albeit diminishing extent, colonial outposts of British—and mainly English—institutions. This background, together with his network of European correspondents and the pivotal role of his fieldwork in relation to Durkheim's account of primitive religion, gave him unparalleled scientific authority at a time when anthropology had a significant influence on the administrative arrangements through which the changing dynamics of the relations between white and black Australia were played out.

These took distinctive forms governed by the logic of settler colonialism, which, as Patrick Wolfe reminds us, is best understood as a structure rather than as an event, and one that persists, taking different forms in different historical moments.[58] Since the primary object of settler colonialism is possession of the land rather than the surplus to be derived from mixing indigenous labor with the land, it aims at the elimination of the indigenous population. In the Australian case, Wolfe argues, this structure has taken three forms: frontier confrontation aimed at the annihilation of the colonial population; incarceration pending the inevitability of the Aborigines' extinction faced with competition from a superior race; and assimilation via managed programs of epidermal and cultural integration with the white population. Beliefs in the "unimprovability" of Aborigines figured prominently in the second and third stages where they operated in accordance with the imperatives of biopower according to which the power to "make live" by improving the health and conditions of life of the population is counterbalanced by the right to "let die" by eliminating "the biological threat to the improvement of the species or race."[59] It is for this reason, Foucault suggests, that evolutionism played such a key role in nineteenth-century colonial practice: "Whenever, in other words, there was a confrontation, a killing or the risk of death, the nineteenth century was quite literally obliged to think about them in the form of evolutionism. If you are functioning in the biopower mode, how can you justify the need to kill people, to kill populations, and to kill civilisations? By using the theme of evolutionism, by appealing to a racism."[60]

Evolutionary accounts of the mechanisms through which habit is translated into instinct provided a warrant for the exercise of biopower where, in the case of "primitive" peoples, the regular functioning of these mechanisms had been blocked. For the form of repetition that this embodies generated what Pitt Rivers called the insuperable problem of sequence: "Or two nations in very different stages of civilisation may be brought side by side, as is the case in many of our colonies, but there can be no amalgamation between them. Nothing but the vices and imperfections of the superior culture can coalesce with the inferior culture without break of sequence."[61]

It was this problem of sequence that Maudsley had in mind when querying the rationality of attempts to enforce the habits of higher levels of civilization on people of a lower level. Yet he goes on to suggest that the very attempt to civilize savages constituted a kind of ruse in which nature and culture conspire to translate the imperatives of competition into their inevitable outcome.

However, as the thing is persistently and pertinaciously done by the higher people moved by a holy impulse to confer the blessings of their civilization and religion, albeit at the cost of the destruction of the lower peoples, we may conclude that the disintegration of the social structure inevitably produced and the demoralization of the people by the disorganization of the cerebral reflexes constituting their mental fabric and serving their needs are the ordained needs by which nature degrades and finally eliminates the weaker races of men and promotes the survival and growth of the stronger races. And although the lower peoples may not feel happy to serve only as organic steps to build up a higher people, yet there is no help for it; they must suffer and die that the race may live and be strong.[62]

It is often rightly objected that Foucauldian accounts of governmental rationalities pay insufficient attention to the more variable, muddied, and muddled administrative arrangements that result from their translation into actual political programs and policies.[63] Maudsley's text was written in 1902, a year after the Federation of Australia, after which the earlier logics of settler colonialism progressively gave way to that of assimilation in the context of the development of a national governmental project and the associated formation of what Tim Rowse calls "an Aboriginal domain" that aimed to integrate the Aboriginal population within the state.[64] This was, however, no simple transmission, with, after 1901, a significant variety of administrative arrangements continuing to order the relations between white and black Australia.[65] The same was true of the discursive mediations of white/Aborigine relations that continued to draw on the mixed legacy of nineteenth-century polygenetic and evolutionary conceptions. However, two tendencies stand out. The first consists in the progressive marginalization of those nineteenth-century missionary and philanthropic initiatives that, in some cases with government support, had aimed to civilize Aborigines, or to help them civilize themselves, by providing means for them to gain access to the resources of Christian and European civilization.[66] The second consisted in the exercise of new form of biopower that aimed, through the strategy of assimilation, to breed out the race by separating "half-castes"—now viewed, in a new light, as improvable on the grounds that their mixed bloodlines meant that they no longer posed an insuperable problem of sequence. "Half-castes" were to be civilized in special stations designed for their improvement, and intermarriage between them would lead to the progressive dilution of the race across generations. In the meantime, "full-bloods" were to be left to go their own way as decaying survivals.

Of course, there were many aspects to white accounts of Aboriginal backwardness: the fragility of their social and cultural forms, the morally and physically deteriorating consequences of their susceptibility to the "vices of civilization," and so on. It is, however, in the frequent reference to their inability to adapt, to their inertia, that the historical force of the habit-instinct nexus, and its racialization, was evident in the new twist it gave to earlier discourses of unimprovability. The most influential conduit for the translation of this nexus into administrative programs was Baldwin Spencer, whose work as a museum director and anthropologist drew substantially on the work of Pitt Rivers. Although initially opposing the separation of half-castes, Spencer later came to endorse and, indeed, implement such programs in the 1920s during the period he was responsible for the administration of Aboriginal affairs in the Northern Territory.[67] The continuing effects of this evolutionary habit-instinct nexus are also evident in the formulations of the anthropologist A. P. Elkin. In 1932—expressing a view he was later to revise—he attributed the failure of Aborigines to adapt to the requirements of a more advanced culture to their inherited racial constitution: "We are almost forced to realise the possibility that the aboriginal race may have been so completely adapted biologically as well as mentally to its own cultural environment that it cannot adapt itself to a culture of a different type, or, in other words, that it lacks the 'ethnic capacity' to become civilised."[68]

We can hear here the legacy of a very peculiar, and deadly, set of relations between liberal modernity and imperial Britain that reached far beyond Britain's shores and outlasted the imperial phase proper. Its logic as a form of governmentality depended on a particular ordering of the relations between habit, will, and instinct that, instead of functioning as a coercive mechanism at the heart of liberal forms of self-rule, laid out the relations between races in ways that organized the exercise of a distinctive form of biopower. The opposition that habit was caught up in here was not one in which Aborigines were to be subjected to the mechanisms of drill and discipline rather than be treated as persons capable of self-governance through the exercise of will. This set of options was no longer on the agenda. The issues were rather posed in terms of survival, with the habit-instinct nexus and its role in relation to the problem of sequence, defined in terms of bloodlines, guiding where the dividing line should be drawn between where the powers to "make live" or "let die" should be exercised.

8. Entertainmentality!

*Liberalizing Modern Pleasure in the Victorian
Leisure Industry*

Peter Bailey

Foucault and company may never have played the London Coliseum or
Hackney Empire, but their identification of various forms of social discipline—governmentality—operating at large in a modern liberal society suggests how the entertainment business also worked to construct a
distinct regime of pleasure and cultural power. An improvised term to
be treated with the qualified indulgence extended to the show biz hype
considered below, "entertainmentality!" is taken to denote both a certain
structural and normative mode of governance in everyday life and the
mentalité or emotional economy it constructs in the modern subject.[1] A
prototype modern entertainment business, the Victorian music hall and
its leading players exemplify the industrial restructuring of capital, labor,
artifact, and consumer that produced entertainmentality and its rationalization of pleasure in a liberal society greatly exercised by issues of social
freedom and the problem of leisure. This rationalization was a combined
discursive and material operation, the shaping of affect and appetite by
language, symbolism, and logistics. Discursively this was secured in the
course of an intense debate over the legitimate claims of leisure in the
realization of a liberalized good life and the open and benevolent embrace
of pleasure and desire, distilled in an all-purpose rhetoric of "fun." In a
second, closely related process rationalization was triumphantly inscribed
in the material fabric and practice of the corporate music halls of the late
century as the industry channeled the new language of pleasure in its own
potent modern aesthetic.

Considered here first, the debate on leisure that both contested and fertil-
ized its capitalist exploitation was long running and extensive in discourse
and application. A precipitate of industrialization and urban expansion,
modern leisure was the largely unexpected and less than wholly welcome

child of modernity. Emerging in the first half of the nineteenth century, this newly compartmentalized locus in time and space was quickly registered as a threat to social and political order. Middle-class vigilantes regarded the new leisure zone as dangerously unpoliced frontier territory where the new work disciplines of the factory would dissolve and the moral disciplines of their own culture might crumble. Obliged by their liberal principles to acknowledge the freedoms justly claimed for leisure—"Free trade and free self-culture are all bound up in the same bundle"—yet subject to severe evangelical strictures on play and public amusements, middle-class reformers sought to construct a regime of "rational recreation." Modern leisure was to be measured and purposive, formalized in a new range of institutions and practices from a reformed athleticism to that remarkable phenomenon the pub with no beer. Rational recreation was "re-creation, the creation anew of fresh strength for tomorrow's work." Gladstone exemplified the new ideal, declaring recreation to be nought but change of employment, refreshing himself for the toils of high office in the arduous pleasures of tree felling on his country estate.[2]

Yet any overt pleasure derived from this new improved leisure remained circumscribed by the priorities of the work ethic and residual guilt at any shortfall of its purposes. Gladstone's biographer, the Liberal politician John Morley (perhaps with his hero in mind) deplored the utilitarian emphasis of the new sports, undertaken for the good of the body (national as well as personal) rather than for enjoyment. "As one set of objections to pleasure loses its hold," he observed in 1867, "others spring up. . . . [J]ust as we have ceased to believe that pleasure is fatal to salvation, people persuade us that it is fatal to getting on in the world." Hence, he concluded, "the truly earnest are as hostile to pleasure as the truly pious." While softening somewhat in their objections, churchmen were still likely to be both earnest and pious. "Pleasure," allowed the Reverend Henry Haweis, a prominent contemporary of Morley, "is a legitimate incident in life, but not a legitimate end." At all times, moderation was to be its proper measure, urged by Samuel Smiles in *Self-Help*, among many similar voices.[3]

Catching up with pleasure, the first edition of the *Oxford English Dictionary* in 1884 took due note of what it called an "unfavorable" sense of the word: "Sensuous enjoyment as a chief object of life, or end, in itself . . . sometimes personified as a female deity." This echoed an ancient Platonic distinction between serious and corrupt pleasure, the latter identified as the feminine threat to masculine reason and self-discipline. Such unfavorable associations were intensified in the English translation of the most common Latin word for pleasure, *voluptas*. Neutral enough in the original, *voluptuousness* now signified pleasure in its most dangerously sensual form. Thus pleasure came with a considerable historical baggage, its deadly temptations still conspicuous in the sizable fraction of middle-class male voluptuaries pursuing lordly decadence in the disreputable pleasures of the "fast" life of drink, gambling, and sexual marauding. No wonder admonitions of constraint and self-discipline continued to make a powerful impression. John Maynard Keynes's father once smoked a cigar and enjoyed it so much he vowed he would never do it again.[4]

Yet by the end of the century proscriptive caveats were losing their leverage in a new leisure that had become more stabilized and assured, structurally and normatively. Capitalism could now safely concede its workers more frequent and regular breathing space, with standardized installments at the end of the day, the new "English week-end" and, ideally, the end of the year, when an annual summer holiday clinched the trade-off between work and leisure. There were significant gains in earnings, as average per capita incomes rose from the slender margin of 25 percent above subsistence in 1870 to a comfortable 150 percent above in 1914.[5] At the same time, changes in the workplace—the subdivision of labor and the introduction of scientific management in the service as well as manufacturing sectors—further reduced the satisfactions of work, giving leisure an enhanced saliency in the emotional economy. Thus social expectations were increasingly focused on "life off the job," while what before had been offered conditionally was now claimed as a just entitlement. To one wryly perceptive cleric, leisure now constituted "a sort of neutral ground which we may fairly call our own."[6] To the *Women's Industrial News*, championing shop assistants' struggle for better working conditions, it was a natural right of citizenship, "the right in fact, of the free man or woman to absolute control, not over labour, but over leisure."[7] Charles Booth's final survey of the London poor in 1903 registered a major change in attitudes for both sociologist and his subjects: "To what we shall eat, what drink and wherewithal shall we be clothed?" must now be added "how shall we be amused?"[8]

The debate on leisure turned to its greater fulfillment within a larger discourse of betterment, seeking to match the material advances of the age with equivalent social and cultural enrichment. In *Evolution of Modern Capitalism* (1894), J. A. Hobson observed "a people moving along the line of progress, seeking an evermore highly qualitative life," to be realized in intellectual and artistic goods appreciated not for any increase in volume but for their capacity to stimulate individual "thinking and feeling." True fulfillment in leisure required education in its proper aesthetics, the aim of middle-class philanthropic schemes inspired by similar Arnoldian ideals, working for class unity through an elevated common culture of "social citizenship."[9] Socialists too gave attention to the cultivation of leisure as a vital part of a new social order. William Morris and followers believed its regeneration would follow the restoration of craft production and the organic unity of work and play. In the Fabian utilitarian mode, the Webbs spoke of "collectivising the kitchen of life that all may have freedom for the drawing room of life," suggesting an ideal of refinement and good manners. In revulsion at the coarseness of proletarian life and its entertainments, Graham Wallas, a fellow Fabian, declared, "Every child should be brought up a nobleman." Decidedly less elitist were the various associations set up by Robert Blatchford's *Clarion,* the movement's best-selling newspaper. Aiming for the integration of politics and leisure through "the revolutionary use of joyfulness," *Clarion* choirs and rambling and cycling clubs generated a strong sense of fellowship if no great political returns. However convivial, Blatchford's romantic vision of a reborn Merrie England was hostile to what he denounced as the spurious pleasures of commercialized entertainments. The socialist vicar, Stewart Headlam, instituted the Anti-Puritan League within the Fabians, defending music hall and the theatre as worthy pleasures of the people, but most schemes for improved leisure combined a prejudice against existing popular culture with an obtrusive didacticism.[10]

It was the conspicuous new aggregations of mass pleasure seekers, seemingly both manic and sedated, that created most alarm. The Liberal politician and social commentator C. F. G. Masterman combined aesthetic revulsion and deep political unease at what he called "the new civilization of the Crowd," exemplified in the Saturday football spectators in the manufacturing towns: "that congestion of grey, small people with their facile excitements and little white faces inflamed by artificial interest." Masterman attacked the suburban lower middle classes for their susceptibility to "the huge ignorance of the music hall and the yellow newspaper" while worrying that "extravagance and excitement are common to all classes." Hobson identified the same disturbing symptoms in the ultra-patriotic hysteria of music hall audiences. The radical journalist W. T. Stead branded the Boer War "a Music Hall war," its "colossal ineptitude" attributed to entertainment he reviled as "drivel for the dregs."[11]

Sexualized display and exploitation was the target for the National Vigilance Association (NVA), moral reformers battling permissiveness in a variety of ancient and modern forms. In 1894 a female commando from the NVA, which was caricatured as "Prudes on the Prowl," led a campaign against the halls, attacking the seminude tableaux of "Living Pictures" and the parade of prostitutes working the fashionable promenade of the Empire in Leicester Square. Together with the Oscar Wilde trial and Max Nordau's attack on European decadence in *Degeneration* in 1895, this issue provoked feverish public debate over sexuality, morals, and the threat of national meltdown. The Aesthetic Movement of the eighties was charged with beginning the rot with its reprehensible "new gospel . . . urging us to ransack life for pleasurable sensations, to live and enjoy the uttermost."[12]

A prominent evangelist for this new secular gospel was the ardently progressive Darwinian philosopher and novelist, Grant Allen, who proclaimed the "The New Hedonism" in a notorious article in the *Fortnightly Review* in 1894. For Allen, the new hedonism, or "shedonism," meant the pursuit of aesthetic beauty manifested in an idealized free love that escaped the imprisonment of conventional marriage. This would, he claimed, afford a fuller realization of life's pleasures, effected by an inversion of the old morality. "Be virtuous and you will be happy," was to be rewritten as, "Be happy and you will be virtuous." Self-development was to triumph over self-sacrifice.[13] Wilde supported Allen, prophesying "a new Hedonism that was to recreate life and save it from that harsh uncomely Puritanism having its curious revival." Another supporter was the poet Richard Le Gallienne, an accountant and lay preacher from Liverpool who had moved to London, Frenchified his name, and adopted Wilde's flamboyant persona. "The new spirit of pleasure," he claimed, "blows from no mere coterie of hedonistic philosophers but comes on the four winds." As anthem for the cause, Le Gallienne embraced "Ta-ra-ra-boom-de-ay!" the sensational music hall song and dance hit by Lottie Collins that fueled the charges of decadence against popular as well as high culture.[14]

"Ta-ra-ra-boom-de-ay" was "fun," a property of pleasure awarded exalted status by the Edwardian literati in reaction against Victorian high-mindedness. Fun was celebrated as an instinctive capacity for joy, encouraged as an antidote to the tensions of an overheated civilization. Its elemental cleansing properties were rooted in the spontaneous play of childhood, a potentially spiritual resource in a more joyous secular theology that privileged laughter as a divine gift, even a form of grace. As humor it was urged as a necessary act of social rebellion, in anticipation of Freud's interpretation of the joke. And fun was suddenly a hot property in the commercialized literary market place with its philosopher wits like Shaw and Wilde.[15] The newly lauded fun was to become a rhetorical stock-in-trade of the era's thrusting leisure entrepreneurs.

Big-city pleasure seekers were now served by a constellation of new leisure products and amenities controlled by an aggressive nexus of closely related corporate interests in entertainment, catering, retail, and the press. London in particular offered a concentration of the new sites of leisure consumption—cafés, restaurants, grand hotels, department stores, exhibition halls, music halls—as well as refurbished staple attractions in handsome new pubs and theatres.[16] In varying degrees the new spaces answered to modern priorities of order, efficiency, and rational conduct. Increasingly under corporate direction, these were secured through the more specific differentiation of product or function within purpose-built premises organized and promoted in pursuit of greater numbers and corresponding profits. This then was the new rational recreation—shorn of the reformers' missionary earnestness, plausibly respectable, invitingly pleasurable.

Initially a rogue and unorthodox branch of liberal capitalism and still under attack from moral reformers and other critics, music hall in its most advanced sector was, from the 1880s, rapidly consolidating as the dominant entertainment business whose corporate structure and operations reproduced or surpassed those of mainstream manufacturing industries.[17] By 1906, through new construction and amalgamation, Moss Empires could well bill itself "The Largest Amusement Organisation In The World," with nearly forty outlets countrywide subject to its centralized management and nationally integrated programming. Something like a third to a half of all remaining halls were under some form of syndicate control. Production values in these newly branded "theatres of variety" were as much about productivity as style in operations that corresponded to the modern practices of scientific management being urged on industrial manufacture. The sprawling offerings of the early halls were now uniformly packaged into twice-nightly programs with an ordered sequence of precisely timed acts closely monitored by house managers committed to schedules prescribed weeks in advance by the head office. Performers on the new circuits complained of "time sheet worship" and the "get through and done" priorities of local management.[18] Other perceived abuses led to the resistance of an alienated professional labor force in the performers' strike of 1907. The performers' trade paper typified the halls as "a great industry . . . One huge machine from the Managing Director to the call-boy."[19]

Orderly consumption, if still a little rough around the edges, was as much a management imperative as orderly production. Within a generation or so the increasingly numerous modern pleasure seekers who peopled the new music halls had been converted into mostly eager, compliant, repeating citizen consumers. The mobile, recomposing, demonstrative crowd of the midcentury halls had submitted to a battery of new price, time, and space controls, together with policed restraints on conduct. Admission by purchase of a refreshment check exchangeable in full or in part for drink had been superseded by a direct cash charge. Casual "drop in" attendance for any time or duration during the nightly performance was abruptly curtailed by precise and regular showtimes. Audiences were now funneled expeditiously in and out of the standard twice-nightly houses by an increased number of carefully planned entrances and exits. In turn, these gave controlled access to specific classes of seats, defined by physically demarcated zones and price differentials. Some halls experimented with turnstiles in the 1870s.

In contrast to the more open plan of the early halls, with audiences of a wide social mix facing each other across round tables or trestle seating at right angles to the stage, allowing standing room and welcome perambulation, the late-century spectator was stabilized in fixed and assigned individual tip-up seats facing the front. In-house transfers between different price zones, a practice much beloved of those keen to demonstrate an aspirant gentility by trading up, were discontinued, or made conditional on a correct dress code. Though complementary passes were issued to some business customers, the free entrance of regulars and other insiders hitherto accustomed to "going in on the nod" or the privilege of a "face pass" was eliminated. The office of chairman, there to monitor the program and its performer, invoke the traditional protocol of "order and decorum," and ensure ample breaks for drinks encouraged by his own conspicuously congenial example, also disappeared.

The timed entrance and exit of performers was now subject to curtain control under the direction of the stage manager, each act announced by illuminated numbers at the side of the stage ("your number's up!") corresponding to those in the printed programs now on sale. The programs provided the names and short descriptions of the numbered acts, commoditized items set amid several columns of display ads for local businesses and brand-name products. In the leading chains drink and its servers were phased out of the auditorium, quarantined in foyer bars. Most notably, audiences and performers alike were denied the spontaneous bonus of the encore, a traditional singalong that could throw the timetable off and encourage loose two-way banter across the footlights. To guard against further license, house rules forbade the performer's "direct address" of the audience. There were additional warnings against "offensive allusions" to public notables from the Royal Family down, any mention of religion, "the political song nuisance," or sexual indecency, on pain of fine or dismissal. Patrolling officials enforced the encore ban and evicted the more demonstrative audience members, for an excess of clapping no less than the traditional negative of hissing, condemned as "unseemly sibilation." Policemen hired by management quelled any other disturbances and screened the crowd for prostitutes.[20]

For their money and compliance, the modern leisure public could enjoy the unprecedented opulence and comfort of the splendid new variety theatres, grandiose engines of spectacle, abundance, comfort, and conformity. A sustained boom in construction from the 1880s produced halls of greatly increased capacity and well-ordered logistics. As the leading theatre architect of the day, with over a hundred new or modernized music halls across the country to his credit, Frank Matcham—"Magnificent Matcham"— defined the ideal design, executed with dispatch, efficiency, and scrupulous attention to both budget and local government safety regulations. A new technology of cantilevered steel construction allowed for more tiers and greater depth to each level of the auditorium. Supporting columns on the ground floor were eliminated, clearing sight lines and adding to capacity in all parts of the house, accommodating the maximum audience in any given space. "Not only all can sit, but all can see," was the claim, boasting a new freedom of enjoyment secured through fixed emplacements of both sitting and seeing. Seats, well upholstered, were now single, numbered, and ticketed, securing the individual a personal but contained territory within the crowd, gregarious yet "segregarious," we might say. The more directional configuration of the auditorium with its fixed front-facing seats and raked floors concentrated greater attention on the stage, reinforced in the 1880s with the new practice of dimming the (electric) house lights. The stage became an isolated cube of brightness fixating the gaze of the viewer and producing a notable muting effect on audiences.[21]

The new Matcham model halls not only served significantly larger audiences with greater functional efficiency but also exercised their own enchanting genius of place, suggested by Max Beerbohm's tag, "garish temples of modernity."[22] The soaring vertical space of extravagantly decorated and dramatically lit interiors generated an auratic if secularized religiosity. The grand elevated style of the exteriors echoed the monumentality of a new generation of city center municipal buildings. Thus did the music hall syndicates bid for establishment status, while such astute conflation of the epiphanous and the portentous conferred a certain dignity on their public.[23] The calming dialectic of the formal and the familiar, together with the oblique visual dynamics of the crowd in relation to each other, generated a variant of the soft technology of control exercised by other self-regulating modern assemblies in contemporary museums and exhibitions.[24]

In other ways the configuration of looking and seeing had changed. The "great and gaudy" plate glass mirrors that had flanked the walls of halls of the previous era were now gone from the auditorium. Their removal greatly reduced the distraction of self-admiration and display and the flirtations of refracted visual exchanges that had provided earlier audiences with their own show and encounter in a virtual laboratory of social styles.[25] Mirrored bars and crush rooms preserved something of the same incitement to the scrutiny of self and others, though now displaced to separate enclosures on the margins of the hall. Such amenities were part of a more generous scale and specialization of appointments in what the French termed *democratization du luxe*. Carpets served notice on spitting and spittoons. The smells of stale beer and tobacco were expunged by regular cleaning and counter-scents of carbolic and patchouli. Matcham halls boasted efficient heating and ventilation, some with sliding roofs guaranteeing "music without asphyxia." The new palaces of the people provided proper, sometimes quite splendid toilets—*pompe de merde* English style. Beholding the extensive faience tiles lining a Matcham auditorium, the comedian Dan Leno pronounced it "the sanitary varieties."[26] The modern leisure public was being house trained by house-proud managements.

In its bid for numbers and revenue, the new industry deployed a rhetoric of amiable yet discriminatory inclusion. Much of the business between proprietors and performers was still conducted in the language of friendship, eliding the specifics of cash and contract with the lubricants of drink and good fellowship. Invocations of a wider community of friends remained in the address of an increasingly more numerous audience—"We're all pals at the Palace"—together with a higher level of equalizing rhetoric in the invocation of the quasi-national community of the "people," a title extensively adopted by larger halls in the industrial towns. Burton's Royal Casino in Manchester, "*The* representative concert room of the provinces," changed its name to the People's Hall in the early 1860s.[27] Elsewhere this usage was parsed in the euphemisms of a class society. In 1873 the Oxford music hall in London's West End installed new stall seating ("fauteuils"), advertising as "The Patrician Lounge and People's Hall of Entertainment." Such hyperbole was typical of the industry's blithely simultaneous address of the few and the many, representing itself as socially select yet democratically gregarious, contriving a dual snobbery, adverted and inverted, at once inclusive and exclusive. The Oxford was "the only Grand Music Hall where the public can enjoy *Otium cum Dignitate* and can, without vexatious constraint [a free people's dig at the licensing authorities] Sup, Drink and Smoke at Pleasure." Across town a major rival claimed "to combine the manners of the drawing room with the conviviality of the true music hall," while Hobson's in Leeds offered "the comfort of a Club with Amusements for the Million."[28] Within its populist envelope the grand music hall dispensed its product to an artfully constructed, freely differentiated public.

As the fairground barker hailed and constructed his audience from the passing crowd, so too did the modern showman bid for custom in a distinctive form of address personified in the radiant yet complex social presence of the publican-entrepreneurs, or "caterers," who promoted the "grand" music halls of the first boom years of the 1860s and 1870s. For all the expanded scale and numbers, the successful proprietor maintained the personal touch, mixing with his customers in the customary convivialities of drink and good fellowship. A beneficent figure in the local community, the caterer combined philanthropy with a sharpened business acumen while still often enmeshed in the world of "the sporting and dramatic," a less than respectable set of affinities with the fast life and that corner of the popular press that reported it.[29] Charles Morton, later ennobled as the "Father of the Halls," sought the patronage of families and womenfolk at his Canterbury hall in Lambeth in the 1850s as a warrant of respectability for what he advertised as "rational and refining recreations." With artworks on the walls and operatic selections onstage, he promised a "Feast of Reason and Flow of Soul." For all his later image as the industry's Mr. Clean, Morton remained an inveterate and conspicuous gambler.[30] Billy Holland, who followed Morton into the Canterbury in 1868, paraded himself onstage as "Emperor of Lambeth" in mock-heroic emulation of his earliest idol, Napoleon III. Promoter of George Leybourne, "The Original Champagne Charlie," and other celebrity exponents of the lordly good time, Holland himself was renowned for his liberality while claiming to banish impropriety and promote public service and improvement. A subsequent Holland persona was that of "The People's Caterer," a second "People's William," not only benevolently Napoleonic but also Gladstonian, identifying with the paragon of Liberal fiscal prudence who had nonetheless delivered a popular bounty in his budgets, reducing tariffs on champagne and tobacco, symbolic accessories of the good time and material plenty.[31] Gladstone himself, the virtuous hedonist, recorded "dropping in" to the Metropolitan music hall on Edgware Road one summer evening in 1877, noting somewhat astringently, "The show was certainly not Athenian."[32]

In the plausible conceits of its rhetoric, mid-Victorian music hall aligned itself with a new mainstream of liberal capitalism affording its working-class subordinates a fuller sense of membership through a greater share of its economic surplus and the extension of the franchise in the Reform Act of 1867. Meliorist incorporation, however limited, acknowledged entitlement in a democratized regime of pleasure that fused a traditional utopianism with the vision of a more permanent and assured world of progress and plenty, shorn of the moralizing and conditional gradualism of official dispensation. Contemplating the expansion of popular leisure in 1860, the *Times* discerned the makings of "a great revolution[,] . . . great displacement of the masses, momentous changes of level."[33] This was capitalism with a beaming human face, an ironic utopia celebrating provision as much as consumption in a world of otherwise grossly unequal resources.[34]

With the extension of corporate control and the new Matchamized and modernized building type of the late century, the People's Halls gave way to Palaces, Hippodromes, and Empires, attracting significant additions of middle-class patrons. At the same time, the populist proprietor with the common touch was superseded by a hierarchy of company managers. Most numerous across the country were the Empires, the brand name of the Moss Stoll combine. The name not only signified but also manifested imperial grandeur and spectacle, providing vicarious consumption of the trophies and exotica of empire exemplified in the plaster elephants, oriental deities, and pagoda-like domes of Hackney Empire, Matcham's 1901 suburban triumph.[35] In the seductively disciplinary configurations of their designs, Moss Empires colonized their own indigenous peoples. As managing director, Oswald Stoll pursued modern business priorities of greater efficiency and profitability with tighter controls on contracts and aggressive expansion of sites. Puritanical and abstemious, Stoll eschewed personal contact with performers and public, yet proved dangerously vulnerable to his own imperial ambitions. Hence the hubris of Stoll's London Coliseum, an independent personal venture and further imperial conceit, built by Matcham (the court architect) in 1904 to surpass the metropolitan superdromes of his rivals. Based on the volume of commuter traffic he observed in Charing Cross station, Stoll scheduled four shows a day in the massive interior, featuring high-end attractions such as Elgar, Max Reinhardt, and Sarah Bernhard and spectacular effects from the latest technology, all dispensed under the house motto of *pro bono publico,* with Stoll as caterer turned pro-consul. The Coliseum's first career was short-lived, destroyed by a succession of misfortunes and miscalculations, great and small. An electric chariot designed to ferry royalty from the grand foyer to their box broke down with the king aboard, the three-level mechanized revolve produced an inadvertent human sacrifice with the death of a jockey in a stage simulation of the Derby, and a schedule of four performances a day was economically disastrous. The company went bankrupt, and the

American stage manager committed suicide. In anticipation of music hall's more general decline over the next generation, an older liberal altruism was destroyed by imperial overreach.[36]

The one triumphant signifier amid the clamor of music hall's climacteric and the West End's emergence as a leisure theme park was "fun," the newly intellectualized pleasure mode now becoming the modern showman's primary address to the consumer subject. In earlier meanings fun denoted foolery with a fraudulent purpose, the use of humor or practical joke to cheat or hoax. Thus the traditional trope "all the fun of the fair" included exposure to its tricksters, con men, and general sharp practice. From the midcentury such associations were gradually displaced by a less contaminated sense of pleasure, yet fun was still not wholly innocuous. Arnold divided society between "the heirs of the Puritans" and "the devotees of beer, gin and fun," the latter most numerous among an untamed and riotous working class, the embodiment of anarchy. This was the boozy saturnalian fun of license and excess that reformers sought to eradicate, still in evidence in the late 1880s when George Gissing witnessed the "imbecile joviality" of the Bank Holiday crowd at the Crystal Palace. It was in this context that Moore and Burgess, proprietors of London's longest-running minstrel show, launched their slogan, "Fun without vulgarity," in the 1870s, and the new model fun was soon everywhere. The sensational new London Pavilion music hall of 1885 that dominated Piccadilly proclaimed itself "The House of Fun"; Fred Karno, agent for the young Charlie Chaplin and entrepreneur of the popular stage, operated out of his Fun Factory in South London. The Franco-British Exhibition in London in 1908 (the greatest of its kind since 1851) advertised its White City location as Fun City. Explaining the formula for his new musical comedy shows at the Gaiety Theatre, the impresario George Edwardes listed "pretty music, pretty dances, pretty women, pretty dresses and plenty of fun." In the Gaiety's 1909 hit, *Our Miss Gibbs*, the shopgirl heroine and pals take a day out at the White City's pleasure ground where they "Frolic, flirt and spoon/ Ride on the cars, pay at the bars." "So," the song concludes, "the upper and middle classes/Will join the merry masses/We'll all have fun before we're done/So come along everyone."[37] Liberal fun promoted an inclusive, universalist charter that all might buy into, a redrawn modern liminality with its carefully managed contract of gratifications and tolerances.

Fun retained a more elastic and ambiguous currency in popular discourse as code for sexual pleasure, from tepid to torrid, specious to authentic, hetero- to homosexual, serving simultaneously as invitation and disclaimer. "Just for fun," "It's only fun," "A little bit of fun," combined self-evident validation with implicit claims to a cultural right or entitlement, to be defended against the enemies of popular pleasure. By 1911 this was an especially compelling need for the modern young working woman who reportedly "aches for vanities and laughter and pretty clothes and all that she comprehensively terms fun."[38] According to the advertising, much of this was on offer in the new department stores whose messages alchemized shopping from a woman's chore to a lady's pleasure, part of an enjoyable day out it was suggested, to be combined with a theatre matinee and refreshments in one of the new chain tea shops. The new-style musical comedies set their stories in this heterosocial world of leisure whose smart new sites of distraction and display were the ready settings for romantic encounter. Offstage the modern girl about town had to be wary of male harassment and any "funny business," the term for unwelcome sexual attention that echoes older, more discomforting usages. But this was the "naughty nineties," when "naughty" licensed sexual mischief under cover of tolerant reproof in language echoing the nursemaid and the prostitute, of a piece with "gay," another faux-naïf imprimatur of the era.[39]

Advertising and the contemporary media did the work of the fairground barker. Part of the new glamorization and exposure of women as showgirls and leisure time adventurers, Dudley Hardy's sensational posters of the Gaiety Girls were endlessly reproduced and imitated in a blizzard of publicity for the new attractions, carried on hoardings, omnibuses, newspapers, and the new picture postcard. A Rip van Winkle character in a 1908 Arnold Bennett novel confronted with London's streetscape after forty years' seclusion is astounded by "gigantic posters . . . in every available space." "All had to do with food and pleasure," he exclaims in wonder. "Endless invitations to debauchery with ham, tea, and beer[,] . . . and an astonishing quantity of pleasure palaces that offered you exactly the same entertainment twice over on the same night."[40]

Entertainmentality may thus usefully denote this modern amalgam of open-ended invitation and schematized conformity, a mix of license and containment that well served the emergent modern leisure industry. Yet its operation was neither wholly novel, secure, complete, nor finite. In the first place its subjects were no strangers to orderly assemblies at play, given the extensive associational world of pub-based secular clubs and societies that had since the previous century been popular sites of festive sociability and communally generated entertainment. The historic "free and easy" model of these meetings was a self-policing yet expressive mix of the demonstrative and the decorous, channeled in the music hall cliché "order and decorum."[41] While the leisure crowd outside might at times still be unruly, something of the ritualized sociability of club culture fed through into the new, more impersonal assemblies of the early halls, as too did the habit of dialogue and engagement between performer and audience. While this feature has been unduly fetishized in nostalgic projections of the Victorian and Edwardian halls, it remained a persistent part of their operation if variously reinflected. Though the most intrusive of audience voices, the claque of theatrical tradition and its duplicate in the "gallery boys" and "chirrupers" of the halls, had been mostly suppressed by the turn of the century as part of the tighter policing of audiences, a good number of independent music halls remained untouched by the disciplines of conduct and performance enforced in the syndicate halls.[42] And artists and audiences in the new-model variety theatres still interacted, working a more coded, knowing exchange of meanings under the radar of the new controls. While hardly radical, the new music hall public preserved a critical counterpoint to official values and the dominant cultural order. As Vladimir Lenin, the émigré student of revolution, noted in 1907, "In the London halls there is a certain satirical or skeptical attitude towards the commonplace, an attempt to turn it inside out, to distrust it somewhat, to point up the illogicality of the everyday."[43]

Despite some protests, the smaller, mostly pub-based music halls with their more highly charged social spaces succumbed to opposition from moral reformers and local councils wielding new safety and licensing regulations in preference for, and in some cases alleged collusion with, the new corporate giants.[44] The opulent new variety theatres ensured that those in search of familiar entertainments were now literally cushioned against any significant resistance to the passing of the old order.[45] This too was a public increasingly habituated to a wide array of structural disciplines, from railway timetables to state schooling to other modernizing cultural institutions. And while civility may have replaced a more overt sociability, the new halls offered their own welcome social ambience. Thus the curved lines of seating and fan-shaped contours of a typical Matcham music hall afforded a peripheral but significant sense of company. Fired by the complicit promptings of the practiced performer, this could bloom into an ad hoc community of enjoyment, producing a paradoxical but well-attested experience of warmth and intimacy in an otherwise vast and cavernous shell. It was on such evidence that a cadre of bourgeois litterateurs and journalists, in marked contrast to the critics of modern culture, wrote in celebration of late-century music hall and the robust and instinctual pleasures of its modern folk.[46] There had nonetheless been a remarkable transformation in the conduct and modeling of its public.

Though "the problem of leisure" was far from exorcised, liberal culture had by the late century negotiated a viable accommodation of leisure to a modern lifestyle, moving on to address the more volatile question of pleasure not just as a top dressing but as an inherent bonus of the fully acknowledged good life. Amid the debasements of the new mass culture, a range of voices and interests sought to rescue and reconsummate pleasure as a personal and social good, variously an enrichment of the self and a collective bond. These were the justifiable freedoms of a liberal society, as the worldly voice from the 1860s had allowed: "Free trade and free self-culture are all bound up in the same bundle." "Free trade in pleasure" proclaimed by the multiple restauranteur and corporate showman Joe Lyons was the generous pledge of the new leisure and entertainment industries.[47]

Yet the fun that was the prime sign and commodity of the new order was constrained within a regime of measured dispensation that was becoming the norm of a modern cultural and emotional economy. Rational recreation was rationed recreation. In an 1892 editorial the leading national trade paper, the *Era*, deplored the persistence of encores in the music halls: "It works mischief by satiating those who get more than they bargained for, and who are not likely to come a second time when they have had all they wanted, and more than they were entitled to on a first visit."[48] Thus modern pleasure was fundamentally compromised. Consumers got much less even as they got much more. With continuous production in manufacture secured through the imposition of an industrial work discipline and the extinction of older spasmodic or seasonal patterns of production, a more proactive commercial capitalism bent its energies to ensuring continuous consumption in a popular culture still haunted by the crude typology of feast or famine, a fitful pattern of scarcity punctuated by episodes of prodigality. In selling its (twice) nightly entertainments as a modern leisure industry, music hall represented its pleasures as a feast, including sexual appetizers. It had therefore to maintain the relish of the seasonal feast day now advertised for every day of the week, reconciling the appeal to traditional associations of license, the carnivalesque and open-ended plenitude—all this and more! as we are still told—with modern norms of orderly and measured consumption. Entertainmentality! was a sensationalized but carefully managed exercise of simultaneous stimulation and containment that heightened expectations, yet threatened to flatten out the rewards, a calculated reworking of the elastic parameters of freedom and constraint, access and equity, discipline and desire in a modern liberal society. It was indeed a funny business.[49]

9.   Same Difference?

Liberalism, Modernity, and Governance in the Indian Empire

Gavin Rand

This chapter explores the intersection—and interconnectedness—of modernity and liberalism in imperial Britain. Taking liberalism principally as a technology of governance, it examines how nominally liberal rationalities of rule were adapted and evolved in colonial India. Much of what follows is concerned with the colonial city, which I suggest was integral to and expressive of novel forms of governance that developed from the mid-nineteenth century. While recent work has done much to extend understandings of urbanization and governance, the colonial city has only recently become the subject of significant scholarly investigation.[1] The role of empire in animating liberal technologies of rule in the metropole, like the impacts of liberal rationalities in colonial cities, remains in need of further unpicking, as do the coterminous histories of empire, liberalism, and modernity in Britain.

Like modernity, liberalism's analytical utility may be attenuated as its uses proliferate.[2] The same could equally be said of some of the debates regarding empire and its influence on Britain.[3] Rather than pursue a forensic analysis of these deficiencies, however, this chapter surveys recent work on the history of the colonial city to situate empire, modernity, and liberal governance within a common analytical field.[4] It focuses on the congruence of liberalism and empire in shaping a sense of the modern, before considering how notions of modernity have inflected understandings of and justifications for empire and imperialism. In arguing for the interconnectedness of liberalism, modernity, and empire in British history (and historiography), it questions the extent to which several distinguishing features of Britain's imperial modernity were *liberal* in their operation. Important studies of the colonial city indicate that it was the contingent and problematic modernity of colonial urban form—rather than its liberal, disciplinary effects—that was vital to the administration of imperial spaces. In attempting to chart the complicity of liberalism and the colonial modern by examining how the tensions between empire's universalist and exclusive imperatives were balanced through the planning and administration of colonial urban space, this chapter invites a series of questions about the relationship between empire, liberalism, and the colonial city: What role did the city play in projecting colonial authority and elaborating specifically colonial subjectivities? How did imperial hierarchies and imperatives influence colonial urban form, and what does the colonial city tell us about liberalism and modernity in Britain's empire? In assessing the forms of subjectivity elaborated for those who lived through Britain's liberal imperial modernity, the concluding discussion emphasizes the limits of colonial governmentality, suggesting that, as an animating force for colonial strategies of rule, liberalism's capacity for "governing at a distance" was proscribed by the ideologies that sustained colonial hierarchies and by the differential operations of colonial law.[5]

Empire helped to distinguish what was unique about Britain and Britain's historical development at the same time that it provided a metric by which the other defining features of British preeminence—commercial and maritime supremacy, political freedoms—were measured.[6] From at least the eighteenth century—and the debates on expansion in the East and abolition in the West—empire played a key role in influential formulations of the nation and its historical development.[7] The historiographic roots of English exceptionalism were nourished on imperial self-confidence, as much as by metropolitan liberalism and constitutionalism (concepts that often drew forcefully on imperial signifiers).[8] Moreover, empire quickly transmitted itself back to the metropolis, shaping the discursive and figurative frameworks through which Britain's industrialization and urbanization were explained and rationalized, so that by the mid-nineteenth century metropolitan commentators borrowed tropes from travelogues and missionary literature to emphasize the alienness of life in the poorer parts of British cities.[9] In the same period, the reconstruction of Whitehall as empire's administrative hub made possible the reform of the state just as the grandeur of the new Foreign and Commonwealth Offices worked to instantiate Britain's role as imperial power within the metropole.[10] Empire was thus inscribed in Britain's urban spaces at the same time that it provided languages and intellectual frameworks that helped make sense of the growth of the metropolitan city.[11]

Paradoxically, while empire was frequently held up as a measure of Britain's historical progress, this marker of British supremacy was also, potentially, a portent of manifest or imminent decline. The moral and material progress of empire was also a measure of British national vitality, and material progress was frequently reckoned in terms of the expansion of "modern" technologies and infrastructure. The massive programs of colonial construction inaugurated from the mid-nineteenth century— when British imperialism in India was appropriated as a state project—are testament both to this wider process and to the specific ways in which it was manifested.[12] The Gothic transformation of Bombay following the appointment of Governor Bartle Frere in 1862 is only one of a number of examples demonstrating how the material was harnessed in the service of empire in this period.[13] If Gothic was, in part, a cultured and critical response to *the modern*, it was also, as its imperial uses demonstrate, a means of instantiating and projecting the modern power of British colonialism. This was most clearly demonstrated in Bombay, where a thirteen-foot statue of Progress was erected above the city's Victoria terminus, arguably the finest example of Victorian High Gothic architecture anywhere in the world. Similarly, if more obviously, the classicism that supplanted Gothic as the preferred imperial style was equally Janus-faced: it proclaimed the modernity of British power by harking back to Rome. [14] As I discuss below, liberal rationalities of rule, like liberal histories and political theory, were similarly refracted through and tested in empire's urban spaces.[15]

URBAN SPACE AND COLONIAL RULE

The networks of colonial infrastructure and administrative buildings that were developed across the subcontinent from the mid-nineteenth century—the Gothic Himalayan hill stations, the hubris and splendor of Lutyen's New Delhi, the many thousands of administrative buildings erected in India's major towns and cities—are suggestive markers of the way in which colonial governance necessitated and was inscribed in material form. These interventions, of an unprecedented scale, also reflected the local and particular exigencies of colonial rule: the rebellion of the Indian Army in 1857 precipitated the formalization of colonial rule under the crown and encouraged performative demonstrations of imperial authority, frequently in material form. The centers of the rebellion—especially Lucknow and Delhi—were therefore subject to extensive reconstruction guided by the twin imperatives of security and majesty. Elsewhere, the codification of British rule after 1857 was reflected in a series of material interventions in India's urban spaces, including Frere's remodeling of Bombay.[16] A central influence on this project was the decisive impact that the rebellion had on the debates surrounding the liberal, reformist nature of the empire in India.[17] In place of the reformist ambitions of the 1830s, when evangelical influence led to the opening of India to missionaries and the organized campaign against suttee, a more pragmatic approach underwrote the reconfiguration of colonial rule after the rebellion. A reified sense of Indian cultural and societal alterity was reflected in many of the infrastructural projects undertaken in the century following 1857, during which the "rule of colonial difference" worked both to circumscribe the limits of colonial ambition regarding the possibilities of remaking Indians as modern subjects and to emphasize the importance of monumentalizing the modernity of colonial rule through urban form.[18] While it is important not to overstate the role of difference in animating colonial rule—which always depended on finding and establishing functional relations of similarity as much as on codifying hierarchies of difference—the specificities of imperial governance endowed colonial urban form with a particular governmental significance. As Veena Oldenburg's account of the rebuilding of Lucknow after 1857 makes clear, modern attempts to engineer the "free flow" of subjects through the city were to coexist alongside material provision that aimed to foster the loyalty and prestige of certain local notables.[19]

The imbrication of urban form and colonial governance is most clearly reflected in the history of New Delhi. Unquestionably the grandest scheme of colonial engineering, the new capital of British India was devised with an eye to India's "tradition" of imperial subjugation. In relocating the imperial capital from Calcutta, the government of India endeavored to distance itself from the tumultuous opposition to British rule that had developed in the province following Curzon's partitioning of Bengal in 1905. As well as reversing the earlier partition, the king's 1911 announcement of the new capital was a concession to and an attempt to marginalize the increasingly influential Bengali *bhadralok* (educated professional classes and vocal critics of colonial rule). The relocation of the capital at Delhi was informed by specific imperial imperatives, deliberately referencing the historic rule of the Mughals and responding to the pressures of an emergent Indian nationalism.[20] The modern and liberal axes of British rule in India thus drew directly on the intersection of older imperial histories and contemporary political struggles: when the Home Minister wrote to the viceroy to propose a new imperial capital, "he emphasised that it would also be regarded as 'an exercise of sovereign power, such as oriental people expect and admire.'" Similarly, the secretary of state declared that "the ancient walls of Delhi enshrine an imperial tradition comparable with that of Constantinople, or with that of Rome itself."[21] The new capital was thus conceived as a manifestation of Britain's imperial power: in Stephen Legg's terms, New Delhi was to be "one of Britain's most spectacular showcases of imperial modernity[,] . . . embod[ying] the rationality of imperialism in its aesthetics (refined, functional classicism), science (a healthy, ordered land-scape) and politics (an authoritarian, hierarchical society)."[22] New Delhi's peculiar modernity was a product of the historical circumstances in which it was devised: conceived as a new imperial capital—and marked by this act of conception as peculiarly modern—the new capital was also profoundly shaped by specific concepts regarding India's tradition, history, and cul-ture. The neoclassical style that Edwin Lutyens adopted for New Delhi won out over alternative Indic styles, which some felt better balanced the "best" of Indian craft traditions and styles with modern scientific meth-ods, in large part because the former was deemed more appropriate for an *imperial* capital.[23] Thus a form of adapted classicism, in which various sty-listic concessions were made in order to reflect the local environment, was adopted.[24] In spite of such embellishments, however, it remained clear that the new city was intended to monumentalize the power of the British as imperial rulers: as the king's private secretary, Lord Stanfordham, wrote to Lord Crewe at the India Office, "We must let [the Indians] see, for the first time, the power of Western science, art and civilisation."[25]

The performative and dialogic elements of this project reflected the tenor of colonial administration in the post-1857 period. This interrelation of old and new can be readily traced, in spatial terms, in the formation and organization of the new capital relative to the old city.[26] In addition, while New Delhi was conceived as a spatial manifestation of British authority, the layout of the new city encoded various assumptions about the nature of authority and power in precolonial India. Stanfordham's correspondence with the India Office emphasized the importance of ensuring that the vice-roy's residence "dominate" both the surrounding terrain and the buildings of the old city.[27] As H. Jyoti has noted, New Delhi thus wrote large the spatial and symbolic divisions that were represented in microcosm in the imperial durbars of 1877, 1902, and 1911, at which the new capital was announced.[28] As in the durbars, the representation of authority in the city reflected an amalgam of ideas about sovereignty and subordination that (mis)appropriated Mughal idioms in the service of colonial power. At the symbolic center of the city, the viceregal house, ministered by its secre-tariat buildings, sat sovereign over the city, much as the representatives of the crown did in the imperial durbars. Similarly, the King's Way, the ceremonial promenade that emanated from the viceregal house and was flanked by the administrative buildings of government, was also used to stage "forceful demonstrations" of British authority, involving the procession of imperial troops.[29]

If these spectacular aspects of the new capital reflected a similar aesthetic rationale as Ruskin's advocacy of Gothic, the new imperial capital also provided for more encompassing interventions in daily life.[30] New Delhi's residential quarters thus reflected the hierarchies of colonial life: farthest from the grandeur of the administrative center were housed the lowest-ranking Indian workers (to whom were allotted the smallest spatial units), and the intervening space was divided, according to status, between the various ranks of civil servants who would administer the government in the new capital. Although New Delhi was intended to represent the modernity of Britain's liberal imperialism, the racial hierarchies that overdetermined the distribution of this space clearly indicate some of the limits on that project.[31] Moreover, residential segregation of this sort was not the only form of spatial division reflecting colonial hierarchies of race. The distribution and policing of Delhi's urban spaces was repeatedly circumscribed by the specific rationalities of colonial rule. Hence there was disproportionate investment in policing the white quarters of the city and securing the health of its white inhabitants.[32] While the "problematizations" of the colonial city involved comparable sanitary, moral, and social imperatives to those in the metropole, it remained the case that the governance of the former was always underscored by the fact of imperial domination. As Prashant Kidambi has shown, Bombay's 1902 City Police Act granted senior police officers wide-ranging and draconian discretionary authority to regulate the conduct of the city's (Indian) inhabitants in thoroughly illiberal ways, empowering the commissioner to prohibit, among other things, "the public utterance of cries, singing of songs [and] playing of music" that might "inflame" communal tensions.[33] Though fears of "the mob" were key to the policing of metropolitan urban space through the nineteenth century, spatial and material interventions in the colony were shaped by the specific logic of imperial sovereignty, as the examples above suggest.

The overriding priority for the planners and administrators of India's urban spaces remained the safety of the European population and the security of imperial prestige. Accordingly, the Delhi Municipal Committee devoted significant attention to interventions that, it was thought, would secure either the health or the safety of the European population. These concerns typically drew attention not just to the organization of space within New Delhi but also to the interactions of the old city with the new.

Continuing a trend that had begun after 1857, when the city walls were breached to allow for better railway access and marshlands near the cantonment were drained to improve the health of colonial troops, various attempts were made to neutralize the environmental dangers the old town was seen to pose.[34] Here, however, colonial racial hierarchies were, once again, apparent. As with security and policing, governmental concern for the city's European minority over and above its indigenous inhabitants is indicative of the limits that constrained the emergence of "biopower" in the empire. [35] The legal and strategic differentials that animated colonial strategies of rule and dictated the ways in which urban space was to be governed were also evident in the preparations made ahead of the announcement of the New Delhi project at the 1911 durbar. A series of additional bylaws were established to provide additional powers of arrest and detention in the protection of the white civil lines, thereby proscribing a range of undesirable behaviors within the European quarters. Like the durbar at which it was announced, the spatial policing of New Delhi also reflected imperialism's racial hierarchies: police powers were codified more rigorously in defense of European space (and the protection of the European subject) than they were in defense of Indian spaces or subjects. Even from the moment the project was announced, New Delhi was both a testament to colonial ambition and a stark indictment of the limits that marked colonial rule. The clear hierarchies evident in the layout, policing, and defense of colonial urban space expose the universalist aspirations of colonial liberalism.

MODERNITY, SUBJECTIVITIES, GOVERNANCE

If notions of colonial alterity were integral to ideas of British progress and modernity—and these hierarchies were reflected in the administration of the Delhi municipality—the lived reality of the city always destabilized the opposition of the old and the new. This further problematizes colonial claims regarding the liberal, pedagogic function of empire and also calls into question the extent to which liberal rationalities of rule animated colonial governance. The penetration of European space by the indigenous population—through their appropriation of "European" styles and incursions into "white" landscapes, as well as through the ubiquitous presence of Indian servants—constantly reworked the divisions and organizations of space devised by colonial planners and architects.[36] Some of these changes reflected the inherent contradictions in colonial ideologies, while others were a product of the shifting balance of political power as India moved toward diarchy and finally independence. As Indians came to occupy the higher posts within the civil service and the municipal administration, there followed a spatial destabilizing of the city's racial boundaries, as senior Indian civil servants increasingly assumed the occupational and residential spaces previously reserved for European officers and administrators. Even at the inauguration of the city in 1931, however, the neat divisions of space projected in the plans for the city proved impossible to realize. When the original plans for New Delhi's residential accommodation were completed, some 5 percent of the total housing stock was allocated to so-called unorthodox quarters, bungalows built in the European style but to be inhabited by Indian clerks. These were intended to provide for those Indians who preferred European accommodation to the "traditional" styles that constituted the majority of Indian accommodation. In fact, however, demand for "unorthodox" quarters rapidly outstripped supply, so that by the end of the 1930s more than 20 percent of the housing stock comprised such dwellings.[37] Far from showing themselves wedded to "tradition," as colonial planners anticipated, many of New Delhi's Indian civil servants had chosen to adopt the "unorthodox" European domiciles. From the outset, New Delhi struggled to realize the neat and expressive divisions of space that its planners had devised so carefully.

The universalist rhetoric of colonialism was also exposed by the unease with which Indian "progress" toward modernity was regarded. In penetrating European spaces and appropriating European domiciles in "unorthodox" ways, New Delhi's Indian inhabitants might have been lauded as the products of empire's pedagogic labors. Instead, the (re)colonization of the colonial city by Indians was problematic not simply because their actions disturbed the spatial boundaries encoded in the city's plans but also because the adaptation of Indians to the city destabilized the logic of difference through which colonial rule operated. This paradox bound liberal strategies of rule in the colonies, a fact that Indian critics of colonial rule readily emphasized.[38] For example, when some of New Delhi's Indian clerks were upbraided for subletting rooms in their accommodation—a response to marked increases in rents, which reflected the shortage of housing in the new city, a further indication of the shortcomings of colonial urban planning—they protested that colonial attempts to proscribe the right to sublet, intended to prevent unsanitary overcrowding, infringed on the "personal liberty" of the would-be subletter, adeptly appropriating a colonial rationale as a means of critiquing the differential operation of colonial law.[39] Alternative but functionally similar arguments were articulated in the opposite register of difference when indigenous communities framed their opposition to colonial spatial interventions—for example, the clearing and traversing of "slum" areas for new arterial thoroughfares—by emphasizing the importance of existing deployments of space for "native" cultural practices.[40] Difference, and similarity, thus provided a range of resources that Indian subjects deployed to critique various colonial projects. If this agonism parallels some of the tensions that animated the "rule of freedom" in Britain (between the watched and those watching) and those in India (between the colonized and their liberal, colonial tutors), whereas in Britain progress could be projected in terms of the respectability of disciplined, clean, sober subjects, these examples also suggest how the reformation of Indians as modern subjects was often, in itself, deeply problematic.[41] While Macaulay had anticipated an educated, improved, and Anglicized "native public opinion," when the expansion of the civil service began to turn out such subjects in the late nineteenth century colonial society looked on aghast at the parody of the modern British subject manifested in the form of the "babu." Thus while the governmentalization of India and her population could be projected in liberal terms, its realization, even in these idealized terms, was always problematic and greeted with ambivalence. [42]

As a hybrid and contested space, the colonial city—like the babu—reveals the tensions and contradictions of imperial rule. From this perspective, the emergence of the urban *bhadralok* and the penetration of New Delhi's European quarters suggest not only an example of the "warrening from within" of the colonial city but reaffirms too the importance of the city as a domain of colonial rule.[43] However, this is not simply about the "warrening out" of a liberal, Western urban space: not only was empire central to the coherence of this notion—present at its birth, as it were—but the organization and administration of such space was always dependent on the Indian intermediaries who made up the administrative spine of the empire. Even in the hill stations—spatial enclaves where Gothic nostalgia and other dreams of Europe were given freest rein—the European reliance on Indian staff and servants ensured the ubiquitous and problematic "intrusion of the other." The bazaar at Simla—characterized by Kipling as a "rabbit-warren" in which the power of police could easily be evaded—was the necessary but nonetheless threatening corollary of the station itself.[44] Thus while the schematics for the colonial city expressed liberal visions of empire and the hill stations projected a fantasy of Europe relocated, the transmissions and hybridities realized in colonial urban environs—and in other administrative locales, including the civil service and the army—were often profoundly destabilizing to imperial hierarchies.[45] Although a liberal rhetoric of empire could conceive of Indian progress through the creation of modern cities, and of quasi-modern subjects in the form of clerks, soldiers, and engineers, a survey of these intermediaries also reveals how problematic each could be.

The mimicry that destabilized colonial hierarchies was also, as we have seen, the explicit justification for, and the implicit objective of, Britain's imperial mission. This tension is reflected in the anxious comments of colonial officers who noted that as Indians were exposed to and became more familiar with the operations of colonial administration, so the "awe" engendered by the modernity of that rule was diminished. As Legg notes, the Home Department wrote to the viceroy on 26 June 1912 to bemoan the lack of respect demonstrated by Indians who had grown accustomed to colonial technology: "Replacing the deference to the white man was an insolence that was 'significant of the true inner feelings of Indians who have some education if the restraints of official gear or favour are not operating, or if the relations of host and guest, or of personal friendship, are in question.'"[46] It is no coincidence that in those administrative localities where contact between European superiors and Indian subordinates was most frequent and prolonged—especially in the civil service and the military—Indian mimicry of the colonial self was mocked, as in the stereotyped babu, but this mockery cannot disguise how destabilizing such mimicry could be. Through their (mis)appropriation of European styles of dress and language, as well as their expansion into the European sectors and domiciles of the city, the Raj's Anglicized Indian civil servants tested the limited ambition and delicate sensibilities of colonial statecraft.

As key intermediaries, civil servants and sepoys were integral to colonial administration, and yet what is most striking about British responses to these colonial subjects are the very different terms in which their subjectivities were evaluated. In contrast to the colonial distaste for the urbanized and Anglicized babu, the typically rural and illiterate recruits to the imperial military were held in comparatively high esteem.[47] Here again the imperial claim to liberal pedagogy is exposed: the "loyal" Sikhs, Gurkhas, and Pathans whose ethnography was thought to make them well suited to a soldiering life were regarded as proverbially stupid.[48] In this, they could be accommodated in colonial rationale much more easily than could the educated babu. The hardening of a sense of Indian ethnographic alterity in the late nineteenth century was reflected in the fantastical ethnographies of India's martial races as it was in the plans of colonial architects. In commemorating the loyalty of Britain's native allies during the rebellion, the statues of Gurkhas, Sikhs, and Afghans, erected alongside representations of "loyal princes" in the great quadrangle at the

India Office in London, indicate how material form and colonial history were brought together to lend coherence to colonialism's sense of its own modernity.[49] If the martial sepoy can be seen as an idealized colonial subject—loyal, simple, and requiring leadership—his subjectivity was hardly modern.[50] Nevertheless, it was the martial sepoy and not the "liberal" and "improved" babu who was more comfortably incorporated into the structures of British colonial administration, and this disjunction became all the more striking as nationalism developed during the twentieth century.

In spite of Gandhi's vision of the village republic, the growth of Indian nationalism did not prompt a wider rejection of colonial *technē*. In fact, urban space remained as expressive of and central to governance after independence as it had been in the colonial period.[51] The conscientiously modern inheritance of Nehruvian India is nowhere more evident than in the planning and construction of Chandigarh, the new capital for Indian East Punjab, conceived in the wake of Partition to replace the surrendered provincial capital of Lahore. Le Corbusier's role in the planning and construction of Chandigarh is well known, and the modernist aesthetics of the city and its capitol complex are striking. However, Chandigarh's modernity was functional and administrative as much as aesthetic. As with New Delhi, the new city was intended to provide an administrative center, and, as with the older imperial capital, Chandigarh was also a material response to profound political and social upheaval. As for the planners of New Delhi, Chandigarh was to represent *and* facilitate the rehabilitation of the governance that would emanate from the city's buildings. As in the earlier case, so Chandigarh's planners woefully underestimated the likely growth and expansion of the city.[52] Both cities, then, shared common origins in the particular dislocations and imperatives of colonial and postcolonial history. For all that its origins were shaped by history, it was explicitly to the future that Chandigarh was to be oriented. Inaugurating the city in language that inverted and yet was also resonant of his colonial predecessors, Nehru implored, "Let this be a new city, unfettered by the traditions of the past, a symbol of the nation's faith in the future."[53] Oriented to alternative coordinates but mapped according to the same rationale, Chandigarh shares more fundamental similarities to New Delhi than its aesthetics alone permit us to grasp.

The temporal reorientation toward the future, and to putative improvement, is characteristic of much that sought to stake a claim to the modern. It is this (re)orientation that animated many of the material and administrative projects discussed above. Even where these projects were explicitly directed to ideas of tradition, or to a lost glorious past—as in

Ruskin's Gothic, or in Lutyens's and Baker's invocations of Rome—it was toward improvement and the future that administration was reoriented. As bounded and contradictory as colonial projects of improvement undoubtedly were, it was the temporal logic of improvement that distinguished the range and ambition of Britain's imperial modernity. This was evident in responses to the poor at home, as it was in responses to the colonized in the empire, just as it is clear that it was the imperial context that provided some of the supplementary referents through which ideas of the modern and of progress were articulated. The extent to which these ideas were informed by liberal governmental rationalities is questionable. If the colonial circuits noted above were more important to the origins of metropolitan liberalism than has sometimes been acknowledged, there may be further grounds for querying the centrality of liberalism in animating modern governance. The palingenetic promises of fascism, in which many of the theatrical and performative impulses noted above are also evident, encode similar temporal logics regarding improvement. The ostensibly universalist aspirations of liberal imperialism and of postcolonial nationalism seem, in this sense at least, to mirror the "mood of Aufbrach" that was central to fascist attempts to realize a new modernity in the mid-twentieth century.[54]

In surveying some of the recent literature on imperialism, liberalism, and the colonial city, I have emphasized the various ways in which the apparent modernity of urban form framed imperial rule (as well as some critiques of that rule) in India from the mid-nineteenth century. My purpose has not been to recuperate a bounded or stable notion of "modernity," much less to suggest that a process of "modernization" illuminates the history addressed in the works examined here. Rather, I have tried to emphasize how "the modern" provided a means of justifying and legitimizing the manifest inequalities of colonial administration at precisely the same time that colonialism helped to define its own sense of modernity. In explaining the relationship of past, present, and future shaped by and expressive of colonialism in India, the apparent modernity of the imperial project justified colonial claims to legitimacy while simultaneously working to disable various critiques of colonial rule. If this notion of modernity was principally a claim to "modernness"—rather than a singular set of attributes, historical phenomena, or responses to either or both—we should not underestimate how important this means of framing historical relationships of power proved to be. It was the productive juxtaposition of Britain's history, the colonial present, and India's future that enabled Victorian commentators to legitimize the fact of colonial expropriation, just as it was the same juxtaposition that provided nationalists with the epistemic resources to critique and ultimately defeat formal colonial rule. In these terms, this paradoxical and contradictory notion of modernity thus provided both the rationale for the construction of New Delhi and the most potent weapons for critiquing the inequalities manifested in its streets, buildings, and administration.

In addition to emphasizing the role of "the modern" in shaping colonial administration in India, this chapter has attempted to question the extent to which liberal rationalities of rule animated colonial governance. In part, I have tried to emphasize how important the notion of colonial modernity was to definitions of nineteenth-century liberalism. More substantively, I have suggested that the ambivalence evident whenever colonial pedagogy seemed to realize the "improvements" it ostensibly sought might reveal the limits of Britain's colonial mission in India. The hostility directed toward the maligned babu and the surprise with which colonial planners greeted the "unorthodox" housing preferences of New Delhi's Indian inhabitants expose liberalism's claims to universality and direct our attention to the operative limits of liberalism as a rationality of colonial rule. From this perspective, it may be more difficult to regard liberalism as the key motor animating power's capacity to operate "at a distance." As with colonialism's claims to Indian modernity, the limits that bound liberalism's rationalities of rule in India (and elsewhere) now require more precise delineation. Such a project promises to reveal more about the transmissions between liberalism and Britain's imperial modernity.

10. Paternalism, Class, and the British Path to Modernity

Jon Lawrence

This chapter explores the peculiarities of Britain's path to liberal democracy across the nineteenth and twentieth centuries. It offers a corrective to accounts of Britain's embrace of modernity that tend to overlook the persistence of older, more paternalist modes of thought and practice. I argue that the persistence of entrenched ideas about supposedly natural social hierarchies, combined with paternalist styles of political leadership, structured the history of liberal democracy in Britain in distinctive ways.[1] Outwardly, Britain possessed the characteristic markers of a liberal polity: equality before the law, representative government, a broad (and ultimately democratic) electorate based on the individual subject, mass political parties to mobilize that subject, and the triumph of opinion over influence. But, at least down to the 1950s, British practice tended to deviate radically from this liberal ideal—so much so that it might be more fruitful to think in terms of "conservative" rather than "liberal" modernity in the British case. The persistence of hierarchical thinking meant that neither the law nor civil administration was class-neutral, while within the polity, corporate identities, patrician idioms, and the politics of influence all continued to flourish. Power rested on the assumption that an educated, and supposedly disinterested, elite would reconcile conflicting (and less rational) interest-claims from below. Tested first in the governance of the four nations, this elitist version of pluralism became the blueprint for governing the newly assertive "masses" in the nineteenth century, then for containing the nationalist claims of an increasingly restless empire.

I do not wish to pretend that paternalist modes of thought and action went unchallenged. On the contrary, they were profoundly shaken by the social, economic, and political turmoil of the half century between the 1790s and the 1840s. During this period established modes of paternalist

government were eroded from all sides: from below, by a newly autonomous and irreverent plebeian radicalism;[2] and from above, by a powerful
cocktail of Evangelical thinkers preaching doctrines of individual sin and
retribution and economic liberals seeking to maximize the opportunities
for individual endeavor and self-reliance.[3] Together these forces shaped
the New Poor Law of 1834, with its harsh test of "less eligibility" for the
able-bodied poor. This was a clear victory for individualist over paternalist
modes of governance, as both Tory and radical critics recognized at the
time. But the victory was not total: implementation was patchy, and the
law of settlement was not rescinded—paupers were not automatically a
charge on their parish of residence.[4]

Even in the early nineteenth century the paternalist impulse was far
from expunged. The backward-looking, agrarian-minded Evangelicals who
supported "less eligibility" hoped, thereby, to see the restoration of a
properly functioning, hierarchical society structured around patrician
obligation and plebeian deference, with private philanthropy as its vital
social cement.[5] Just as importantly, there was a strong strain of both Whig
and Tory politics that continued to adhere to the more communitarian,
classically inflected modes of thought that had shaped both seventeenth-
century civic republicanism and the eighteenth-century Whig Enlightenment.[6] Among Tories this tended to be expressed primarily in terms of the
defense of the traditions of local, paternalist government, though Michael
Thomas Sadler, leader of the Ten Hours movement, was also open to the
innovative use of central state power (as Pitt the Younger had been).[7] Crucially, paternalist-minded Whigs also proved willing to countenance bold
initiatives of state intervention in the name of "the people." According
to Peter Mandler, in the years after the New Poor Law, it was the more
interventionist Whig grandees, rather than the economic liberals, who
made the running as the governing elite sought to contain the challenge
of popular unrest associated with Chartism and the Ten Hours movement
and restore the perceived legitimacy of elite rule.[8] At the level of political
ideas, J. W. Burrow reminds us that linear histories of the rise of liberal
individualism do great violence to the complexity of nineteenth-century
thought, and especially to their deep roots in eighteenth-century debates
about civilization, civil society, and progress, which all worked to con-
strain the claims of individualism.[9] And at the level of political practice,
Jon Parry reminds us that throughout the heyday of Victorian Liberalism,
the dictates of laissez-faire, like those of internationalism, were always
tempered by Liberal politicians' adherence to the ideal of "manly" and

"patriotic" leadership, which presupposed a willingness to use the power of the state in a vigorous manner, both at home and abroad.[10]

If we turn to cultural history, Mandler has stressed the longevity of eighteenth-century "civilizational" perspectives, with their refusal of the radically universalizing implications of Enlightenment rationalism and individualism. According to the civilizational model, both "classes" and "nations" existed at different stages of development on a common path (or "ladder") toward full "civilization."[11] By this reading, only those at the top of the ladder—members of Britain's "progressive but inegalitarian and anti-democratic ruling elite"—possessed in full the qualities of virtue, politeness, refinement, and character deemed necessary to enjoy, not only full citizenship, but also recognition as fully rounded "individuals"—Dror Wahrman's newly conceptualized "modern subjects."[12] But while Wahrman's *Making of the Modern Self* brilliantly traces the genesis of this conceptualization of unified and embodied personal identity in late-eighteenth-century England, it is less concerned to explore how the meanings attached to these markers of social identity were frequently used specifically to deny the *universality* of modern "selfhood."

This, then, is an exploration of the underbelly of liberal modernity in Britain—of its willful exclusions and its creative compromises with older political and social traditions.[13] Indeed, arguably the dominant creed of nineteenth-century British government was a hybrid variant of liberal individualism—a sort of "Tory liberalism." Tory liberalism was premised less on the exclusion of most Britons from full citizenship than on the widespread acceptance of patrician ideas about the merits of elite government and the need to preserve (or as often reinvent) "natural" social hierarchies. Such thinking cut across the dictates of economic liberalism and individualism, which it sought to confine within the limited sphere of the market. Raymond Williams famously termed this the "idea of service," arguing that it was inculcated through elite education and served not only to modify individualism through its emphasis "on conformity and on respect for education" but also "to confirm and maintain the *status quo*."[14] Crucially, under Tory liberalism, the political subject remained essentially corporate rather than individual. Primary identification was with the collective group: the parish, the town, the county, the nation, but also the school, the club, the church or chapel, or, for many workers, "the union." Such corporate blocs were envisaged as ordered, stratified entities, as spheres within which paternalism could still operate, and where the compelling bonds of mutuality were powerful, yet unequal, in the obligations they implied (this was no less true of trade unions, even if the figures of authority were not "born to rule"). It was the long survival of these impulses that shaped Britain's distinctive path to modernity, a path that is perhaps better captured by the idea of "conservative" rather than "liberal" modernity.[15]

CORPORATE SELVES

The persistence of corporate alongside individualist conceptualizations of identity and subjectivity can be traced through many facets of modern British society and politics. Recently, Keith Snell has explored the deep attachment to historic parish identities that survived late into the modern period, and Marc Brodie has demonstrated the centrality of parish-level Anglican loyalties to the popular Conservatism of London's East End before World War I.[16] One might also cite Patrick Joyce's pioneering early work on the rise of a new urban paternalism in the factory politics of Lancashire, or the strong emphasis on the subordination of self to group in the ethos of Victorian public and grammar school education, and even more in the ethos of the armed forces. Here, as in the ethos of organized labor, the individual was subordinated to a hierarchically organized collectivity that valued obedience and loyalty above the dictates of reason.[17]

But then the constitution itself was strikingly slow to register the claims of the individual, liberal subject. Not only was full adult suffrage not granted until 1928 (and one-person-one-vote delayed even longer, to 1948), but throughout the nineteenth century the representation of *interests* remained as important as the representation of individuals. Indeed, down to 1918 the eighteenth-century argument that nonvoters were "virtually represented" by voters—for whom the franchise was not a right but a public trust—remained widely deployed as a bulwark against full democracy. The Whig architects of the 1832 Reform Act explicitly saw themselves as redressing the balance of interests at Westminster. By transferring seats from decayed ancient boroughs to the counties and new urban centers of population, they sought to dilute the personal influence of the crown and new money, in favor of more settled and organic forms of influence rooted in the agricultural, industrial, and commercial interests of specific localities: for example, the metalworking trades of Birmingham and Wolverhampton, the leather trades of Walsall, the cotton trade of Manchester, or the shipping interests of Gateshead and Tynemouth. But if voters were still defined primarily by corporate (rather than individual) identities, the 1832 act nonetheless accentuated the distinction between voters and nonvoters (by creating the first registers of electors) and inscribed sharper socioeconomic meanings on that distinction.[18]

Thereafter, the balance gradually shifted toward more individualized conceptions of voting and voters, but the idea of representing "interests" was never wholly superseded. In 1867 male householders (i.e., ratepayers) below the £10 threshold were admitted as a class, rather than as individuals, apparently in an attempt to construct a more defensible bulwark against a fully democratic franchise. On the other hand, the underlying logic of the move was to identify a class of voters who would display the *individual* personal characteristics deemed necessary to exercise the public responsibility of citizenship: reason, forethought, and, above all, "manly" independence.[19] Constituencies continued to be radically unequal in size—recognition both of the historic claims of specific communities and of the continued salience of representing local interests (the pronounced pattern of regional specialization associated with Britain's early industrial development helped reinforce this logic).[20] In the big cities minority interests were to be represented by ensuring that electors cast fewer votes than the number of MPs to be elected. It was already clear that here "interest" essentially meant "party," although one could argue that in many respects party was, in turn, a vehicle for corporate interests—especially the rival religious interests of Church and chapel.

But voting as a public ritual in which "manly," independent citizens acted as disinterested trustees of wider public interests did not long survive the Second Reform Act. In the face of widespread concern about disorder and corruption at the 1868 election, both open public voting and public nomination were abolished by the 1872 Secret Ballot Act (though not without a determined rearguard defense of classical models of open, *public* citizenship).[21] Thereafter voting became a purely private act, conducted in secrecy away from the public gaze; but it did not thereby become a purely *individual* act. On the contrary, the manner of workingmen's admission to the franchise in 1867 helped strengthen older ideas about the "virtual representation" of nonvoters. Male ratepayers were presented as respectable, domestic patriarchs—as responsible fathers and husbands whose social progress vindicated the "civilizational" model, and who could now be trusted to represent the interests not just of their wives and children, but of all unenfranchised workers.[22] It was, in effect, the trickling down, not of liberal individualism, but of the rights and privileges of the hierarchical, paternalist old order. One might reasonably argue that this logic was widely contested by the 1870s, notably by radicals who held out for universal suffrage and by advocates of female suffrage who mercilessly unpicked the hypocrisies of "virtual representation," but one still finds the concept being mobilized as late as 1918, when it was used to justify the decision not to enfranchise most women under thirty. Whether anyone really believed that younger women would be "virtually represented" by their older sisters must be doubted, but the concept still retained enough residual credibility to be mobilized as a coherent rationale for a rather shabby compromise.[23] The 1918 act also preserved the representation of corporate interests alongside full male democracy: the number of university seats (where graduates could cast a second vote) was raised to fifteen, and the plethora of historic property franchises was rationalized into a single "business vote." The epitome of "conservative modernity," these reforms helped to sustain plural voting for another generation.

Moreover, as the British state finally ended men's corporate interest in gender-exclusive political rights, it simultaneously encoded gender at the heart of the embryonic new system of *social* rights. As Susan Pedersen has shown, during the war the state had stepped in to shore up the patriarchal, male-breadwinner model of citizenship both economically, through the payment of dependents' allowances to servicemen's families, and morally, through attempts to police the behavior of their errant wives.[24] Key elements of this system became grafted on to postwar state responses to mass unemployment, which from the outset treated the claims of married women, youths, and single men much more harshly than those of male "breadwinners."[25] Nor was this simply the imposition of a cunning state strategy of "social control." On the contrary, the claims of the paterfamilias were deeply embedded in both labor politics and popular culture. Between the wars trade union suspicion toward the campaign for family allowances was rooted as much in fears that the movement represented a critique of working-class male respectability and familial responsibility as in fears about the reform's likely impact on wages.[26] And, inserting a personal note, my mother recalls that into the 1950s her bus-driver father insisted that his entire family should vote Labour while they lived under "his roof."[27] It was the anti-individualist logic of the trade union block vote writ small, and as such a powerful testimony to the residual strength of corporate over individual conceptions of the self in twentieth-century Britain.

One might also argue that, besides party self-interest, one of the most important factors behind the retention of majoritarian, first-past-the-post voting in British parliamentary elections has been the argument that this system best secures the representation of distinct and meaningful "communities." Indeed, even where more proportional voting systems have been introduced, representatives' explicit links with geographic constituencies have been retained. On the other hand, the claims of locality have certainly been compromised. From 1885 large cities were broken up into smaller subdivisions with no distinct historical or communal identity. True, the boundaries of the new, single-member constituencies were to be drawn to reflect the "pursuits of the people," but this still represented a challenge to broader civic identities. This trend was accentuated in 1918 when, for the first time, the law decreed that constituencies should contain roughly equal numbers of voters, although the boundary commissioners were still instructed "to segregate adjacent urban and industrial areas" (only in 1944 was this stipulation finally dropped).[28] But, as recent work on so-called villa Toryism reminds us, even such "artificial" constituencies could generate powerful new collective identities, thanks in part to the creative efforts of local newspapers.[29]

Perhaps significantly, as Britain finally embraced a democratic franchise in 1918, so the political elite began to flirt with extraparliamentary versions of corporatism as possible solutions to industrial unrest and political instability. And while many of these ideas foundered on the wreck of the Lloyd George Coalition, throughout the remainder of the interwar period figures from across the political spectrum floated schemes for institutionalizing Britain's corporate economic interests in new ways. In Labour and trade union circles there was much talk of creating a separate "Industrial Parliament" where employers and unions could meet directly to resolve their differences. In turn, many Conservatives began to have deep misgivings about the ability of liberal democracy adequately to represent (and reconcile) powerful economic interest blocs. Some were explicitly drawn to the totalitarian versions of corporatism flourishing in fascist states, but most envisaged adapting corporatism to British traditions of representative government and evolutionary change: in short, making it compatible with the central tenets of "conservative modernity."[30]

LIBERAL EXCLUSIONS

Liberal exclusion was not just a question of political rights: the exclusion of the majority of adult Britons from the formal rights of citizenship until 1918 and the denial of full equality between the sexes for another decade. These exclusions are familiar enough, though no less important for that, but they were merely the constitutional expression of a deeper governmental logic that held that most adults remained confined to the "civilizational" slow lane and, as such, were incapable of living up to the ideals of liberal selfhood.

But this was not an unchanging story. In the 1840s most British Liberals had shared the conviction of their continental counterparts that "freedom" and "democracy" were incompatible, at least on European soil. However, attitudes began to change during the 1850s and 1860s. Among both moderate Liberals and old-style Parliamentary Radicals there was a perceptible rapprochement with notions of democracy and popular sovereignty—a rapprochement that ultimately created the basis, not just for mid-Victorian franchise reform and labor legislation, but also for the development of a distinctively liberal version of state-directed social reform in the early twentieth century. Many factors shaped this politics: Liberal engagement with popular nationalism in Europe and democratic government in America, Radical disillusionment with purely parliamentary conceptions of sovereignty, and the local importance of Liberal alliances with plebeian radicals. [31]

But the Liberal rapprochement with popular democracy was only partial. Most mid-Victorian Liberals remained profoundly uncertain about both the limits of popular sovereignty and the virtues of untrammeled democracy. Indeed, the heady optimism of the 1860s quickly turned to disillusionment as Liberal intellectuals confronted the vulgarities of mass politics and a revitalized Conservatism. [32] In turn, plebeian radicals remained uncertain about Liberalism, fearful that the strong influence of conservative-minded Whigs and Liberals within the party would always act as both a restraint on reform and a barrier to genuine popular government. Moreover, while Gladstone's moral rhetoric and his appeals to "the people" breathed new life into the demotic underbelly of British popular politics, the late Victorian state he helped to shape remained strongly stamped by the hierarchical, class-inflected logic of the "civilizational" model (it was no accident that his cabinets were packed with aristocrats).

Whilst Liberal governments challenged Tory/Anglican privileges in the armed forces, the universities, and the civil service, they were slower to challenge class-inflected biases in the state, the law, or the provision of public services. Class differences were registered, but the aim was to contain them within established hierarchical modes of governance rather than overthrow the established status order. Hence in the field of education Liberals introduced reforms that consolidated a three-tier system mapping all too closely on to the model of Britain as a static, hierarchical class society of "upper," "middling," and "lower" orders. The 1868 Public Schools Act oversaw the reform of elite education, encouraging public schools to introduce curricula suited to preparing upper-class children for the ancient universities, civil service examinations, the armed forces, and imperial administration. In turn, the 1869 Endowed Schools Act oversaw the transformation of ancient "grammar" schools from institutions intended to provide free education to the children of the poor into fee-paying schools intended to prepare children of the middle classes for business, the professions, and university. Finally, the 1870 Education Act created municipal elementary schools for the mass of poorer children destined for apprenticeships or dead-end jobs in early adolescence.[33] At first social mobility between classes was almost wholly discounted, and even well into the twentieth century the preferred model of mobility remained the "ladder," with mechanisms created to facilitate the educational advance only of the most exceptional children from disadvantaged backgrounds.[34]

As Paul Johnson has forcefully argued, class thinking was also deeply embedded in the Victorian legal system, even in economic spheres such as the law of contract where one might expect liberal doctrines to predominate.[35] Johnson contrasts Victorian laws on bankruptcy and small debt and concludes that the stark differences between the lenient treatment of the bankrupt and the harsh treatment of small debtors reflected strong class prejudices about the different moral character of each group. Workers were assumed to be incapable of acting as responsible, autonomous agents; they were "childlike" and needed different, more draconian, legal disciplines to regulate their behavior. But this was not about teaching them how to be free, liberal agents—rather it was premised on the logic that they existed at a stage of intellectual and moral development below that necessary for liberal freedom.

David Vincent's work on secrecy shows the same logic at work within the machinery of government. Here an informal gentlemanly code based on notions of personal "honor" sufficed to police the flow of secrets until the expansion of the state bureaucracy, coupled with more "meritocratic" procedures for appointment, brought new, less privileged cohorts into the heart of government. These new recruits tended not only to be of "low" birth but also to be self-educated, which meant they were assumed to lack the socializing, character-building influences of school and university deemed necessary to instill a proper sense of gentlemanly "honor" and loyalty to the group (i.e., the right "corporate" ethos). Attempts to restrict the flow of sensitive information to the higher ranks of the civil service failed to prevent frequent leaks to the popular press, and with the Official Secrets Acts of 1889 and 1911 the state turned to legal sanctions rather than moral exhortation to protect its hidden workings from public scrutiny. Even then, the old gentlemanly code survived at the heart of the secret state, as the postwar scandals surrounding Burgess, Maclean, and Philby amply illustrated.[36]

The history of censorship and the law of obscenity present a similar story. Again, the "masses" were considered childlike and incapable of acting as fully autonomous liberal subjects, whereas members of the educated elite were assumed to be invulnerable to moral corruption. In the field of publishing, the result was that the authorities moved swiftly to suppress books aimed at a mass audience but tended to view expensive editions intended for an upper-class market more leniently (extending even greater license to private, subscription-based publications).[37] The theatre worked under a similar regime. Public performances were subject to prior approval by the Lord Chamberlain's office, but private theatre clubs were allowed much greater freedom to stage not just controversial but even banned plays for "a minority audience."[38] Genuinely submerged cultures, including radical underworlds, were also given considerable license, not least because prosecution would bring them dangerous publicity. But when an underworld culture threatened to become mainstream, liberal tolerance rapidly gave way to stern paternalist intervention, as when the state moved against revolutionary socialists at the end of World War I, or against the radical counterculture movement around sixties journals such as *Oz* and *IT*.[39]

But by the sixties the paternalist, "civilizational" mind-set was already under full-scale assault. A key landmark in its defeat was the obscenity trial against Penguin Books for publishing D. H. Lawrence's *Lady Chatterley's Lover* as a mass-market paperback. Both the prosecution and the presiding judge made much of the fact that Penguin had already printed 200,000 copies and that at 3s 6d they would be "available for all and sundry to read." Speaking for the prosecution, Mervyn Griffiths-Jones famously asked, "Is it a book you would even wish your wife or your servants to read"? (though three of the jurors were women), and talked of how it might deprave "the young girl working in a factory."[40] The defense countered by arguing that Penguin Books existed to challenge the class hypocrisy that said "it is alright to publish a special edition at five or ten guineas" but not to make the same works available to all; the hypocrisy that said that judges, lawyers, and jurors could all read a book without becoming "depraved and corrupted" but that others, servants, factory girls, and the like, were morally weaker and must be protected.[41] In many ways the trial was as much about challenging Britain's traditions of authoritarian paternalism as it was about upholding the right to freedom of expression.[42] How fitting, therefore, that the book at its center was as much about class as sexual transgression.

THE PERSISTENCE OF PATERNALIST LEADERSHIP

The challenge to patrician authority posed by the *Lady Chatterley* trial was part of a wider crisis of paternalism caused by the political and psychological fallout from the debacle of the Suez intervention in 1956 and the growing recognition of Britain's ebbing global and imperial power. Many social and cultural trends reinforced the challenge to paternalism, including the more irreverent tone of print and broadcast journalism, which culminated in the satire boom of the early 1960s, the growing critique of authoritarian practices within the professions, the rising expectations about choice and personal autonomy associated with the so-called affluent society, and the corrosive effects of debates about national "decline" on the prestige of the political elite. But no less important was the elite's own crisis of confidence in the wake of Suez. Just as abroad the pretensions to global power and empire were swiftly wound up over the next decade, so at home politicians began to question the deep-seated assumption that government really did know what was best. As Mark Jarvis argues, Conservative governments of the late 1950s initiated many reformist policies that prefigured the so-called permissive revolution of the 1960s. Macmillan talked of politicians needing to stop treating the people like "children" and argued that individuals must henceforth be able to make their own moral choices.[43] Indeed, the *Lady Chatterley* trial sprang directly from this moment, since it was largely made possible by the 1959 Obscene Publications Act, which replaced the old Common Law offense of obscene libel. Jarvis demonstrates that Conservative leaders were always uncertain liberalizers, wary of the demoralizing effects of "affluence" and quick to retreat to more traditional, authoritarian positions when faced by the social consequences of liberalization, but the edifice of insouciant patrician power could not be rebuilt.

But before tracing the death throes of paternalism in the late twentieth century, we should perhaps pause to ask why paternalism and hierarchy remained so long entrenched in the British political and social system given that, from the 1860s, the country had a mass (if not fully democratic) franchise and from the 1920s one of its main political parties (Labour) was officially committed to the overthrow of class privilege in all its forms. I have already identified two key factors here: the contested status of individualist and laissez-faire doctrines in the nineteenth century and the power of "civilizational" models, which held most Britons to be incapable (for now) of living as fully autonomous liberal subjects. To this one must also add the role of imperial conquest, military success, and fairly consistent socioeconomic progress in legitimating the existing order. If, as Bernard Porter insists, imperialism was always strongly stamped by the impress of class, with the British upper classes viewing imperial rule as a natural extension of noblesse oblige, it follows that while the imperial project flourished paternalist leadership was enhanced domestically as well as globally.[44] Similarly, David Edgerton's argument about the balance between warfare and welfare within the twentieth-century British state reminds us, not only of the adaptive qualities of Britain's "natural" rulers, but also that victory in war entrenched their position at the heart of the British polity.[45]

But paternalism was also sustained by the culture of British public life, and in particular by the persistence, deep into the twentieth century, of patrician models of political leadership. This was about more than the fact that money and/or birth long remained prerequisites for a successful political career, even on the radical left. It was also about the structure of political interaction in Britain: the tolerance of plebeian disorder and irreverence at elections, the indulgent attitude toward the "pleasures of the people," and, crucially, male politicians' embrace of the gentlemanly ideal of self-control, good humor, and reasonableness.

Turning first to the persistence of disorder in public politics, perhaps the most salient points to stress are, first, the uncharacteristically indulgent attitude of the authorities toward disorder, vandalism, and even violence at elections down to 1918, and, second, the frequent involvement of politicians in such disorder, either as clandestine organizers or as public apologists. At elections the Victorian and Edwardian public, in particular unenfranchised adult males, were given license to cause mayhem both in the streets and at candidates' public meetings. It was as though Britons possessed a constitutional right to abuse, shout at, and even manhandle their political masters. But these dramas of symbolic social leveling were both tightly scripted (for instance, the gentlemanly ideal did not demand forbearance if one's "honor" was impugned) and served to emphasize the gulf between politician and public, thereby affirming the right of the political class to rule over their less "civilized" fellow countrymen.[46] In essence electioneering was a sort of bastardized *"carnevale"* during which the barriers of class were suspended, if not inverted, and the spirit of "misrule" indulged.

But all this changed very quickly after World War I, not because politics became more peaceable (though in many places they did), but because widespread social and industrial unrest, coupled with Labour's dramatic electoral breakthrough, transformed the class dynamics of public politics. Westminster was no longer a gentleman's closed shop—the barriers of class and sex had been breached—and elections now seemed as likely to undermine as affirm the social order. Disruption and disorder came to be seen as symptoms of an incipient class war rather than as the innocent horseplay of an unruly populace that knew no better.[47] But if most politicians now shunned association with disorder, this did not mean that they retreated altogether from street politics and face-to-face contact with the irreverent public. On the contrary, election meetings continued in rude health down to the 1950s, bringing voters and politicians together in public rituals of accountability that drew their power, like the old nomination hustings, from the symbolic disavowal of the gulf between governors and governed. Some politicians took this further, using overtly populist techniques to portray themselves as men (or occasionally women) of the people, but as Martin Francis reminds us, even on the left there was deep distrust of those who sought to appeal to the "irrational" emotions of the masses.[48] Instead, late into the twentieth century the dominant style of public politics continued to valorize restraint, self-discipline, and moral earnestness in order to perpetuate the mystique of elite leadership and power.[49] Baldwin's genius between the wars had been to convey these qualities to the masses via the new media of radio and film, and to do so in a more homely, less austere manner than his Victorian forebears.[50] Writing in 1961, Raymond Williams lamented how the mass media connived in the idea that democratic leadership should be about "man-management" rather than the frank and open discussion of issues. It was, he argued, "the tactic of a defensive autocracy"—adding caustically, in an apparent swipe at Labour, "and people do not have to be born into an autocracy to acquire its habits."[51]

Indulging the "pleasures of the people" was also central to the paternalist idiom in British politics. "Cakes and ale" Toryism, with its roots in the raucous electioneering of the eighteenth century, long remained a staple of Victorian party politics. Indeed, its purchase increased from the late 1860s with the broadened franchise and the growing clamor for temperance reform. Tory politicians stressed the putative historic rights of the "free-born Englishman" to enjoy his "sparkling warm ale"—though they were generally careful to couch this in terms of the defense of his right to a quiet pint rather than a riotous binge.[52] The aim was to expose the class fault lines running through the Liberal commitment to liberty but to do so while retaining a veneer of paternalist respectability.

Beer was not the only plebeian pleasure to be celebrated in party politics. Late Victorian and Edwardian politicians often cultivated close ties to popular sports such as football and horse racing. In Black Country towns like Walsall and Wolverhampton both professional and amateur football were closely linked to local Conservative politicians, but elsewhere the

Liberals also played this card. Even Labour politicians could be attuned to the politics of pleasure. David Howell may be right to suggest that within the Independent Labour Party (ILP) the "tory-socialist" tradition of Hyndman and Blatchford ultimately lost out to the more ascetic traditions of chapel socialism, but, even so, there was always a minority streak in Labour politics that embraced the people and their pleasures "warts and all."[53] But the dominant Labour view insisted that workers' prioritization of immediate pleasures held them in thrall to their social and political masters. In seeking to purge British politics of the distracting, even debasing, "politics of pleasure," Labour leaders merely rejected one facet of paternalism for another. For patrician indulgence they substituted education and moral improvement, with themselves, naturally, cast in the role of the enlightened educators who would lead their people to the Promised Land.

Many Labour politicians came to see their first task as reforming not the system or the state but rather the workers, who had to be educated and moralized to make them fit to build the socialist New Jerusalem. There was a sociocultural dimension to this story: most early Labour leaders came from, or moved into, a distinct autodidact subculture, from which it was all too easy to see the workers and their distracting, increasingly commercialized leisure culture not as a resource for building socialism but as a major impediment to its realization. Although Chris Waters argues that Labour leaders had developed a more pragmatic approach to popular culture by 1914, the work of Stuart MacIntyre, Jeremy Nuttall, and Lawrence Black suggests that the impulse to reform the people remained powerful long after the party leadership had passed from the autodidact pioneers to a new generation, among whom university-educated professionals such as Attlee, Dalton, Gaitskell, and Jay loomed increasingly large—men steeped in the gentlemanly codes of Oxbridge and the paternalist ethos of adult education and the university settlement movement.[54] Indeed, Raphael Samuel argues that the same "paternalist" spirit also infused the politics of Britain's post-Suez New Left, whose activists, he recalled, "did not doubt that they were missionaries or ambassadors of high culture."[55]

True, Labour leaders still understood their mission as being to "set the people free"—but they remained convinced that many of the chains that bound the people were of their own making. The epitome of this attitude was Douglas Jay's famous observation that, when it came to questions such as education, nutrition, and health, "the gentleman in Whitehall really does know better what is good for people than the people know themselves."[56] During the heady days of the "People's War" these tensions receded into the background; many Labour leaders convinced themselves that war socialism had wrought a cultural revolution in the people. Their dramatic electoral breakthrough in 1945 seemed ample proof of the revolution in popular attitudes. But faced by the difficult challenges of power, Labour leaders soon reverted to a more pessimistic assessment of "their people." The party quickly found itself in conflict with the more individualist and instrumental strands of popular culture. Earlier attempts to reach out to the aspirant and affluent were largely forgotten, and the party retreated into a narrow conception of "its" people that more closely resembled its opponents' caricature of the party as sectional and divisive. From the heroic experiences of war and reconstruction Labour leaders constructed an idealized "working class"—selfless, solidaristic, and instinctively socialist. Many lived up to these ideals, both within and without "the movement"—this was what gave power to Labour's vision of "its" people—but nonetheless, judged by these standards, it was perhaps inevitable that as many would be found wanting.

Labour also embedded many paternalist assumptions at the heart of its "welfare" state. Most strikingly, means testing was retained for all those not entitled to contribution-based national insurance benefits, thereby weakening the sense of universal entitlement. Little was done for vulnerable but politically marginal groups such as the disabled, while the fiercely judgemental, paternalist notion of the "problem family" became enshrined in postwar state social work practice.[57] But given the powerful strand of paternalism running through Labour politics, it was perhaps inevitable that the shadow of the "undeserving poor" would not be wholly eradicated, especially when it also had deep roots in popular culture, as Robert Moore discovered in his ethnographic study of Methodist miners in postwar county Durham.[58]

Perhaps this is why the institutions of Labour's "welfare" state survived the defeat of 1951 largely unscathed. In many ways Labour politicians were as patrician in their outlook toward "the masses" as the politicians they opposed across the floor of the Commons, or the civil servants who advised them on policy. Hence the constant lament during the 1950s that Labour's supposedly "natural" electoral majority could not be mobilized. Labour's vision was a noble, inspiring one; it was much less exclusionary than its critics suggested, and its promulgation did more to elide ideas of "nation" and "people" in British political discourse than either nineteenth-century Liberalism or interwar Baldwinite Conservatism.[59] But even so, it left Labour pledged to set the people free on terms dictated by the party, not the people themselves. For Labour, it was thus a travesty that just three years after it had won power, pledged to realize the hopes and ideals of a "People's War," it should find Churchill successfully rallying anti-government sentiment under the slogan "Set the People free"—a slogan that would go on to become central to the Conservatives' postwar political revival.[60]

But the Conservative party of Churchill, Eden, Macmillan, and Home had a similarly narrow conception of what it meant to "set the people free"; relaxing controls, lowering taxes (a little), and gradually ending rationing was one thing, but fundamentally challenging hierarchical and paternalist traditions was quite another. Despite their post-Suez wobble, Conservative leaders such as Macmillan and Home remained unmistakably patrician figures presented to the public as men "born to lead." They recognized that imperial retreat and economic "decline" had tarnished the image of Britain's traditional gentlemanly leaders, prompting an unprecedented outpouring against "the Establishment" and the "class system,"[61] but they sought to ride the storm by offering decisive leadership—that is, by deploying Williams's demonic arts of "man-management." It is probably no accident, however, that it was at this point that British political leaders finally lost confidence in their ability to proclaim the pieties of public religion to the masses. Until the 1940s Britain had regularly proclaimed official National Days of Prayer, but when the idea was mooted in the wake of the Suez crisis of 1956 ministers proved decidedly lukewarm. Thereafter British political leaders, many of whom remained deeply religious in private life, largely purged their public discourse of the language of religious exhortation. It was a decisive moment in the disintegration of "conservative modernity" in Britain.[62]

Responding to the changing public mood, Harold Wilson, Labour's leader from 1963, sought to cultivate a self-consciously "modern," forward-looking image, characterized by an informal, even folksy, "man of the people" demeanor. In this he was doubtless encouraged by private polling evidence suggesting that a clear majority of voters would prefer someone who had "risen by ability" over someone born into the political class.[63] Wilson's cultivation of a simple, provincial image epitomized by his proclaimed love of HP sauce, gannex raincoats, and Huddersfield Town F.C., nonetheless reflected the declining power of traditional notions of paternalist leadership. But his claim to power and authority still rested on the idea that he was the ordinary boy *made good*—that he possessed the technical skills, in particular the grasp of macroeconomics and planning, and the political authority to enable him to transform the lives of ordinary Britons from above. [64]

But patrician leadership was not easily repackaged. Alongside the counterculture radicalism and industrial militancy that dogged the governments of Wilson, Heath, and Callaghan throughout the sixties and seventies, there was also a less dramatic but nonetheless inexorable growth of assertive individualism that hollowed out the institutions of Britain's corporatist civil society. By the early 1970s, when second-wave feminism was mounting an excoriating critique of the very concept of traditional male authority, many began to question whether Britain was still "governable." Perhaps significantly, when John Goldthorpe tried to explain the industrial militancy of the period he stressed the vital role played by "the decay of the status order," by which he meant belief in "natural" hierarchies of prestige and reward. This, Goldthorpe argued, had weakened the "constraints" and "inhibitions" that had historically acted to limit the assertiveness of Britain's disadvantaged groups.[65]

Britain's "conservative modernity" had survived the doubt and disillusion of the interwar period, thanks in part to Baldwin's genius for bringing out the inclusive and democratic facets of a still essentially graded, hierarchical worldview.[66] Victory in the People's War, and Labour's electoral landslide in 1945, had ushered in further democratization (including strict one person one vote), without fundamentally challenging the patrician assumptions at the heart of the British system. Not only were the symbols of old power—monarchy, empire, Church, and even the Lords—sacrosanct, but paternalism was written into the fabric of the new welfare state, just as it was written into the dominant style of Labour politics. Britain's "conservative modernity" began to unwind only in the 1950s and 1960s. These decades witnessed an accelerated retreat from empire, the decision to abandon Commonwealth kinship ties in favor of European markets, the softening of patriarchal authority within the home, and public arguments over immigration that exaggerated the dilution of Britain's ethnic homogeneity.[67] The bulwarks of "conservative modernity" were undermined from within and without. But until Thatcher, most political leaders remained in denial of these changes. Like Baldwin between the wars, they sought to conserve an essentially paternalist system by modernizing its "image": tweed was out, folksy was in.

But with Thatcher, both "Tory" and "Labour" versions of paternalism came to an abrupt end. Largely unintentionally, Thatcherism unleashed a more radical transformation in British political culture than either the "permissiveness" of the 1960s or the militancy of the 1970s. Thatcher's populist espousal of economic liberalism and the acquisitive society, which contrasted sharply with Conservative anxieties about the corrosive effects of "affluence" a generation earlier, coupled with her constant war against the entrenched "liberal establishment" that had supposedly presided over decades of national decline, legitimated precisely the sort of radical individualism that Macmillan and his associates had recoiled from in horror in the early 1960s. Though herself a staunch opponent of liberal attitudes to personal morality and sexuality, Thatcher's political style eroded most of the remaining bulwarks of paternalism and moral authoritarianism in British public life. At the time, left-wing commentators such as Stuart Hall believed that exactly the opposite was happening. With good reason, they focused on how Thatcher sought to harness reactionary moral populism on immigration and crime to bolster an unpopular right-wing assault on the unions and the welfare state.[68] However, with hindsight we can see that the popular, iconoclastic social forces that Thatcher mobilized in her struggle to remake both Conservatism and the British state were not easily corraled behind her broader agenda of social conservatism. On the contrary, her neoliberal championing of "freedom" and "liberty" in economics licensed precisely the sort of radical break with the constraints of tradition and social conformity that British politicians of both left and right had been determined to prevent throughout the twentieth century. Finally, the barriers erected to corral possessive individualism within the confines of the cash nexus were torn down, the corporate loyalties and the "idea of service" that had once restrained its power in civil society and polity now counted for nought.

No doubt Thatcher was working with the grain of history here. She did not create consumerism and the mantra of "choice," any more than she caused the increase in divorce or "illegitimacy" rates. Her genius was intuitively to grasp that rapid social change, coupled with national "decline" and the end of empire, had already eroded the bulwarks of the old politics of elite paternalism. But her plain-speaking, populist style raised a previously subterranean popular culture of irreverence and robust plebeian individualism to the status of the new "official" culture of the nation. As Thatcher's government declared war on the surviving claimants to moral and political leadership that had once been the backbone of "conservative modernity"—the Established Church, the BBC, the professions, even the monarchy—the demotic culture that had for so long simultaneously chided and cherished these symbols of life in an "old country" became instead the new High Court of opinion and taste. In short, the historic foundations of "conservative modernity" were finally dismantled by a Conservative government convinced that it needed to mobilize the people against an "Establishment" that had supposedly presided over decades of national "decline."

11. Government and the Management of Information, 1844-2009

David Vincent

Whether as tragedy or farce, the invasion of Iraq in 2003 was a repeat of history. If nothing else it brought together the themes of this book, an imperialist endeavor undertaken in the name of liberal democracy designed to promote modernity in a backward political culture. Its domestic consequences are being played out in many registers, not least the control of public information. The war was undertaken on the basis of espionage about weapons of mass destruction and the subsequent inquiries into its origins and conduct have been fraught with conflict over the use and misuse of official secrecy.

The line that divides the past from the present in this regard is the Freedom of Information Act of 2000, which came into force in January 2005, after the war began but in time to frame the debate about its causes. Until the acts of 1889 and 1911 there was no written legal definition of the state's powers to manage its information. The 1911 Official Secrets Act, passed during a manufactured panic about German aggression, acknowledged the existence of government secrets but left it to ministers and senior civil servants to define what these were. The 1989 Official Secrets Act for the first time attempted a classification of what could and could not be communicated, but only at the beginning of the twenty-first century was the public formally given ownership of the information held on its behalf by those it had elected. By this time most Western democracies possessed some kind of legislation, and it was only when the new Labour government accepted the European Convention for the Protection of Human Rights that British exceptionalism in the management of public information became untenable. This did not prevent Labour from subsequently making a virtue out of necessity. In the view of the minister of justice, Jack Straw:

> The Freedom of Information Act has profoundly changed the relation-
> ship between citizens, and their elected representatives and the media
> on the one hand, and the Government and public authorities on the
> other. It has, as intended, made the Executive far more open and
> accountable. The Act provides a regime for freedom of information
> which is one of the most open and rigorous in the world.[1]

Once more the United Kingdom could define its liberalism against less
advanced political cultures. Not only does it stand out against regressive
tyrannies such as Saddam Hussain's Iraq, but it also carries the beacon
of progress among modern democracies. As was the case in the first
public controversy about official secrecy in 1844, the issue is essentially
comparative.

The drama of that year was ignited when Peel's administration was
caught opening the correspondence of Italian exiles in England at the
behest of the Austrian government, a regime held by progressive opinion
to be the leading opponent of European liberalism.[2] Giuseppe Mazzini took
his complaint to Parliament where the sympathetic radical MP Thomas
Duncombe protested at the introduction "of the spy system of foreign
states," which was "repugnant to every principle of the British constitution, and subversive of the public confidence, which was so essential to
a commercial country."[3] Already the interdependence of capitalism and
a particular mode of governance was recognized. The liberal state stood
charged with a double betrayal of its principles. Not only was it aligning
itself with the old reactionary European order, but it was refusing public
debate of its actions. Rather than either admit or deny the allegations, the
Home Secretary, Sir James Graham, declined to discuss them at all. He
responded to a petition submitted on behalf of the Italian exiles by discov-
ering an unwritten convention of not exposing government surveillance
to public scrutiny of any kind. This led Duncombe to mount the first modern attack on official secrecy: "if a Secretary of State, or the Government,
were justified in screening and sheltering themselves behind this official
secrecy, he wanted to know what became of that responsibility of which we
heard so much when any measure was submitted giving more extensive
powers to the Secretary of State or the Government?"[4]

The narrative of liberalism assumes progress. Not only has the United
Kingdom passed through the stations of change ahead of less advanced
nations, but the journey is not reversible. The passions unleashed in 1844
derived energy from the apprehension that the pressures of domestic disorder and international revolution would undo the achievement of the
Reform Act settlement of 1832. Just two years before the controversy

Duncombe had presented the second Chartist Petition to Parliament and it was uncertain how far the Conservative administration was prepared to go to preserve the interests of the newly enfranchised in the face of mass working-class protest. His opponent, Sir James Graham, had been an enthusiastic Whig supporter of the Reform Bill and had served as First Lord of the Admiralty in Grey's administration. He had become a Tory only in 1837, and a persuasive reading of his silence in 1844 was that he was seeking to avoid overtly committing his government to a formal abandonment of the reform agenda. Instead he adopted a particularly British compromise to the dilemma of protecting both order and progress. It was unpalatable to be seen to associate with the forces of European reaction, but it was irresponsible to abandon reserve powers of protection against the agencies of domestic protest whose threat to the propertied classes in the early 1840s was impossible to calibrate. The solution was a double negative that informed British politics at least until the end of the following century. In the words of Henry Taylor's mordant guide to statesmanship of 1836, "A secret may be sometimes best kept by keeping the secret of its being secret."[5] Declining to communicate the control of communication reconciled the confidence of liberalism with its fears.

Jack Straw's endorsement of the new regime of written rights of communication also occurred at a particular moment of uncertainty. In the aftermath of Al Qaeda's attack on the United States in September 2001 and the United Kingdom in July 2005, the tension between civil liberties and national security was under fierce scrutiny. The management of official communication was at the center of the debate. It had been more than a decade since the eager new Labour administration had committed itself to legislation in the White Paper *Your Right to Know: Freedom of Information*. The document contained a preface by Tony Blair, accompanied by a photograph of the young prime minister wearing a shirt that symbolically still displayed the creases of the box from which it had just been unpacked. "The traditional culture of secrecy," he wrote, "will only be broken down by giving people in the United Kingdom the legal right to know."[6] But in the following two years, partly under the influence of Jack Straw in his first manifestation as Home Secretary, the bill had been watered down and then strengthened again in the face of fierce protest by the freedom of information lobby. Once passed, a cautious Whitehall had waited another five years before permitting the act to take effect, and by early 2009 it was still too early to gauge its long-term effect.[7] The first information commissioner, Richard Thomas, expressed a mixture of nervousness and hope in his retirement speech in June 2009:

The Freedom of Information Act has been seen as a somewhat fragile flower for most of its lifetime. It has now come of age and moved centre stage—a permanent fixture and a core part of the fabric of public life. The recent uproar over MPs' expenses has cemented FOI's reputation as a success story. Over the last four years a much wider range of other information has been disclosed up and down the country. It is a key channel for securing substantially improved transparency and accountability. The surprise is no longer the nature and extent of disclosure. What is astonishing is how much was previously treated as secret.[8]

The balance between apprehension and expectation was captured by the twin issues of public interest and ministerial veto. During the debate over the White Paper, the government had managed to insert class exemptions covering defense, international relations, law enforcement, commercial interests, the economy, and the frankness of internal discussions or the "effective conduct of public affairs,"[9] but the capacity of government to block information without judgment or appeal was curtailed. Maurice Frankel summarized the key achievement of his lobbying campaign: "I think the critical thing was, they agreed to make the public interest test mandatory. Although they retained the ministerial veto, that fundamentally shifted the organisation of the bill, so, what was then a gigantic class exemption to do with policy formulation, for example, became subject to a statutory test of whether on balance disclosure was in the public interest or not."[10]

The Iraq war for the first time set the public interest test against the ministerial veto. In December 2007 a request was made for the release of cabinet minutes and records relating to meetings held between 7 and 17 March 2003. These covered the two key cabinet meetings on 13 and 17 March in which the attorney general's legal advice on the military action in Iraq was debated. The request was refused by the Cabinet Office, citing clause 35(1) a and b of the act, which gave exemption to material relating to the "formulation of government policy." It argued that "if Ministers and officials knew or thought that once a decision was reached, information pertaining to the process by which they reached that point was to be revealed, they might be less willing to engage in full and frank discussions of the issues. Their candor in these discussions could be affected by their assessment of whether the content of these discussions will be disclosed."[11] It made a further confidential submission to the commissioner outlining "the specific damages that would arise from the disclosure of this information."[12]

In the first major assertion of his authority, the commissioner ruled against the government in February 2008. He invoked the public interest clause that could override a class exemption, on two grounds. First, he appealed to the special significance of the issue under discussion. Where once national security had been the overriding argument against disclosure, now he argued the reverse: "The Commissioner considers that a decision on whether to take military action against another country is so important, that accountability for such decision making is paramount."[13] Second, he asserted that the value of openness in the democratic process did not stop at the door of the cabinet room.

> To more fully understand this particular decision of the Cabinet, the Commissioner believes that disclosure of these minutes is necessary. Release of the minutes would therefore serve the public interest in respect of transparency and public understanding of the relevant issues in this case. This would enable the public to be made aware of what was officially recorded about any evidence and argument the Cabinet considered and then the process the Cabinet followed in making a decision.[14]

In response the cabinet exercised its right to appeal the commissioner's decision to the Information Tribunal, which published its decision on 27 January 2009. By a majority of two to one it decided that the public interest balance fell in favor of the release of the minutes, arguing that "the questions and concerns that remain about the quite exceptional circumstances of the two relevant meetings create a very strong case in favour of the records being disclosed."[15] Faced with a doctrine that could breach cabinet secrecy at just the point when ministers would most wish to preserve it, the government chose neither to accept the decision nor to pursue a further appeal but instead for the first time exercised its right of veto under section 53 of the Freedom of Information Act. Jack Straw was able to speak with some authority on the matter in his capacity not only as the minister who had passed the act and was now invoking its fallback clause but also as the foreign secretary to whom the attorney general's advice had been given in spring 2003. The Campaign for Freedom of Information described the decision as "extremely retrograde" and pointed out that in Australia the Labour government of Kevin Rudd had just introduced a bill to remove the veto from Australia's Freedom of Information Act in accordance with a 2007 manifesto commitment. Once the bill was passed, ministers would lose the right to veto disclosures that might damage security, defense, international relations, or policy formulation.[16]

The issue of the continuing requirement of Westminster politicians to assert or defend their actions in the context of an assumed league table of international liberalism is the first point that emerges from the transitions between the initial and the latest of the controversies provoked by the management of state secrets.[17] In the high tide of Victorian imperialism, Europe represented the negative other, the realm in which the behavior of civil servants had to be controlled by written codes and the liberties of subjects were compromised by state espionage. The empire was the source of innovation, especially in the case of the Indian Civil Service, which pioneered the selfless, exam-based civil service, conducting its administration through systematically composed and recorded correspondence.[18] The postwar reconstruction of Europe and the emergence of self-confident Commonwealth countries led to new forms of comparison that no longer flattered the domestic version of liberalism. With the reluctant accession of the United Kingdom to the European Community in 1973, the unwritten tradition of civil liberties was increasingly challenged by the European Convention for the Protection of Human Rights, backed up by the European Court of Justice. And in 1982, while the Thatcher administrations were enthusiastically extending their surveillance powers over trade unions and other domestic foes, Australia, Canada, and New Zealand passed Freedom of Information Acts that stood as critical touchstones for British reform for the remainder of the twentieth century.[19]

The second point is the way in which the debate is shaped and reshaped by the interaction of political and communications revolutions. The axis between liberal democracy and transparency in the communication of information was established by the first Whig administrations of the Reform Act state. In a linked series of interventions they set about removing the obstacles to ignorance about the practice of politics and, more broadly, in the conduct of social relations. They were especially concerned to ensure that those who had the vote would be able to exercise it in an informed manner and that those who were as yet excluded from the franchise would set their feet on the path toward earning full citizenship by demonstrating their capacity for rational intercourse. In 1833 the government committed itself to making a literate population through the grant of a subsidy to elementary education and laid the foundation for the measurement of progress through the creation of the statistical department of the Board of Trade; in 1836 it legalized the political reading of the people through the reduction of the newspaper stamp to a penny; in 1838 it promoted access to the parliamentary process by putting *Hansard* on sale and established the Public Record Office to preserve and make available state documents; and in 1840 it sought to create a society linked by written communication through the costly introduction of the penny post.[20]

The postal espionage scandal of 1844 derived much of its drama from the apprehension that the promotion of personal communication through the written word might be transferring new powers to government rather than to the electorate. Letter opening had a history as long as writing itself, but with the launching of the penny post and the commitment to the creation of a society networked by the written word, the state was acquiring an unprecedented capacity to gain access to the thoughts and feelings of its subjects, whether or not at the request of foreign governments. Despite the claims by commentators from Bentham to Straw, transparency was not the inevitable concomitant of the liberal enterprise. The question was not so much whether a liberal polity could possess secrets or could act in secret, but whether it was safe to permit the exercise of that secrecy itself to be secret. With much strain, the second communications revolution, the telephone, introduced in 1875, was absorbed within the structure of informal controls that had built up around the management of correspondence, but the third revolution, the personal computer and the internet, forced a new era of legislation, which included the Data Protection Acts of 1984 and 1998, the Interception of Communications Act of 1985, the Privacy and Electronic Communication Regulations of 2003, and the Environmental Information Regulations of 2004.

In his final *Annual Report* the first information commissioner drew attention to "a much wider agenda of social change." "People are better-educated than ever," he wrote, "and no longer expect to be kept in the dark. There is a suspicion of secrecy and cover-up. Modern communications mean that the public expect instant access to what is going on."[21] As in the first communication revolution, the balance between individual liberties and state responsibilities was continually destabilized by the information skills learned by citizens and the communication devices to which they had access. He went on to cite the recent report of the House of Lords Constitution Committee: "The expansion in the use of surveillance represents one of the most significant changes in the life of the nation since the Second World War . . . and continues to exert a powerful influence over the relationship between individuals and the state."[22] The controversy over the use of the veto was in this regard something of a throwback to an older, slower world. The question of what happened to the written record of a cabinet meeting discussing the written legal advice of a government law officer belonged to a former century. Jack Straw drew attention to the minority report of the Information Tribunal, that "publication would . . . be more likely than not to drive substantive collective discussion or airing of disagreement into informal channels and away from the record.

This would over time damage the ability of historians and any inquiries, if constituted, to reconstruct and understand the process Cabinet followed in any particular instance. And it would not be conducive to good government."[23] The warning was met with mockery by commentators long critical of Tony Blair's sofa government,[24] but there was substance in the apprehension that debate and decision making were in danger of being driven beyond the reach of democratic access. The real point, however, was not whether the public interest provision of the Freedom of Information Act was being used too freely but whether its long-delayed introduction was too late to deal with an information universe that had changed out of all recognition since reform was first broached in the 1970s.

If there was no immutable balance between liberalism and transparency, attention is forced onto the third issue to be addressed in this chapter, how a workable and peculiarly British compromise was achieved and how far its legacy informs or is illuminated by current contested practice. My concern is with liberalism not as a set of principles but as a culture and practice of governance embodied in the lives of citizens over time. In particular, this chapter will use the Iraq cabinet debate and its antecedents to examine the extent to which the opposition between formal legal constraints and informal cultural discipline within liberal governmentality is not given but always negotiated and unstable, and how far the twenty-first-century settlement represents a significant reformulation of the nineteenth- and twentieth-century regime of managing public secrets.

The compromise that was reached following the uproar over Mazzini's correspondence required a deliberate substitution of culture for law. Sir James Graham wrapped his refusal to admit or deny postal espionage in unwritten constitutional precedent. He and subsequent Home Secretaries declined either to inform MPs or to accept the need to bring the practice of surveillance within a legal framework. For as long as possible they resisted legislating and thus incurring parliamentary debate and scrutiny. The practice of excluding the management of information from public scrutiny was sustained by appeal to the concept of honorable secrecy. The emerging political system was not in fact especially secretive. In terms of direct spying on the domestic population, as far as can be ascertained the cloak of confidentiality had nothing inside it at all for the three decades or so following the crisis of 1844. But ministers and a growing civil service had in their possession information that they might desire not to communicate. And in the British version of a liberal state this secrecy was embodied as a cultural form. Unwritten regulation was used to smother controversy by ancient tradition. But it was also consciously deployed to manufacture a new cultural form specifically appropriate to a state that considered itself on the leading edge of constitutional change. The ambition to keep secrecy secret foregrounded the requirement of trust that any blocked communication imposes. There was no legal framework for the civil service in general, or for its right to withhold official information or interrupt its flow. As a consequence, the ethical basis of government and its professional servants became a central feature of liberal governance. In the words of Sir George Cornewall Lewis:

> One of the first qualities required in the clerks of a public office is trustworthiness. In many public offices, papers containing information respecting pending questions of great importance, and of deep interest to private individuals, to companies and associations, to the public at large, and to the whole civilised world, necessarily pass through the hands of clerks in their successive stages of preparation. The honourable secrecy which has distinguished the clerks of our superior offices, and their abstinence from communicating information to interested parties or public journals, cannot be too highly commended.[25]

The notion of "discreet reserve"[26] informed the behavior of the public servant. It combined the emerging self-discipline of the professional ethos with a reworked tradition of gentlemanly self-restraint.

There was being invented what much later in the twentieth century would be termed a culture, a set of values and behaviors that existed outside formal regulation. In its mid-nineteenth-century manifestation this construction was seen by successive governments not as an evasion or a dilution of the rigors of a legal framework but rather as a more robust and effective form of democratic accountability. The management of official information foregrounded the issue of character, which Patrick Joyce has rightly seen as a key issue in the development of liberal governance. "The preservation of secrecy," wrote its first theorist, "is something so unstable; the temptations of betrayal are so manifold; the road from discretion to indiscretion is in many cases so continuous, that the unconditional trust in discretion involves an incomparable preponderance of the subjective factor."[27] The answer to this challenge for those constructing the apparatus of the modern British state was to see honor not as the victim but the guarantor of secrecy. To borrow a concern from Tony Bennett's chapter in this volume, the habits of a reconfigured social and professional elite guaranteed the ethical handling of blocked communication. The Reform Act state represented the accommodation of the landowning elite to the rising middle class, and in the same way the new spirit of public service combined the self-restraint of the gentlemanly ideal with the self-discipline of the professional ethos. The modern rationality of rule required a modesty of government. Liberalism, as the introduction to *Foucault and Political Reason* states, was "not about governing less but about the continual injunction that politicians and rulers should govern cautiously, delicately, economically, modestly."[28] In the same way a civil servant acted not in pursuance but in denial of his personal interest. His silence on matters of state was a form of abnegation rather than aggrandizement.

The revolution in mass communication that the Reform Act state sought to promote was at once a British and a global event. If the invention of the steam engine, the railway, and the penny post were all domestic achievements, every state with any pretense to modernity possessed by the middle decades of the nineteenth century a structure of flat-rate correspondence and a rail network to carry the letters. The generally state-owned postal and railway organizations rapidly became the largest civilian employers. While there were variations in the pace of progress, most European countries embarked on educational campaigns designed to inculcate their growing populations with literacy skills at least sophisticated enough to compose and decipher a short letter.[29] In 1875 the Universal Postal Union was formed to promote an international flat-rate postal service.[30] By 1914 all but a handful of countries were embraced in a worldwide communication network irrespective of distance, language, and form of government. Everywhere correspondence enlarged the private sphere, and in every country it equipped governments with unprecedented powers of surveillance. As the realm of domestic secrecy expanded beyond the physical limits of oral intercourse, so the opportunities for its exposure by the secret agents of the state increased. The clumsy and time-consuming practice of overhearing conversation could be supplemented by the large-scale opening of letters in the centralized, government-controlled post offices. Liberal modernity was defined neither by mass communication nor by official secrecy. The issue was not whether but how communication was blocked. In the emerging British compromise, the sanctity of the private sphere was guaranteed by the private ethical code of a gentlemanly professional elite. By declining formally to communicate how communication was controlled, the reserve powers of the state could be maintained without unsettling the liberal balance between what should be transparent and public and what needed to be enclosed and private.

A robust base for the new culture of honorable secrecy was established by the linked reforms to civil service recruitment, accelerated by the Northcote-Trevelyan Report of 1854, and to the public schools to enable them to instill not only gentlemanly ethics but also the intellectual skills required to pass examinations. However, the settlement was constantly threatened from below. As the early Victorian state expanded to meet the needs of empire and domestic arenas such as education, policing, and poor relief, it began to draw into its ranks more and more employees from outside the gentlemanly professional elite. The increasing number of low-born clerks could not be assumed to possess the character traits of self-denial or to display the right habits of mind. Still worse was the prospect of women who were brought into government offices by the introduction of the typewriter from the 1880s onward. These employees were the best products of the new structures of inspected elementary schooling, whose mission was to instill the same instincts of self-denial and self-discipline that it was assumed their social superiors acquired from their birth and training. In practice, when it came to matters as critical as public secrets the state could not bring itself to trust those whose acculturation was so thin and so recent.

Governments remained disinclined to expose the issue of blocked official communication to public debate. The reluctance to permit the House of Commons to discuss official secrecy after the first Reform Act was reinforced by the second and, in particular, the third Reform Acts, which paved the way for the election of members who might lack anything recognizable as an appropriate education. But when in 1878 a ten-pence-a-day Foreign Office copyist, previously employed in the dog-licensing department of the Inland Revenue, leaked for private gain the draft of a secret treaty with the Russians to the *Globe*,[31] it became apparent that this "cheap and untrustworthy class of people"[32] required more formal control. The problem was then compounded by the emergence of new external threats to the state with the eruption of Fenianism on mainland Britain and then the rise of German militarism. It thus became necessary to go to Parliament to seek a legal sanction for controlling official information. The Official Secrets Acts of 1889 and 1911 contained a minimum of detail and were rushed through both Houses with scant debate. An initial draft of the 1889 act was titled "Breach of Official Trust Bill," which conveyed the focus of the concern.[33] The final version exposed civil servants to prosecution for communicating any document to any person who "ought not to receive it," without otherwise defining the document or the person.[34] The acts were designed not to defend the public from government, but government from the growing numbers of its employees who were beyond the influence of the code of gentlemanly conduct. The initial settlement suffered a kind of defeat, but its lineaments survived in the new order of formal control. Under the terms of the 1911 act, senior civil servants, who were still drawn from the public schools and universities, remained free to authorize the communication of official information themselves. It was the lower ranks who were policed by the ceremonial (and in legal terms meaningless) ritual of "signing the Act" and were occasionally made the subject of symbolic prosecutions.

The achievement of the doctrine of honorable secrecy was that it foregrounded the need for ethical standards in public administration. As nineteenth-century liberal states gained the apparatus of raising and spending tax revenues, the absence of pecuniary corruption in the British civil service was a genuine mark of distinction. In this sense the public servants were engaged in a denial of self-interest that in turn sustained an informal culture of regulating official secrets. Trust was everything. It required confidence in conduct that could not be seen, could not be policed, could not be rendered to public account except through the figure of the minister in Parliament, whose position on secrecy was protected by Sir James Graham's convention of not ever discussing its exercise.

In turn, the twentieth-century decline in honorable secrecy was located in a slow erosion of confidence in the ethics of public service. The Suez invasion of 1956 was the turning point. As with the Iraq invasion half a century later, a foreign policy disaster called into question both the competence and the integrity of the liberal state. The machinery of government was deeply implicated in the deception and misjudgment that informed the desperate attempt to halt the final collapse of British imperial power. A decade later the failure to sustain Britain's position in the international economy raised additional questions about the competence of its managers. At the same time the expansion of the welfare state was placing new strains on the ownership and communication of official information. The doctrine that depended on the cultural traditions of a small administrative elite could not adapt to the multiplying transactions between officials and citizens. A state apparatus for generations celebrated as the best in the world was under increasing scrutiny by a growing body of journalists and academics no longer patient with its silences. "Of all the governments in the free world," wrote Bernard Crick in 1964, "the British administration is certainly the most restrictive in giving access to information about its operations to either scholars or journalists: this I take to be not just the old arrogance of an administrative and political elite, which is used to minding its own business, but a new uncertainty about the efficacy of the new system."[35] The Fulton Enquiry into the Civil Service, whose findings were published four years later, addressed multiple forms of closure ranging from class bias in recruitment to resistance to new ideas and for the first time attacked the secrecy surrounding the administrative process.[36] In the event, the Wilson and Callaghan administrations failed to legislate, leaving the civil service at the mercy of Mrs. Thatcher who combined a contempt for its traditions with an unprecedented enthusiasm for deploying the now-discredited Official Secrets Acts to prosecute unauthorized leaks of information.

"The culture of secrecy," a phrase never used at the time it might have had a positive meaning, now stood as the shorthand for all that needed changing. In one of his first speeches as prime minister, Gordon Brown told *Liberty*, "FoI is the right course because government belongs to the people. . . . There is more we can do to change the culture and workings of government to make it more open. . . . We should have the freest possible flow of information between government and the people."[37] The information commissioner himself says that he was "the first to acknowledge that FoI does amount to a major challenge to a culture of unnecessary official secrecy and our job involves tackling that need for cultural change head on."[38]

The nature and outcome of this head-on challenge remain deeply unclear. Nikolas Rose has written that the "links between the political apparatus and the activities of governing are less stable and durable than often suggested: they are tenuous reversible, heterogeneous."[39] After a prolonged period of decline in the nineteenth-century settlement, what is now being attempted is a wholesale reversal. Rather than the values and traditions of a governing elite standing in for formal regulation and justifying its absence, now a complex formal bureaucracy is attempting to create the conditions within which a new or revived set of ethical standards can flourish. At the time of the debate over the 1997 White Paper and the drafting of an apparently much weaker Freedom of Information Bill, critics were greatly exercised about particular exemptions being written into the legislation, including the reserve power of veto. What they missed was the construction of a new kind of administrative infrastructure to police the flow of information. The information commissioner now runs an office of 282 staff that oversees more than 115,000 public bodies covering not only central government but also schools, universities, health trusts, local councils, and the police. Each of these bodies in turn has had to appoint and train its own specialized freedom of information officers to comply with the act. In his 2008–9 report, the information commissioner welcomed "the new requirement for every government department to identify a Senior Risk Information Officer."[40] These staff members are required not only to ensure observance of the law but also positively to promote its purposes by drawing up schemes of publication and actively advising and assisting those seeking information.[41] The Information Commissioner's Office runs its own helpline, which received 112,767 calls in 2008–9. The consequence has been an estimated half a million requests for information under the act since it came into operation at the beginning of 2005.[42] Many of the arguments that now surround the office are those of bureaucratic efficiency, with the Campaign for Freedom of Information protesting that it is taking an average of 19.7 months for complaints about the act to be resolved and the commissioner responding that his resources are failing to keep step with his growing responsibilities.[43]

"There is now," claimed the commissioner, "a recognition that legislation is irreversible and a determination on the vast majority of politicians and public servants to make the best of the law and to take it seriously."[44] Trust remains fundamental to the process but is now seen as the objective of regulation, not the alternative. It is a concept more easily invoked than measured, but with the new bureaucracy has come a range of devices for calculating outcomes. An opinion poll taken each year during the period 2004–8 asked respondents to assess the "benefits of being able to access information held by public authorities." The response to the question of whether it "increases trust in public authorities" rose consistently, from 51 percent in 2004 to 72 percent in 2007 and 75 percent in 2008.[45]

The apparent transformation perhaps reflects the sheer scope of the public sector, which is so much more extensive and heterogeneous than it was when the Victorian culture of secrecy was constructed. Citizens may believe that their local school or hospital is behaving more ethically because of the increased transparency of their deliberations, and in terms of the quality of their daily lives this can be the crucial change. There is scant evidence, however, that such generosity of sentiment is being extended to central government. At one level it can be argued that Labour is suffering from a kind of injustice. If we stand back from the current debates, the record of New Labour contrasts favorably with the first majority Labour government under Attlee, which managed to launch a nuclear weapons program without consulting Parliament or informing the electorate, or the Wilson and Callaghan governments, which passed up golden opportunities to reform the already indefensible 1911 Official Secrets Act. The Conservative administrations from 1979 were forced by cases at the European Court of Human Rights to place phone tapping and the Security Services on a legislative footing, but their reform of the 1911 Official Secrets Act had done little to disturb the state's control of its own information.[46] There is a case for arguing that whatever its doubts, Labour has been cautious about using its reserve powers since the act came into operation. In his announcement of the deployment of the veto over the cabinet minutes, Jack Straw was able to point out that between 1 January 2005 and September 2009, "in approximately 78,000 cases where the requested information was held by Government Departments, it has been released in full."[47] Labour is now paying the price for its initial indecision between 1997 and 2000, when having set out a vision of reform, it then panicked and had to be dragged back toward its original intention by means of fierce lobbying inside and outside government. It gave the impression of reforming in spite of, not because of, its core values and instincts, leaving the freedom of information lobby deeply skeptical of government intent. This impression has lately been compounded by the publication of Tony Blair's memoir, *A Journey*, in which he energetically recants his earlier enthusiasm for freedom of information. In part because of the events discussed in this chapter, he now regards the act as "utterly undermining of sensible government." "I quake at the imbecility of it," he writes of his decision. "It was only later, far too late in the day, when the full folly of the legislation became apparent, that I realised we had crossed a series of what should have been thin red lines, and strayed far beyond what it was sensible to disclose."[48]

The most effective critic of Sir James Graham in the 1844 debate over letter opening was Thomas Macaulay. His charge was that silence promoted mistrust. "This was a case," he argued, "beyond all others, in which the Minister ought not to think he had done enough to satisfy a House of Commons, by merely saying that he had the power; he had exercised it; he was responsible for the exercise of such power; but he would give them no account of the manner in which he had exercised it. This was to encourage the suspicion that the power had been abused."[49] The issue provoked debate about the boundary between the private and the public sphere. That a letter had been committed to a government monopoly for transmission did not, in his view, alter its status: "He defied any person to show him the difference between a letter of his being taken from him when in the Post Office, and a letter taken from him out of his desk."[50] Above all, postal espionage and the secrecy surrounding it raised questions fundamental to the indigenous tradition of liberty: "Even if the right hon. Baronet had the power, and said that the power was necessary, and that in these cases it had been properly used, still it was a power that it was most odious to use, and for which strong reasons ought to have be given; for, even if the power were necessary, still it might be obvious that it was one singularly abhorrent to the genius of the English people."[51] The speech was conveyed by a double movement, backward over the centuries through a narrative of freedom and outward to the practices of contemporary continental neighbors. The perspectives were combined most powerfully in a resonant attack on the use of spying and torture in times of national peril:

> There could be no doubt there might be an advantage in breaking open letters. No one denied it; but then was it fitting that it should be done? In the same way, did any one doubt that there was an advantage in having police spies? But then the country did not approve of them. The French had an advantage in having police spies. No one doubted that the spy system enabled them to bring to justice many who must otherwise have escaped. It was the same thing as to torture. There could be no doubt that as long as the English law sanctioned the use of torture a great many crimes were detected by it. It had, too, its advantages [Cries of "Oh, oh."]—Yes; for the instant that Guy Fawkes was shown the rack, out came at once the entire story of the gun-powder plot. Even this torture, as well as the spy system, had these advantages, but then this country had determined long ago that such were pernicious, debasing and dangerous modes of maintaining its institutions. Their ancestors declared that they would rather take the risk of great crimes being committed, than owe their security to that system or those means, which would destroy the manly spirit of the people, on which far more reliance could be placed than all the schemes and decrees that could be invented for maintaining their greatness and independence as a nation.[52]

At the end of the debate the Whigs, then in opposition, lost the division by 206 votes to 162, and in one sense they also lost the argument. The Tory administration and its successors of all parties found a way to combine, not oppose, a structure of secrecy with a modernized tradition of the "genius" and "manly spirit" of the English people. But it remained an unstable compromise. One way to characterize the behavior of successive Home Secretaries down to the closing decades of the twentieth century was a desire not to be exposed to the kind of prolonged public humiliation visited upon Sir James Graham by Macaulay and his colleagues in the Mazzini case.

This chapter has focused on how secrecy was made safe for liberalism and how that settlement became untenable once the high tide of liberal modernity began to recede after 1918. The concern is with the choices taken about the balance between informal and formal regulation. The account argues that the "culture of secrecy," which since the 1990s has stood as a shorthand for all that is antique and repressive in the modern state, was in its original formulation a peculiarly British and consciously progressive means of managing an apparent contradiction in the liberal enterprise. A deliberate absence of openness in the management of official information enabled the state to reconcile its commitment to transparency with its need to retain the capacity for clandestine surveillance. The threats from below after the Reform Act and from outside later in the century made it unsafe to abandon reserve powers of control. At the same time the construction of an ethically based, professionally competent civil service made it possible to demand trust in the exercise of hidden authority.

Three circumstances undermined the tradition of being secret about secrecy. The first was the sheer growth of the state. A critical factor in the liberal modernity of the nineteenth century was the scale of the government apparatus. Progress was delivered through a small domestic civil service bound together by a common social background and education. Its subsequent expansion, accelerated by the liberal welfare reforms of the early twentieth century, rendered the structure of informal controls increasingly unstable. The second circumstance was the successive revolutions in communication. Nineteenth-century liberalism was founded on paper, its storage, its indexing, its recovery, its transmission. The systems of policing the archive were strained by the arrival of the telephone and collapsed in the face of the computer. The third was the erosion of trust in the informal processes of policing the ownership of information and the search, driven partly by the example of former colonies and partly by the rulings of the European Court, for more formal means of controlling management and access.

It might be argued that what is consistent in liberal modernity, even up to this new century, are not the solutions but the problems. Blocked communication is always a contested privilege. Governments must manage the information about their activities if they are to govern, especially at times of crisis. Individuals must control access to information about themselves if they are to function as liberal subjects. The boundaries of legitimate and illegitimate secrecy were policed in the nineteenth century by a private administrative code that in some part is now being replaced by a statutory framework. With the Chilcot Inquiry into the Iraq War due to report at the end of 2011, there is nothing about the present debate to suggest that a durable balance has been achieved.

12. Liberty and Ecology

Resources, Markets, and the British Contribution to the Global Environmental Crisis

Chris Otter

> The bourgeoisie, during its rule of scarce one hundred years, has created more massive and more colossal productive forces than have all the preceding generations together. Subjection of Nature's forces to man, machinery, application of chemistry to industry and agriculture, steam-navigation, railways, electric telegraphs, clearing of whole continents for cultivation, canalization of rivers, whole populations conjured out of the ground— what earlier century had even a presentiment that such productive forces slumbered in the lap of social labour?
>
> KARL MARX AND FRIEDRICH ENGELS, *The Communist Manifesto*

For Marx and Engels, the modern era witnessed the triumph of "that single unconscionable freedom—Free Trade," epitomized by the 1846 repeal of the Corn Laws, which Marx called "the greatest triumph of Free Trade in the nineteenth century."[1] Yet, as these oft-quoted lines from *The Communist Manifesto* suggest, the rise of capitalism and free trade was not just an economic transformation: it was also an ecological transformation. The emergence of capitalism and economic liberalism required a radical reconfiguration of the natural world. In the mid-nineteenth century, this reconfiguration was arguably most pronounced in Britain and its empire.

The literature on "modern" British liberalism, however, largely ignores this environmental transformation. Patrick Joyce has made some imaginative connections between liberalism and the built environment, but historians of liberalism have generally remained within the ambit of ideas, discourses, and politics.[2] Conversely, British environmental historians have been relatively quiet about liberalism, despite substantial discussions of institutions and policy.[3] As Stephen Mosley has recently argued, they have also been rather reticent about integrating their work with that of social historians.[4] Within British history, environmental history remains somewhat disconnected from other subfields, with the important exceptions of the histories of science, technology, and medicine.

In this chapter I use the examples of coal and wheat to argue that significant historical connections exist between the emergence of liberalism and environmental transformation. Consumption of both commodities was clearly rising during the early modern period, well before the advent of liberalism. However, the economic liberalization evident from the late eighteenth and early nineteenth century, along with interrelated phenomena such as the transportation revolution, dramatically transformed the scale of this consumption. The ecological consequences of this were manifold: smoke, acid rain, industrial waste, deforestation, energy-intensive agriculture. Rising consumption and ecological degradation have not, obviously, been unique to modern, liberal societies, so the precise environmental significance of liberalism requires some elucidation. In the final sections of this chapter, I argue that the British combination of economic liberalization, fossil fuels, empire, and global markets created an especially pervasive modality of development, as the later examples of postwar American hegemony and neoliberalism demonstrate. The web of relations between liberty and ecology revealed by the nineteenth-century British case, then, has historical significance reaching beyond both the nineteenth century and Britain.

Before beginning, a note on terminology. *Liberalism, liberty,* and *freedom* have multiple meanings.[5] I focus primarily on one form of freedom treasured by nineteenth-century Britons: *freedom of trade.* This can be simply defined as a belief that trade was best regulated by individuals and markets rather than states or other political institutions: it thus closely accords with Karl Polanyi's *economic liberalism.*[6] I also occasionally allude to a second form of freedom: *individual liberty,* or, in post-Foucauldian parlance, "liberal subjectivity."[7] By *ecology,* I mean the totality of relations between living beings and their surroundings, a meaning similar to Haeckel's original definition.[8] Since living beings include humans, and surroundings can be inorganic and artificial, the concept of ecology can plausibly be extended to include precisely the technological apparatus Marx and Engels highlighted. Historical analysis of free trade and individual liberty, then, need not be limited to the realm of ideas or social relations: it can be productively extended to analysis of how particular economic and political systems transform human interactions with energy, food, and other natural resources.

COAL

> Unfettered commerce, vindicated by our political economists, and founded on the material basis of our coal resources, has made the several quarters of the globe our willing tributaries.
>
> w. s. JEVONS, *The Coal Question: An Inquiry Concerning the Progress of the Nation, and the Probable Exhaustion of our Coal-mines* (1865)

It was, declared Jevons, "the Age of Coal."[9] In 1800 over 80 percent of world coal was produced in Britain, a figure still over 50 percent in 1870.[10] Britain remained the world's heaviest coal consumer until 1905, when it was surpassed by the United States.[11] Coal was "the material source of energy of the country—the universal aid—the factor in everything we do."[12] It produced domestic heat, powered industries, and, when distilled, produced coke and coal gas. Its by-products fueled Britain's expanding chemical industry. Successive inventions (the separate condenser, the high-pressure engine) made steam power considerably more efficient and coal use significantly more cost-effective.[13] Coal was "the motor and the meter of all nations," essential for commerce, industry, war, progress.[14] In *Coal and Civilization* (1925), Edward Jeffrey argued that coal remained society's most essential resource, as evinced by the comparative prosperity of coal-rich nations like Britain and coal-poor ones like France and Italy.[15] "The consumption of coal *per capita* of the population," he declared, "supplies a very reliable indication of the wealth and prosperity of a nation."[16] Cheap coal's centrality to Britain's industrial revolution has seldom been doubted. As E. A. Wrigley argued, coal made possible an escape from an "organic economy," in which land was the source of almost everything humans used, to a "mineral economy," which drew on the vast reservoirs of energy buried beneath the British Isles.[17] This transition to nonrenewable energy sources was an epochal world historical event, a "great transition" akin to the Neolithic revolution, shattering a solar energy system that had endured well over ten millennia.[18]

In 1830 coal entering London was subject to a baroque mélange of duties.[19] A contemporary report found these and other duties "utterly inconsistent with every just principle of political economy."[20] Liberalization followed: an 1831 act declared the London Coal Exchange "a free and open market for the sale of coals brought into the port of London," and import duties were also commuted.[21] Export duties were reduced, stimulating coal exports: Britain had an 85 percent share of the world seaborne coal trade by 1900.[22] This was, Jevons argued, essential to Britain's balance of trade, filling ships that would otherwise have lingered in port waiting for cargo or sailed half-empty.[23] Coal relieved pressure on land, the ultimate cause of organic, Malthusian, crisis.[24] Taxing this "universal aid" was anathema to economic liberals. Coal taxes, declared Robert Bald in 1812, would "unnerve the very sinews of our trade, and be a death-blow to our flourishing manufactories," and Jevons argued that since everything was effectively produced from or moved with the aid of coal, to tax coal was to tax everything, from bread to light.[25] Economic life, he suggested, was increasingly unimaginable without coal.

This was especially true for transportation. The Stockton and Darlington Railway (1825) was created to transport coal, which remained the most important rail freight across the nineteenth century. By 1913 British locomotives burned 15 million tons of steam coal annually.[26] In terms of its function and how it was governed and imagined, the railway network had several dimensions that can plausibly be described as "liberal." Railways were almost entirely funded by private capital. Successive British governments pursued policies of minimal regulation, allowing companies to construct lines where they wanted, speculate and compete, and ultimately amalgamate and form monopolies.[27] Inspection and safety regulations were quite hesitantly applied.[28] The railway network, with its speed and predictability, largely liberated commerce from climatic forces and geographic obstacles, leading to falling freight rates, price convergence, market integration, and transcontinental speculation. Railways, then, allowed economic liberalism—uninhibited, regular, transnational circulation, capital accumulation—to be engineered into existence. The rapid rise in passenger transit also created a very corporeal form of personal liberty. In one week in summer 1850, over 200,000 people left Manchester on excursion trains. According to Michael Freeden, the *Economist* described the railways as "the *Magna Carta* of the poor's motive freedom" in 1851.[29]

Steam power also had an imperial dimension. William Huskisson considered steam power a "great moral lever," which would spur acquisitiveness among "savage nations," producing "an improvement of their condition."[30] Railways were technologies for integrating imperial territory into a broader transcontinental economy. Indian railways were designed to funnel raw materials to ports, to be carried to Britain for processing, domestic consumption, and reexport. John Chapman of the Greater Indian Peninsular Railway stated in 1848 that Lancashire cotton merchants considered the line "nothing more than an extension of their own line from Manchester to Liverpool."[31] The Indian railway network, again, was almost wholly built with British capital. It guaranteed profits to its investors, and it embedded and made durable the commodity flows perpetuating British economic power. It also introduced structural asymmetries into imperial economic relations, later formalized in Naoroji's "drain theory."[32]

This apparatus of extraction also had multiple environmental consequences, from polluted rivers and slag heaps to the embankments and cuttings that radically transformed the British countryside's appearance. Here I want to concentrate on air pollution. Complaints about smoke long predate the modern period, but they intensified after 1800. In 1919 William Bone estimated that nearly 10 million tons of smoke and soot entered Britain's atmosphere annually.[33] In 1922 Simon and Fitzgerald blamed domestic fires for three quarters of national atmospheric pollution.[34] Sulfur compounds released on combustion formed acid rain, a term coined by Robert Angus Smith in 1859, who found British urban air sufficiently acidic to sometimes redden litmus paper in ten minutes.[35] Mancunian rain, it is estimated, had a pH of 3.5 around 1900.[36] The 1920 Committee on Smoke and Noxious Vapour Abatement found urban industrial areas receiving up to 20 percent less sunlight than rural areas.[37] The fossil-fuel economy effectively superimposed a new climate over an old one: on weekdays smoke clouds expanded from 6:00 A.M., peaking around 11:00 A.M.[38] This industrial mediation of climate was registered linguistically ("smog" was first used in 1902) and chemically: historians of climate estimate that carbon dioxide emissions slowly rose throughout the nineteenth century.[39] It was also evident in the rising incidence of urban respiratory disease, which became especially noticeable as the incidence of "filth" diseases like typhoid declined after 1870. The obliteration of sunlight also accentuated levels of rickets and tuberculosis. Sootier, blackened environments affected other biological communities, for example, through the phenomenon of "industrial melanism," a process whereby darker species or variants come to predominate in given populations. The first example of this was the ascendancy of the black peppered moth in Manchester. This moth was first recorded in Manchester in 1848; by 1898 98 percent of Manchester's peppered moth population were melanic.[40]

The tenets of liberalism, however, limited large-scale governmental intervention in pollution's causes. Nineteenth-century attempts to reduce emissions were timid: environmental issues, inasmuch as they were conceptualized at all, were clearly regarded as "external" to economic ones. The smoke clauses of the 1875 Public Health Act, for example, generated various local prevention regimes, all vitiated by low fines and the problem of proving that a certain factory's effluents caused a certain individual's ailments. Domestic coal use remained exempt from such legislation.[41] Fireless grates epitomized domestic misery, while smoke-free factories meant unemployment. Reformers hoped that more efficient technologies would become sufficiently competitive to oust existing ones. But efficient technologies, as Jevons noted, only promoted greater use (the so-called Jevons paradox) and hence more emissions.

The production of coke and coal gas also generated mounds of waste, especially coal tar and ammonia. Sales of these products to emergent chemical industries produced substances typifying the second industrial revolution: dyestuffs, perfumes, photographic materials, creosote, asphalt, fertilizer, saccharin, detergents, explosives, disinfectants, and pesticides.[42] The chemical industry thus generated a galaxy of new products that were, effectively, made of coal. By 1900 dependence on fossil fuels was becoming far more than a question of transportation, domestic heating, and industry: it was palpably integral to hygiene, warfare, fashion, and agriculture.

For some, this increasing symbiosis of coal and everyday life seemed unproblematic. Reviewing domestic heating systems in 1872, William Eassie declared, "The truth is, we have coal to spare and to waste!"[43] Not everyone, however, shared Eassie's nonchalance. Many reformers castigated the prodigality of the British open fire, up to 80 percent of heat from which vanished up the chimney.[44] Geologists were warning about the potential exhaustion of Britain's coalfields from at least the late eighteenth century. Depletion greatly concerned Jevons, who was the first British political economist to truly comprehend the implications of the shift to fossil fuels. The finite nature of coal set firm, calculable parameters to British economic progress: *"While other countries mostly subsist upon the annual and ceaseless income of the harvest, we are drawing more and more upon a capital which yields no annual interest, but once turned to light and heat and motive power, is gone for ever into space."*[45] Coal provided escape from organic limits set by land but in turn imposed a different set of "mineral" limitations. Political economy offered no solutions to this energy crisis. Importing coal was unrealistic, since it would produce an implausible trade deficit. Increased efficiency generated increased use. When Rowland Hill floated the idea of a coal tax at an 1873 Statistical Society meeting, his idea was ridiculed.[46] A contemporaneous House of Commons Select Committee concluded that rising prices would stimulate greater efficiency.[47] Britain, it seemed, was condemned to follow a very steep trajectory of growth and collapse dictated by her coal deposits: this appeared less a question of individual freedom than of economic, material, and technological determination.

By 1900, then, coal had become integral to the operation of British society, for transportation and industry, not to mention domestic heating, lighting, and cooking. It had acquired, in Thomas Hughes's parlance, a tremendous amount of technological "momentum," meaning that older forms of energy (animals, wind, water) were slowly marginalized, while inventions like solar engines or electric vehicles had to compete against hegemonic carboniferous technologies as well as overcome their own technical challenges.[48] An energy-intensive economy was effectively "locked in," with smoke, smog, acid rain, respiratory disease, and, ultimately, climate change itself as "externalities." As debates about the coal question revealed, economic liberalism appeared to generate conundrums about resources for which it had, ultimately, no easy answers. The large-scale emergence of oil, the automobile, and the petrochemical industry after 1918 would only intensify these quandaries.

WHEAT

> We are born wheat-eaters. Other races, vastly superior in numbers, but differing widely in material and intellectual progress, are eaters of Indian corn, rice, millet, and other grains; but none of these grains have the food value, the concentrated health-sustaining power of wheat, and it is on this basis that the accumulated experience of civilised mankind has set wheat apart as the fit and proper food for the development of muscles and brains.
>
> WILLIAM CROOKES, "The Wheat Question" (1898)

In 1771, 3.7 million Imperial quarters of wheat bread were eaten in Britain. By 1870 this figure had reached 17.1 million.[49] As wheat became Britain's favorite grain, consumption of oats, barley, and rye plummeted. This process followed a geographic pattern, beginning in the southeast and urban areas before slowly radiating across the rest of the British Isles.[50] Wheat bread, moreover, became almost exclusively white. Brown bread was practically extinct in Britain by 1850, with bran used for biscuits and animal feed.[51] However, pace Crookes, there was nothing natural or intrinsically British about this process of "wheatification." It was very much a product of power and history. By the nineteenth century wheat had become the "true and unequivocal symbol of civilization."[52] In the twentieth, its global spread, like that of coal, routinely operated as a material index of development.

Rising British wheat consumption was, and is, routinely associated with liberalization of the grain trade, connecting, as Frank Trentmann argues, "cheap food and open markets" with "a national story of liberty and freedom."[53] In 1800 grain was heavily regulated, with laws controlling its buying and reselling. Millers claimed a toll whenever they ground grain.

Numerous Corn Laws had been passed since the early modern period to regulate the trade and protect domestic markets, culminating in the famous one of 1815. Most important, bread was assized: a standard loaf's legal size was determined by grain's cost.[54] Since bread was the population's staple food, its price was too important to be set by the market: it offers a historical exemplar of the concept of moral economy.[55]

The regulation of grain, and the Corn Laws in particular, consequently became the bête noire of classical liberals. This economic argument was made in numerous ways. Taxing a staple food raised wages. If overseas nations could sell cheap grain to Britain, they would buy more British goods. Macaulay made this argument for reciprocity and international specialization in 1842: were the Corn Laws repealed, he declared, Britain "might supply the whole world with manufactures, and have almost a monopoly of the trade of the world."[56] Moreover, precisely *because* it was the most important foodstuff, its price should not be regulated by government officials. "Can any artificial scheme exceed in providence and forethought that natural arrangement by which sellers supply the market according to the wants of the buyers?" asked Peel in 1845.[57] The repeal of the Corn Laws (and the assize, eradicated 1815–36) was *the* triumph of nineteenth-century economic liberalism.

Repeal, however, had little immediate effect. Domestic wheat production collapsed only after 1870, following poor domestic harvests and falling costs of imported wheat. England imported 20 percent of her wheat in 1841; by 1913 this figure for imported wheat and flour was around 80 percent.[58] The *Economist* noted this trend in 1883:

> People think of the old days when the British harvest really fed the British people. Now we have to go further afield. A good wheat harvest is still as much needed as ever to feed our closely packed population. But it is the harvest already turning brown in the scorching sun of Canada and the Western States—the wheat already ripe in India and California, not the growth alone of the Eastern counties and Lincolnshire, that will be summoned to feed the hungry mouth of London and Lancashire.[59]

Food self-sufficiency was abandoned in favor of a liberal, international division of labor, with America, Canada, Argentina, Australasia, Russia, and India operating as Britain's wheatfields. In 1881 the liberal economist Robert Giffen argued that "if wheat can be grown permanently abroad for a long period at 35s. per quarter, or perhaps a lower price[,] . . . it might be very desirable indeed that no people in this country would be employed in so wasteful a thing as growing wheat at 50s. per quarter."[60] "Wasteful" had a purely economic meaning: Giffen had no comprehension of what we would call "food miles." Market integration, evident in parts of Europe from the sixteenth and seventeenth centuries, was now evident on a transcontinental scale, as British and American prices, in particular, became very strongly correlated by 1900.[61] This was perhaps the world's first genuinely integrated market, and it centered on Britain. By 1860 Britain received 49 percent of total Asian, African, and Latin American food exports.[62] In the interwar period British import prices remained, effectively, "world prices."[63] Wheat, noted one commentator in 1908, was "the greatest distributor of money" on earth, constantly animating trade.[64] Companies who could command grain surpluses (Cargill, Dreyfus, Continental) made immense profits on the incipient global market. By diversifying supply, a global market was held to reduce both prices and the risk of famine, but it had grave geopolitical ramifications: as Avner Offer argues, the benefits of cheap grain must be offset by the escalating cost of naval defense in the years leading up to World War I.[65]

Like the transition to fossil fuels, this switch from a (predominantly) subsistence to a (predominantly) market economy was an epochal, if uneven and temporally distended, event. For most of human history almost all food had been produced and consumed locally.[66] The conversion of substantial parts of Latin and North America and Australasia into large-scale zones producing agricultural surpluses for distribution to overseas markets facilitated the simultaneous urbanization of Western Europe, a process first evident in Britain. Such large-scale agriculture, Marx observed, "reduces the agricultural population to an ever decreasing minimum," producing "an irreparable rift in the interdependent process of social metabolism" and terminating in "a squandering of the vitality of the soil."[67] British farming grew more heavily capitalized. Commercial fertilizers became popular, including superphosphates and ammonium sulfate, a by-product of coke and gas making. The most notable substance was guano, seabird excrement (especially the nitrogen-rich excrement of cormorants, pelicans, and gannets) harvested from numerous islands off the Peruvian coast. Its importation to Britain was, for Marx, tangible evidence that Western agriculture was no longer self-sustaining.[68] Fritz Haber's 1908 development of synthetic nitrate fertilizer was partly designed to reduce such dependence by allowing Germany to feed itself. Instead, it made agriculture more fuel-intensive, something only partly offset by subsequent improvement in efficiency.[69] Nitrogen inputs into British agriculture rose enormously after 1900.[70] Synthetic nitrate fertilizers became central to colonial and postcolonial development projects: they were used in vast quantities during the Green Revolution. The ecological side effects of energy-intensive agriculture have been substantial, including nitrate leaching, increased greenhouse gas emissions, deforestation, and eutrophication.[71]

Wheat is a capitalist foodstuff par excellence. It is, if stored correctly, practically imperishable.[72] It lends itself to accumulation and transportation without requiring complicated refrigeration equipment. Stone-ground wheat flour, however, starts going stale after three months, a process accelerated if bran is present. Millers, who were liable for damaged cargo, were reluctant to transport anything but white flour.[73] They were consequently great supporters of railways, which were quicker and less likely to be delayed by inclement weather. Flour was the first cargo on the Liverpool-Manchester railway (1834).[74] The consumption of white bread, then, was encouraged by energy-intensive transportation, a process that has continued unabated: a quarter of today's British trucks carry food.[75] The production of railway space allowed the simultaneous production of a market economy in grain, with economies of scale, standardized grades, and futures markets.[76] In 1883 the Liverpool corn exchange authorized futures trading, and London's Baltic exchange followed suit in 1897.[77] This was not a pan-European phenomenon: in 1896 the German Reichstag banned futures trading in grains and flour.[78]

Liberalization transformed the economics of British wheat. It also transformed the British bread loaf itself. Before 1846 most wheat consumed in Britain was of the soft variety. Harder wheats, imported from North America and Russia, contain more protein than soft wheat. Their more glutinous flours produce large, light, cakelike breads rather than the denser loaves made with soft wheat.[79] Hard wheats also remain moist for a longer period: when roller-milled, they produce a more durable flour, making integrated world markets more materially feasible.[80] In 1905 the plant breeder Rowland Biffen found "English wheat . . . lacking in 'strength.'" "The flour of English-grown wheat, alone," he said, "will not produce a loaf which is marketable under present conditions."[81] By 1939 most British wheat was used for biscuits, cakes, and animal feed, not bread.[82] The Chorleywood Bread Process (CBP), pioneered in 1961, finally enabled bread to be made with low-protein "soft" British wheat, by using ascorbic acid (among other additives) and high-speed mixing.[83] The resulting white loaf was mass-produced, insipid, standardized. Well before the invention of the CBP, white bread was under attack, particularly from early critics of the food industry. In *Mechanization Takes Command*, Siegfried Giedion assailed "mechanical bread" as uniform and elastic, with "the resiliency of a rubber sponge."[84] Others launched more medical critiques: the doctor Arbuthnot Lane blamed the "white travesty" for an endemic modern condition: constipation.[85]

While some were enduring such diseases of civilization, others continued to suffer from more transhistorical phenomena: hunger and famine. Classical liberals generally blamed famine on governmental intervention, arguing that liberalizing markets would generate perfect distribution. However, as Irish and Indian famines demonstrated, dogmatic adherence to market ideology and self-help could transmogrify dearth into gigantic famine.[86] Hobson observed that by evading the population problem at home, Britain simply displaced it overseas.[87] These famines, which critics have called genocidal, have contributed to a very different myth of liberal Britain, one of utilitarian brutality and callous greed, which has arguably eclipsed the more egalitarian, ethical dimensions of liberalism.[88] Yet by 1900 concerns were being raised that Britain, and its insouciant consumers, might not itself evade dearth indefinitely. Crookes, for example, warned, "The world has become so familiarised with the orderly sequence of demand and supply, so accustomed to look upon the vast plains of other wheat-growing countries as inexhaustible granaries, that, in a light-hearted way it is taken for granted that so many million additional acres can be added year after year to the wheat-growing area of the world."[89]

Crookes concluded that the food supply would "become a very perplexing problem" in the future.[90] In the short term, Crookes was proved wrong. Haber's invention broke the natural limits of the nitrogen cycle: combined with significant increases in agricultural land, this enabled enormous twentieth-century world population growth. However, although Crookes was not exactly conceptualizing a world food crisis, he was articulating the idea that the "orderly sequence of demand and supply" of this giant, transcontinental agro-food system, could not continue indefinitely. As with coal, it appeared that the dynamism of a liberal economy produced only instability, at both the economic and ecological levels. To what extent can *liberalism* itself be blamed for modern environmental problems?

COMPARISONS

> Unfortunately this great change in the nature of environmental problems occurred at a time in world history when economic liberalism was becoming the dominant doctrine, and with it a notion of common good that established itself by allowing the market to sort out the various interests.
>
> JOACHIM RADKAU, *Nature and Power: A Global History of the Environment*

As Marx and Engels suggested and as the history of coal and wheat reveals, liberalism had ecological consequences. International free trade was incompatible with food self-sufficiency; Britain relied on coal exports to maintain its balance of trade. Coal use rose exponentially, producing a society deeply dependent on fossil fuels. Ingenious recycling merely expanded consumption, and increasing material consumption became the most obvious, empirical index of progress. Asymmetries of consumption multiplied, both within wealthy nations in the global north and between these nations and those of the global south (and within these nations too). Environmental problems mounted: smoke, acid rain, exhausted soil, deforestation, resource depletion, climate change. Environmental regulation was limited and, since subjugated to economic imperatives, largely inconsequential. A cursory examination of these environmental ills might produce the conclusion that liberalism, and specifically British liberalism, has caused today's environmental crisis, understood, as Radkau puts it, as "*one* great and global problem" rather than the multiple but less tightly enmeshed environmental issues of the early modern period, such as biological invasions or the intensification of land use, especially on frontiers.[91]

To test this thesis, historical comparison (however cursory) with the environmental records of nonliberal regimes must be undertaken. The environmental dimensions of Nazism, for example, have attracted much recent historical attention. It has been argued that Nazism and conservation have clear ideological affinities: opposition to technological modernity, commitment to *Heimat*, vegetarianism, and so forth. These affinities generated legislation, like the 1935 *Reichsnaturschutzgesetz*, which expanded the scope of German conservation.[92] In *The New Ecological Order*, Luc Ferry generalizes this argument, characterizing environmentalism as fundamentally antiliberal and antimodern.[93] While liberalization meant escape from natural determination, environmentalism means renaturalization: a return to the local, the premodern, the constrained. This argument, however, is historically flawed. The ideological overlap between Nazism and environmentalism was partial and Nazi commitment to environmentalism halfhearted at best, as total war and *Autobahn* construction, for example, demonstrate. Despite the derogatory neologism "eco-fascist," the historical connection between environmentalism and fascism is tenuous.[94]

Nonetheless, the idea that environmentalism is inherently authoritarian (or requires authoritarianism) persists. The right often suspects that environmentalists want to deprive individuals of their freedom; the left sometimes fears that liberal individuals might need coercing into green subjectivity. The example of the USSR, however, explodes any necessary connection between authoritarianism and environmentalism. From the 1918 State Plan for Electrification to Khrushchev's forcible modernization of agriculture, Soviet faith in progress through fossil fuels and mechanized agriculture was unshaken. By 1990 the litany of Russian environmental calamities was long and alarming, from Chernobyl to the vanishing Aral Sea. An area of 2.5 million square kilometers of Russian federation territory was in "an acute ecological situation," and sixteen cities' air pollution was over fifty times the norm.[95] In Maoist China, meanwhile, one finds a similar combination of industrial giantism and belief that authoritarian will could surmount all natural obstacles. The legacy is similarly negative, from technological calamities (554 dams collapsed in 1973 alone), inefficient coal-burning power stations, and pervasive acid rain to famines demonstrably *not* caused by liberalism.[96] Ecological critics of Mao's regime were silenced and punished.[97] Analysis of other authoritarian regimes (e.g., Cuba, Brazil, and the Philippines) has also highlighted varying degrees of ecological degradation.[98] History does not suggest that authoritarian regimes are intrinsically any more environmentally progressive than liberal ones.

No straightforward equation, then, exists between political system and environmental policies or effects. From the perspective of deep ecology, all modern political regimes appear incapable of thinking beyond material growth and resource exploitation: there are many political paths to environmental crisis. Indeed, as Kenneth Pomeranz has argued, the past five hundred years of world history can be characterized in terms of the rise of *developmentalism*, which has assumed multiple forms, not all liberal or capitalist. Developmentalism involves commitment to territorial power, state building, and intensification of resource use. But, as Pomeranz continues, liberalism has been "the most influential such synthesis."[99] This synthesis is built around the market economy, relatively unconstrained private behavior, private property, an assumption that individual material consumption is a key path to happiness, and belief in the power of self-regulation rather than state regulation, at several scales (individual, economic, ecosystemic).[100]

We are perhaps now in a better position to historically situate the relationship between liberty and ecology. In the early modern period Britain, rather like Japan, faced ecological pressures: rising population, increased resource use, limited land, and fuel scarcity.[101] Unlike Japan, however, the British turned toward empire, the mercantile system, the fiscal-military state, and fossil fuels to temporarily escape its organic limits.[102] Over the course of the eighteenth and early nineteenth century, however, the mercantile system and the fiscal-military state were dismantled, or at least reconstructed, according to newer, liberal ideas of economy and government.[103] This plexus of liberal practices and ideas, emergent between 1775 and 1850, produced an enduring modality of developmentalism built on a powerful, multifaceted critique of an ancien régime that limited physical mobility and constrained temporal growth.[104] When one considers Britain's vast coal supplies and its substantial imperial system, this liberal modality of development appears peculiarly significant.[105] The fusion of fossil fuels, free markets, and empire created, quite unintentionally, a loose "model" of growth, or development, with "environmental" issues being almost entirely ignored or "externalized." In escaping from its organic, territorial constraints, Britain thus inaugurated ecological changes with global ramifications.[106]

The enduring historical relevance of this model can be seen by briefly examining the phenomenon of *neoliberalism,* which developed from the 1970s. Keynesianism and welfarism, like the ancien régime, were accused by many of constraining growth: taxes were high, and states redistributed wealth via social welfare programs. Barriers to international trade remained, especially in the realm of agriculture, which was largely exempt from the General Agreement on Tariffs and Trade (GATT) until the Uruguay Round of 1986–93. The dismantling of national and international regulations limiting capital accumulation, the assault on the welfare state, and the revival of corporate power was promoted at national (Reagan, Kohl, Thatcher) and international (IMF, World Bank) levels.[107] Neoliberalism thus marked a revival, although not a repetition, of the liberal mode of developmentalism pioneered in nineteenth-century Britain. The ensuing policies—deregulation, trade liberalization, workfare, commercialization—have taken many concrete forms. The cumulative effect, however, is a form of market-driven developmentalism powered by institutions and corporations operating above the level of nation-states. The environmental effects have been complex but generally negative. Corporations, for example, can evade increasingly stringent Western environmental regulations by relocating polluting industries to the global south, which is also being used as a dumping ground for various forms of hazardous, radioactive, and electronic waste. Such "toxic colonialism" is merely one dimension of neoliberalism's impact on the global environment.[108]

The age of neoliberalism, then, is equally the age of environmentalism. Around 1970, as the neoliberal critique of the Keynesian-welfare state sharpened, "the environment," as concept and policy domain, was being produced and institutionalized.[109] At the 1969 Labour Party Conference, Harold Wilson urged that environmental protection be politically prioritized: the Conservative Peter Walker became Britain's first secretary of state for the environment in 1970.[110] As a concept, the "environment" has escalated in importance thereafter. Roughly contemporaneously, as numerous scholars have noted, "society" (or "the social") lost its salience.[111] In the nineteenth and early twentieth century, the "social" emerged as a capacious domain into which were collected all the problems that economic liberalism created but could not solve (poverty, anomie, work-related injury, unemployment).[112] Today the environmental occupies a rather analogous position, referring to a broader, less anthropocentric set of problems (pollution, resource depletion, climate change) that economic liberalism (and neoliberalism) has generated but appears peculiarly incapable of solving.

If the environmental has waxed while the social has waned, perhaps Margaret Thatcher serves as an especially significant transitional figure. This architect of neoliberalism, who famously declared that there was no such thing as society, did not have a distinguished environmental record as prime minister. Yet in 1989 Thatcher was the first national leader to address the United Nations General Assembly on global warming and ozone depletion, and she continued these themes at the Second World Climate Conference (1990), urging reduced carbon emissions and reforestation.[113] Although the motives behind Thatcher's "greening" can be debated, two things are clear. First, her speech indicated the degree to which the environmental as a political and cultural category had assumed a salience wholly absent twenty-five years earlier. Second, it shows how the environmental is a protean concept, potentially compatible with basic economic imperatives, as recent terms like *sustainable development* and *natural capitalism* suggest. Like France, Britain has become, to borrow Michael Bess's felicitous expression, a "light-green society," in which almost everything has been penetrated by environmentalism, without the underlying liberal economic premises being seriously affected.[114] How unstable or impossible this synthesis is remains to be seen.

CONCLUSION

The history of coal and wheat demonstrates, as Marx and Engels grasped, that a "double environmental break" occurred during the period 1600–1900, and in particular in the second half of this period. This break involved a shift from renewable to nonrenewable fuel sources and from subsistence to market agriculture. The ecological ramifications of this double break have been enormous: pollution, resource depletion, climate change, and ecosystemic transformation. Neither break, obviously, was total. Renewable energy sources and nonmarket production remained, and remain, significant. Neither break, either, can be described as rapid, even when viewed from a *longue durée* perspective: environmental and economic breaks are seldom swift or absolute. Neither break, moreover, was a peculiarly British or Western European affair. Coal, for example, was used extensively in Han China. But by the nineteenth century its economic significance eclipsed that of any previous period. Similarly, the long-distance grain trade was nothing new, but an integrated world wheat market, organized along liberal lines, was a novel development.

Historical explanations of such complex, protracted, geographically dispersed shifts cannot be monocausal. Historians should, and do, speak of nonlinearity and feedback systems.[115] We cannot say that liberalism, much less British liberalism, "caused" this double environmental break in any straightforward way. Many ideologies and philosophies have preached growth and development, and many nations and empires have sought economic and territorial expansion. Other variants of liberalism have been highly "globally" influential at different points over the past couple of centuries, for example, French republicanism in Africa or eighteenth-century authoritarian liberalism.[116] Yet British liberalism, with its particular, fertile fusion of free trade, personal liberty, private religion, private property, material growth, and skepticism about state regulation, has formed a peculiarly enduring model of development. "Development" or "modernization" has usually involved a shift away from burning biomass, producing for pure subsistence and living in rural communities, toward energy-intensive, market-driven, urbanized life. After 1945 the British liberal model clearly informed the thinking behind American hegemony, with urbanizing developing nations fed by American grain surpluses. Although liberalism neither necessarily causes nor has a monopoly on environmental degradation, the global reach of its developmental project, and its tendency to "externalize" all nonhuman elements, has tangibly shaped today's environmental crisis.

Finally, the relationship between liberty and ecology, as demonstrated by coal and wheat, forced some nineteenth-century Britons to reflect on temporality and historicity in historically distinctive ways. Jevons and numerous contemporaries calculated how much coal Britain had left, how fast people were burning it, and how soon it would be before the British economy collapsed. The future would be, temporarily, richer and more materially satisfying. As coal deposits became economically unworkable, the machinery of modern life would grind to a halt and Britain would revert to an organic economy. The future had calculable contours, rates of growth and decay. Cyclicality and finitude were not novel ways of thinking about history, of course, but thinking about cycles, recessions, and even irreversible catastrophes in terms of purely terrestrial process and forces (thermodynamic, economic, environmental) was a product of the age of Kelvin and Jevons.[117] The anxieties surrounding our freedom to use and squander resources have intensified in the 125 years since the publication of *The Coal Question*, as the slew of contemporary books on peak oil makes clear.[118] The question, however, has ceased to be simply about Britain and its economy. It is now an issue affecting everyone, everywhere: it is global. It is also an issue that not only affects human societies, but those bigger collectives we call ecosystems. The age of free trade, fossil fuels, and wheat bread, then, made possible a new style of thinking about the future, in which human liberty and ingenuity appear capable of destroying the integrity of the ecologies that sustain us.

13. Stories We Tell about Liberal Markets

The Efficient Market Hypothesis and Great-Men Narratives of Change

Mary Poovey

Whether in the "classical" form articulated in the nineteenth century or in the post-1970s "neo" version, all liberalisms—and theories about them—contain constitutive contradictions. In nineteenth-century Britain one of the contradictions that gave liberalism its peculiar form turned on exclusion: despite liberal theorists' emphasis on individual character, political entitlement, and personal autonomy, only some kinds of people got to be what Catherine Hall calls "civilized subjects." As the editors of this volume point out, this contradiction became visible in the last quarter of the twentieth century when feminists and postcolonial scholars began to emphasize the inherent incoherence of such a formulation. One of the characteristic contradictions of neoliberalism, by contrast, involves the nature of individualism itself—or, more precisely, the relationship between individual agency and the dynamics of those larger systems in which individuals operate, especially the market. The contradiction follows from the potential tension between the two sites of agency this theory names: on the one hand, individuals are cast as autonomous actors with full agency and self-determination; on the other, the economy is supposedly self-governing as well, and its dynamics are, by nature, rational and efficient. The tension between these two modes of agency has recently veered toward contradiction as people struggle to understand the global financial crisis that erupted in 2007. If individuals are autonomous agents, can we identify the people who caused this mess (or who could get us out of it)? If the market is an efficient, self-regulating system, why did the financial crisis occur? Neoliberal narratives offer few satisfying answers to such questions precisely because they fail to engage the central contradiction I have just identified. Instead, various financial insiders, journalists, and academics continue to publish theoretical accounts of an autonomous financial market *and* histories of the crisis that emphasize individual agents. Until we understand that there is a relationship between the stories people tell about the market—and the contradiction these stories reproduce—and the dynamics of the market itself, it will be impossible to think ourselves out of this situation or to formulate policies that will prevent a recurrence.

In this chapter I explore the tensions between these two kinds of stories: on the one hand, the narrative implicit in theoretical formulations like the efficient market hypothesis, which stress the efficiency and autonomy of markets; and on the other, narratives about the history and implementation of this hypothesis, which emphasize the agency of the "great" men (and they are almost all men) who created and used such (often mathematical) formulations. In order to illuminate the intellectual and institutional conditions in which the efficient market hypothesis and its correlates were generated, I show how the peculiarities of nineteenth-century British liberalism were overtaken (and displaced) by tendencies inherent in the U.S.-centered practices that flourished in the global, relatively unregulated market that emerged after 1970. Along the way, I argue that the efficient market hypothesis not only gave a numerical cast to Adam Smith's trope of the invisible hand but also became an active agent in the very dynamic it purported to describe. The efficient market hypothesis, in other words, along with its theoretical offshoots, actively mediated the relationship between individual market agents and financial markets. In so doing, it "resolved" the paradox inherent in the neoliberal market by making what it claimed to describe come true. In my narrative I try to minimize the kind of account that attributes agency to particular individuals, but, even as I attempt to balance an emphasis on the historical conditions that made these developments possible with the acknowledgment that some individuals deserve mention, I remain equally aware of the power that individualized narratives exert and cautious about the arrogance of many all-encompassing structural explanations.

THE RISE OF THE EFFICIENT MARKET HYPOTHESIS

An early suggestion that markets might be governed by a principle of equilibrium (where various forces balance each other) can be found in Adam Smith's *Wealth of Nations* (1776). For Smith, this phenomenon constituted a paradox that emerged when autonomous individuals banded together into a larger group: in the social state, the individual who labored only for himself inadvertently increased the well-being of his fellow citizens. Smith never referred to a "rational" market, nor did he suggest that quantification was the best way to model this paradox. Instead, he elected to resolve the paradox metaphorically, in a figure that appears only once in the *Wealth of Nations:* "By preferring the support of domestic to that of foreign industry, he intends only his own security; and by directing that industry in such a manner as its produce may be of the greatest value, he intends only his own gain, and he is in this, as in many other cases, led by an invisible hand to promote an end which was no part of his intention."[1]

Smith's embryonic model of market equilibrium was first represented mathematically in the 1870s when a number of European political economists rejected Smith's labor theory of value in favor of a model that emphasized utility. By quantifying utility, these theorists aspired to make political economy a "science" based on mathematics, and, as political economy began to morph into the academic discipline of economics at Cambridge University in the 1880s, the dream of a fully mathematical economic science seemed about to come true. As we will see in a moment, however, mathematics was fully integrated into university-based economics curricula only in the 1970s—and this occurred initially not at Oxbridge but in the United States. At that point mathematics could function as the sign that economists' descriptions of market dynamics were "scientific," and mathematical formulas could be presented as accurate descriptions of the world as well as internally precise models.[2]

The elaboration of the claim that *financial* analysis, as related to but distinct from economic theory, could also have a "scientific" basis was not solely the work of economists. Indeed, the argument that financial matters could be treated "scientifically" was initially yoked to the assertion that *management* was a science in which rational principles obtained. This conviction came from the link already formed between operations research (OR)—the mode of military planning developed during World War II in Britain—and management theory. OR is an interdisciplinary branch of applied mathematics that uses an array of sophisticated modeling techniques to generate optimal solutions to complex problems (like how to integrate an early warning radar system with ground communications and personnel deployment). While initially used in military situations, OR was soon applied to other complex systems, like economies.[3] In the United States, in particular, OR was fused to management theory within the university-based business schools that had been slowly growing in number since 1881, when the Wharton School was created at the University of Pennsylvania. Business schools were placed within universities in the United States both to emphasize the goals that business education shared with other kinds of professional training and to highlight the connections between traditional liberal arts education and sophisticated managerial training.[4] The university affiliation of U.S. business schools constituted a critical departure from the British model of higher education, where business training tended to be institutionally separate from universities.[5] Along with the eventual incorporation of economic principles into the U.S. business school curriculum, these links—between business schools and universities and, within U.S. business schools, between management theory and operations research—provided the crucial infrastructure for many of the postwar theories that were formulated after World War II.[6]

Even before this institutional infrastructure had been fully incorporated into American universities, world events had conspired to push Great Britain out of the center of global finance. A full account of these developments lies beyond the scope of this chapter, but suffice it to say that the power Britain exercised from 1871 through the onset of World War I was based not on the superiority of its universities or economic theorists but on the widespread adoption of the gold standard. During this period, the willingness of other nations to base their currencies on gold, along with London's importance as the leading supplier of credit, gave the British pound (and British monetary policy) extraordinary power. World War I disrupted international credit flows, however, and, in the chaos of the interwar years, the gold standard collapsed (in 1931). As Europe was torn by the forces that culminated in World War II, individual nations began to adopt isolationist policies. Only after the end of the war did a single nation once more assume the responsibilities (and burdens) of centering an international financial system—and this nation was the United States, not Great Britain. The preeminence of the United States, and the implications of this dominance for global financial markets, was made clear in 1944, when the Bretton Woods agreement was signed.[7]

During the 1930s, no single economic model had dominated international policy or theory. Nor was the financial market universally understood to be self-regulating, or "rational." Before any market could be seen as rational, in fact, the analytical methods and data streams capable of depicting an "economy" or a "market" as a discrete entity had to become available. Analytical methods began to appear once U.S. departments of economics began to embrace statistics and to affiliate themselves with the Econometric Society, an international organization founded (in 1930) to explore the intersection of economic theory, statistics, and mathematics. In 1932 the Cowles Commission for Research in Economics was created, and in 1933 the Cowles Commission launched *Econometrica*, a journal that enabled people interested in these fields to pursue common research programs. Reliable streams of easy-to-use financial data also began to become available around 1930: while Charles Dow's stock price averages had been regularly published since 1884, Standard Statistics, the forerunner of Standard and Poor's, began to provide a competing, market-cap-weighted stock index—the prototype of the S&P 500—only in 1923; and in the 1930s the National Bureau of Economic Research began to generate the data that allowed analysts to conceptualize and measure quantifiable entities like the gross national product.

During the two-and-a-half-year lead-up to Bretton Woods, U.S. economists began to formulate a model that depicted the nation's economy as a unified whole and as self-regulating. Equally important, the policies implemented by Bretton Woods laid the groundwork for realizing this model beyond the level of the nation-state—that is, for creating a global economic system that would make self-regulation seem possible. These policies also expressed the preferences of the United States over those of other nations: after Bretton Woods, trade tariffs were reduced, and trading blocs were broken up (enabling the United States to penetrate Britain's imperial preference system); fixed exchange rates were pegged to gold (and mediated by the dollar), which ensured an international balance of trade; and the dollar (whose convertibility to gold was guaranteed by the U.S. government) became the world's reserve currency. In accordance with U.S. wishes, the International Monetary Fund (IMF) did not become a powerful central bank capable of printing its own money. Instead, it was merely a fixed pool of national currencies and gold, and, because all the European combatants were deeply in debt after the war, large amounts of gold were transferred into the United States through the IMF, whose headquarters were located in Washington, D.C.

In the wake of the Bretton Woods agreement, U.S. economists associated with the Cowles Commission began to refine the theoretical model that depicted markets as rational and self-governing—and therefore compatible with both the free market policies articulated at Bretton Woods and the management strategies associated with Operations Research. This model was eventually expressed mathematically (in 1965, by Paul Samuelson) and in complex formulations like portfolio theory (from 1952), the efficient market hypothesis (from 1970), and the options pricing model (from 1973). But what is important about the basic model associated with the efficient market hypothesis is that its success as a theory of value began to influence the dynamics of the market it was intended to describe. In simplest terms, this occurred because the model was so widely adopted by economists and institutional investors, who were in charge of ever larger pools of capital.

We can explain the success of the model, in turn, both by noting that it was compatible with the way that economists, who had begun to populate U.S. business school faculties in 1970, understood their theoretical work (as "scientific") and by recognizing that it gave intellectual credibility and an expressly financial content to OR-influenced financial managers, who also began to identify themselves as members of a professional group in the 1970s. The overlap between the self-interested agendas of these two groups (academic economists and financial managers) largely went unnoticed during this decade because the promoters of the model presented it as simply descriptive: according to its champions, it is simply true that market prices contain perfect (comprehensive) information and that they fluctuate randomly (independently of each other). (If successive prices do fluctuate independently, in theory, they must be responding to some external factor—presumably, an increase in information, which is, by definition, random. And if the market is aggregating this information efficiently, the information will translate into prices.)[8] Paradoxically, then, the success of the claim that the model simply describes facts that actually exist rests on the ability of the model to persuade people to believe that it is accurate, for if the majority of market actors behave as if these claims are true, the principles of an efficient market will be realized in market dynamics. Let me explain this a bit more.

Unlike natural phenomena (the weather, for example), social phenomena (like the stock market) are always affected by the stories that participants tell about them. This is known as reflexivity or performativity, and its characteristic dynamic is the recursive feedback loop. When market actors become convinced that a particular theory of value is a good story, which expresses how to go from value to price, they buy and sell with this theory in mind, and, as they do so, the theory is transmitted into prices, which only *seem* to express facts about an "autonomous" market and the tendency of prices to reflect all the information that is available. While this point may sound like a theoretical critique mounted by a literary poststructuralist, it is actually a commonplace within the financial community. Even the most outspoken champions of the efficient market hypothesis acknowledge the reflexive relationship that links theories to the dynamics of financial markets. Thus Peter L. Bernstein, the author of two important histories of the theories he calls "Capital Ideas," explains reflexivity as an "ironic" (and unproblematic) truth: "It may sound ironic, but as investors increasingly draw on Capital Ideas to shape their strategies, to innovate new financial instruments, and to motivate the drive for higher returns in relation to risk, the real world is on a path toward an increasing resemblance to the theoretical world described in *Capital Ideas*."[9]

Some financial insiders, like the hedge fund manager George Soros, are more skeptical about the relationship between theory and market behavior (although what troubles Soros seems to be the lack of fit between theories and reality rather than the former's ability to influence the latter). "The prevailing paradigm," Soros wrote in 2008, "asserts that financial markets tend towards equilibrium. . . . While it is possible to construct theoretical models along those lines, the claim that those models apply to the real world is both false and misleading."[10] I'll return in a moment to the dangers inherent in the reflexivity of the efficient market hypothesis, but first let me show how this theory, which is typically but not necessarily cast in a mathematical form, was reinforced by developments in the 1970s. By the beginning of that decade, the Bretton Woods agreement had enabled the United States to attain hegemony in the global financial markets; no longer needing Bretton Woods, the United States abandoned its principles in 1971 when it allowed the dollar to float free of gold. Even without Bretton Woods, and with the power of the dollar established, the United States was able to remain the center of global finance. In the 1970s, and in the context of a worldwide crisis in energy production, at least four, interrelated developments reinforced the appeal of the efficient market hypothesis and its correlates: first, finance began to replace industry as the leading source of economic growth in the West; second, economic theorists introduced a new paradigm for investment management, portfolio theory; third, in 1974 the U.S. government passed the Employee Retirement Security Act (ERISA); and, fourth, financial analysts emerged as an influential professional group.

These events were related to each other in the following way: ERISA, which was intended to protect workers against the ruinous effects of corporate bankruptcy, required companies to set money aside to fund retirements, and this dramatically increased the capital in search of investment returns; by law, the huge pools of assets thus produced had to be managed according to current industry standards; the financial industry adopted portfolio theory as its standard, and because this theory (which priced risk at the level of the portfolio as a whole rather than in terms of individual stocks) was more complicated than picking individual stocks, individuals and institutions increasingly sought investment help; and a professionalized group of money managers (or professional investors) presented its members as better trained to satisfy the standards of their industry because they could apply portfolio theory. Professional managers fared better than individual investors because, once the industry identified the portfolio as the most important site of risk, it became important to figure asset diversification and mean variance into investment strategies. Calculating mean variance requires sophisticated mathematical tools, including computer programs, which can figure the covariance (or tendency to move together) of the stocks contained in a portfolio. With such tools at their disposal, financial professionals were able to determine which portfolios most closely approached the ideal ratio of risk and returns, which they denominated the "Efficient Frontier."[11] *Institutional Investor*, a monthly magazine launched in 1968, not only helped investment managers identify themselves as members of a professional group but also helped translate the highly sophisticated mathematics formulated by economic theorists into usable investment strategies.[12] The combination of an economic shift from production to finance, a mathematically expressed investment theory, the legal requirement in the United States that a huge volume of assets be channeled into managed funds, and the availability of a group of professionals trained to implement the theoretical claims of economists helped the efficient market hypothesis become orthodoxy during the 1970s.[13] This model was largely in place by 1980, the year Ronald Reagan became president of the United States and Margaret Thatcher entered 10 Downing Street as Britain's prime minister.

The theory of supply-side economics endorsed by Reagan and Thatcher helped cement the influence of the efficient market hypothesis. Equally important, of course, were specific legislative measures implemented to facilitate the free movement of financial markets. Beginning in the 1980s, nearly every restriction that had been placed on U.S. banks in the 1930s was repealed. Central to the liberation of the banking system was the repeal of the 1933 Glass-Steagall Act, which had established a barrier between investment banking and commercial banks. With the enormous growth in assets and investment opportunities that followed the repeal of Glass-Steagall, investment banks like J. P. Morgan and Bear Stearns began to devise financial instruments that allowed them to trade in new kinds of securities, take advantage of temporary inefficiencies in global markets, and maximize the degree of leverage involved in individual wagers.

In the 1980s U.S. (and global) corporations also renewed their efforts to implement the market principles articulated by the efficient market hypothesis. Such actions were legitimated by agency theory, a paradigm generated by economic theorists that claimed that the interests of company executives should be aligned with those of shareholders. Because market prices were assumed to reflect all available information about the company, this theory also asserted that a company's stock price constituted a consensus about the company's—and its executives'—performance.[14]

One unintended consequence of agency theory was to encourage corporate executives to take more risk, because only by doing so could they enhance the earnings of shareholders.[15] Beyond agency theory, two real-life factors also encouraged company executives to accept the efficient market hypothesis and the risk-enhancing discipline of the market price. First, the threat of hostile takeovers, which had loomed large on the horizon of all "underperforming" companies since the early 1970s, made it seem imperative for CEOs to maximize shareholders' returns (i.e., stock prices); second, once executive compensation was yoked to the company's performance, executives had an even greater incentive to beat the so-called number, the single metric set by Wall Street analysts, which allowed investors to compare the value of different companies.[16] Preventing hostile takeovers required amassing huge amounts of assets on company budget sheets, which meant, in practice, closing even those factories that continued to be productive and loading up on debt. Tying compensation to an executive's ability to make his "number" encouraged CEOs to try almost anything to create the impression (if not the fact) of success. Finally, issuing so much of a CEO's compensation in the form of stock options, which were valued by a corollary to the efficient market hypothesis called the Black Scholes options pricing formula, encouraged executives to assume additional risk, for options pricing favors the volatility of stock prices, not a company's productivity. All these incentives for corporate executives to take more risk encouraged ambitious individuals to become precisely the kind of outsized characters that individualistic narratives were later to chronicle.

During the 1970s and for much of the 1980s, neither the increasing hegemony of the efficient market hypothesis and its corollaries nor the reflexive relationship between investment theory and the dynamics of financial markets attracted much attention outside of the financial community. In 1987 this changed abruptly when a computerized trading program designed to help professional investors minimize risk triggered a huge sell-off on Wall Street. On October 19 of that year, the Dow Jones Industrial average dropped 508 points; at 23 percent, this represented the worst single day in the history of the U.S. financial market. This collapse was sparked by traders' use of a software program that priced portfolio insurance and was created and marketed by Leland O'Brien Rubinstein (LOR). In 1987 LOR directly managed $5 billion in employee pension funds; other money managers, who had licensed this proprietary software, controlled an additional $45 billion. The program was intended to protect clients' portfolios during a down market, but, because the LOR program was keyed to the "pervasive forces" of the market, it was inevitable that a sufficiently large number of positions hedged according to the same algorithm would affect the market. On October 19 this is exactly what happened: the trading model directed fund managers to sell, and, when they all dumped stock at the same time, the Dow plummeted. While U.S. regulators soon outlawed this particular form of portfolio insurance, they did not question the risk model LOR had used or the reflexive nature of the relationship between the model and the market.[17]

The dangers inherent in this relationship also became visible in a model specifically designed to price risk, called "value at risk" (VaR). Adopted in the early 1980s, VaR (which is still used) is a quantitative measure of the (theoretical) amount a portfolio can drop in a down market. Based on the mathematical principle of "semi-variance," models of VaR, like the one marketed by RiskMetrics, are intended to help factor the effects of derivatives and other structured products into the valuation of risk. Like some other theoretical models, however, VaR tends to create the very conditions it is intended to control: since the VaR metric cannot register all the market factors involved in trading, widespread use of it has tended to make markets riskier—precisely because managers' sense that they are controlling for risk has encouraged them to make even riskier wagers. As managers act in concert, moreover, they invalidate the VaR models that direct their decisions. The resulting uncertainties do not conform to VaR or any other available risk models, all of which are based on the assumptions that the market is the stable, closed system described by the efficient market hypothesis and that human actors are, by nature, rational too. In George Soros's view, the use of risk models like VaR (along with the dubious models used by rating agencies like Standard and Poor's and Moody's) continues to misprice both financial instruments and the risk they entail. Such mispricing then feeds back into the recursive loop that can undermine the very nature of what the models claim to describe.[18]

The events of 2007–9 have further exposed the dangers inherent in failing to grasp the implications of model/market reflexivity, as even a brief summary reveals. Essentially, during the 1990s, financial engineers developed two new kinds of investment products, both of which were intended to maximize the profitability of (managing) risk. The first, which consisted of instruments designed to *spread* risk across various investor groups, was epitomized by credit default swaps. In a credit default swap, which is a form of insurance (like the portfolio insurance that proved so disastrous in 1987), one party purchases a guarantee that he will be compensated if a counterparty defaults from a seller who does not expect the counterparty to fail. The seller is willing to assume this risk because he believes that the debt the contract insures is made up of super-safe securities. He assumes this, in turn, because a credit rating agency has given these securities the highest rating: triple-A.

The second group of financial instruments *produced* the securities that the credit default swaps were designed to insure. As a class, these instruments are called *derivatives* because their value is derived from, but independent of, an underlying asset. Because the derivative contract (which is what is bought and sold) is separated from the underlying asset it represents, it is priced independently. One form of derivative was based on mortgage-backed securities—groups of mortgages that investment analysts had bundled together, then sliced into tranches that carried different degrees of risk (and rates of return). Individual mortgages had historically offered little appeal to investors because borrowers could pay them off at any time, but when offered as slivers of a bundled group of mortgage debts, derivatives based on mortgages offered precisely the kind of risk-specific product that large-scale investors had begun to seek. Mortgage-backed securities were only the most notorious tip of an iceberg composed of many innovative derivative products created and marketed in the 1990s: these included collateralized debt obligations, collateralized loan obligations, and various "synthetic" securities created by bundling and slicing all kinds of asset pools—some of which were purely theoretical in nature (i.e., they were based on nothing except the mathematical models by which they had been created).[19]

In theory (and if financial markets were not social—or reflexive—phenomena), the combination of risk-distributing instruments and structured investment products like derivatives could create the market "perfection" postulated by the efficient market hypothesis. Because an infinite number and kind of derivatives could be created in this largely unregulated, global market for financial instruments, in other words, risk could theoretically be distributed so widely, at such tolerable levels, and to parties willing to incur so many levels of risk that equilibrium would be produced in the worldwide financial market. Of course, as we all now know, this is not what happened—because the market is both social (i.e., composed of human actors) and locked into a reflexive relation with the models professionals use to understand it. For mortgage-backed securities to continue to fuel both the credit of hundreds of thousands of consumers and the voracious appetites of institutional investors, the value of the underlying assets (in this case, houses) and the number of mortgage purchasers would have had to continue to increase forever. Once oversupply glutted regional housing markets, however, prices stabilized, then began to fall, and, as mortgage rates began to reset, home owners in the United States and elsewhere began defaulting on their loans. As the number of defaults increased, the assets from which some of even the most highly rated derivatives took their value turned out to be worth less, then just plain worthless; the claims against credit default swaps multiplied; and some of the world's most venerable investment banks found it impossible to borrow money. In fall 2007, in a domino effect made up of cascading defaults, revelations about balance sheets riddled with toxic assets, and desperate governments' ineffectual attempts to intervene, investment banks began to falter, global flows of credit froze, and previously prosperous companies—even some national governments—were forced to declare insolvency.

STORIES WE TELL

Although many economists, financial analysts, and market pundits now agree that the model that claims to describe the financial market actively influences its activity, little attention has been paid to the way that stories about the efficient market hypothesis support this reflexive dynamic. I do not suggest that these stories have had the same kind or degree of impact on the financial market as have economic models like the efficient market hypothesis (if for no other reason than that the people who tell these stories do not typically control huge investment funds). It is the case, however, that by preserving the contradiction inherent in the neoliberal model of agency, these histories continue to blind us to the inadequacy of the theoretical paradigms by which we try to understand and make policy about the financial market.

In the months since the financial crisis began, bookstores and newsstands have been inundated with books and articles seeking to explain the events surrounding the collapse of Lehman Brothers in 2007. The vast majority of these accounts prominently feature outsized individuals—investment bankers, CEOs, hedge fund managers, and Ponzi schemers—whose machinations inflated the bubble of finance, then recklessly blew it up. The sheer quantity of such narratives makes naming them all impossible, but a few examples will make my point. William D. Cohan's inside story of the rise and fall of Bear Stearns features the "hubris and wretched excess[es]" of individuals like CEO James Cayne and the hedge fund traders Matthew Tannin and Ralph R. Cioffi; Lawrence G. McDonald's *A Colossal Failure of Common Sense* hones in on Lehman Brothers' executives Joseph Gregory and David Goldfarb before arriving at the door of Richard Fuld's gigantic ego; as its subtitle suggests, David Wessel's *In Fed*

We Trust: Ben Bernanke's War on the Great Panic highlights the heroics of the Federal Reserve chairman; and Erin Avredlund's *Too Good to Be True* vilifies Bernie Madoff, the arch financial miscreant of our time.[20]

Beyond a desire to help readers understand how the hitherto opaque financial industry works (and to make money in the process), these books (and the dozens more I have not named) share the conviction that readers prefer stories about individuals, stories that assign blame to particular people and identify the supermen who will save our national economies (and personal retirement accounts). In so doing, these books repeat the neoliberal claim about individual agency, whatever the specific politics of individual authors. While sales figures generally corroborate this position and while it is also the case—as I have tried to show—that developments beginning in the 1970s encouraged individuals in positions of corporate power to take the kind of risk that could make them seem larger than life, it is also true that the story of the financial crisis could be (and has been) told in other ways, which do not center so exclusively on individual agents.[21] If one wanted to challenge the claims of neoliberalism, it might be useful to try to figure out why such individual-centered narratives are so popular—and why they coexist so comfortably with theories that also depict the financial market as a rational and self-governing agent. Rather than address this question directly, I want simply to suggest why accepting *either* the individual-centered narrative *or* the narrative about efficient markets in the terms that neoliberals have proposed is naive and potentially dangerous. I also want to argue that failing to see that these two kinds of narratives both pull in opposite directions and are related to each other keeps us from understanding the complex dynamic of social systems like financial markets.

Why do I say that accepting either of the two neoliberal stories is dangerous? First, narratives that assign agency unproblematically to individuals not only oversimplify the complex relationships between will and action and cause and effect; they also encourage readers to believe that responsibility even for complex events can be laid at the feet of a relatively small number of individuals. Such a belief is dangerous for two, apparently antithetical reasons: believing that individuals caused this fiasco imperils the trust that is essential to any market economy; and believing that (some other) individuals can fix the financial system sanctions the ignorance so many investors tolerate, as they (we) cede decision making to experts who claim that their interest coincides with ours. Second, narratives (or economic models) that depict the market as an efficient, self-governing system inevitably simplify this extremely complicated phenomenon—not least because such models fail to capture the countless idiosyncrasies of the human agents who participate in market activity, who literally make the market. The danger inherent in allowing professional investors to trust such models completely—to hand decision making over to software programs and the algorithms they encode—became obvious in 1987 and then again in 2007: instead of managing risk, these models generated a kind of risk so enormous and so unmanageable that it threatened to destroy the financial system itself.

Failing to recognize that the two kinds of narrative that organize so much of the neoliberal discourse pull in opposite directions, finally, tends to divert our attention from the urgent need to develop more sophisticated models to capture the ways individuals are actually related to complex social systems like the economy—in historical and technical detail. Something—some *things*—must mediate the relationship between the individual and the system. These "things" may be institutions, like corporations; they may be regulatory discourses, like law; they may be culturally specific conventions, like habits or beliefs. Such mediations must also have characteristic dynamics: the reflexivity that makes the stories we tell about financial markets affect market activity is one such dynamic; what Michel Callon has described as "framing"—the process by which a system dictates what counts as a legitimate action or "fact"—is another.[22] Whatever the nature of these mediations and whatever kinds of dynamics organize the operations of complex social systems, they definitely exceed the relatively inflexible models that neoliberal theorists tend to use. Stories that emphasize individual agency and models that depict an efficient, self-governing economy both fail to capture the complexity of the financial system we actually inhabit. Continuing to believe that either of these stories is true—or that they fit comfortably together—is merely a desperate attempt to preserve a way of understanding the world whose incoherence threatens to invite more crises like the one we are still suffering now.

Notes

1. Christopher Bayly, *The Birth of the Modern World, 1780–1914* (Oxford, 2004).

2. Jack Goody, *The Theft of History* (Cambridge, 2006).

3. See the work of the Global Economic History Network (GEHN), at the London School of Economics, www.lse.ac.uk/collections/economichistory/ GEHN.

4. This revival, above all in a new conversation between history and the social sciences, is both urged and charted in Patrick Joyce, "What Is the Social in Social History?" *Past and Present* 206 (2010). On the role of materiality in history and the social sciences and on what now amounts to a "material turn," see Tony Bennett and Patrick Joyce, eds., *Material Powers: History, Culture and the Material Turn* (London, 2010).

CHAPTER 1

1. Alexis de Tocqueville, *Journeys to England and Ireland,* trans. J.P. Mayer (New Brunswick, 2003 [1835]); J.G. Kohl, *England and Wales,* trans. T. Roscoe (London, 1844); Karl Marx, *On Britain* (Moscow, 1953); Frederick Engels, *The Origin of the Family, Private Property and the State* (New York, 1942); Max Weber, *The Protestant Ethic and the Spirit of Capitalism* (New York, 1976); Karl Polanyi, *The Great Transformation* (Boston, 1957); W.W. Rostow, *The Stages of Economic Growth: A Non-Communist Manifesto* (Cambridge, 1960); Talcott Parsons, *The System of Modern Societies* (1971); Jürgen Habermas, *The Structural Transformation of the Public Sphere* (Cambridge, MA, 1989).

2. Frederick Cooper, *Colonialism in Question: Theory, Knowledge, History* (Berkeley, 2005), 7–9. Like Cooper we have used the Article First database for this keyword search. Accessed 1 October 2009.

3. Cooper is not alone in considering that modernity is "hopelessly confused by the divergent meanings given to it." *Colonialism in Question,* 10.

4. Cooper, *Colonialism in Question,* 7. See also chap. 5. The year 1995 refers to keynote count.

5. On modernization theory generally, see Michael Latham, *Modernization as Ideology: American Social Science and "Nation Building" in the Kennedy Era* (Chapel Hill, 2000); Nils Gilman, *Mandarins of the Future: Modernization Theory in Cold War America* (Baltimore, 2003); and on Britain, see Joseph Hodge, *Triumph of the Expert: Agrarian Doctrines of Development and the Legacies of British Colonialism* (Columbus, OH, 2007). For books claiming Britain's firstness, Peter Mathias, *The First Industrial Nation: An Economic History of Britain, 1700–1914* (London, 1969); Harold Perkin, *The Origins of Modern English Society, 1780–1880* (London, 1969); A. L. Beier et al., eds., *The First Modern Society* (Cambridge, 1989); Roy Porter, *The Creation of the Modern World* (New York, 2000); Dror Wahrman, *The Making of the Modern Self* (New Haven, 2004); Steven Pincus, *1688: The First Modern Revolution* (New Haven, 2009).

6. This was not just a national conceit. See note 1, above, for a selection of the large numbers of foreign observers who reified the British experience as exemplary.

7. This critique did not begin with the Communist Party History Group established in 1946, but the work of Thompson and Hobsbawm was critical in the twentieth-century. E. P. Thompson, *The Making of the English Working Class* (New York, 1963); E. J. Hobsbawm, *Labouring Men* (London, 1964).

8. With apologies to Thompson, "the working class did not rise like the sun at an appointed time." *Making,* 8.

9. A. J. Mayer, *The Persistence of the Old Regime* (London, 1981); Martin Wiener, *English Culture and the Decline of the Industrial Spirit* (Cambridge, 1981); J. C. D. Clark, *English Society, 1660–1832* (Cambridge, 1985); Philip Corrigan and Derek Sayer, *The Great Arch: English State Formation as Cultural Revolution* (New York, 1985).

10. For two notable exceptions, see John Brewer, *The Sinews of Power: War, Money and the English State, 1688–1783* (New York, 1989); Pincus, *1688.*

11. The literature is enormous, but for characteristic examples, see Clark, *English Society;* Richard Price, *British Society, 1680–1880* (Cambridge, 1999); Harold Perkin, *The Rise of Professional Society* (London, 1989); José Harris, *Private Lives, Public Spirit: A Social History of Britain, 1870–1914* (Oxford, 1993); Susan Pedersen and Peter Mandler, eds., *After the Victorians* (New York, 1994); Becky Conekin, Frank Mort, and Chris Waters, eds., *Moments of Modernity: Reconstructing Britain, 1945–64* (London, 1998); Callum Brown, *The Death of Christian Britain* (London, 2001).

12. For an account that emphasizes continuities that are then dramatically ruptured and transformed, see Price, *British Society.*

13. P. J. Cain and A. G. Hopkins, "Gentlemanly Capitalism and British Overseas Expansion, Part 1, 1688–1850," *Economic History Review* 39, no. 4 (1986):

501–25; Patrick Joyce, *Work, Society, and Politics* (New Brunswick, 1980); David Vincent, *The Culture of Secrecy* (New York, 1998); Stefan Collini, *Public Moralists* (Oxford, 1991); David Cannadine, *Ornamentalism* (Oxford, 2001); Jonathan Parry, *The Rise and Fall of Liberal Government in Victorian Britain* (New Haven, 1996).

14. Among many, see Dipesh Chakrabarty, *Habitations of Modernity* (Chicago, 2002); Timothy Mitchell, *Questions of Modernity* (Minneapolis, 2000); Arjun Appadurai, *Modernity at Large* (Minneapolis, 1996).

15. See, e.g., Kenneth Pomeranz, *The Great Divergence: China, Europe, and the Making of the Modern World Economy* (Princeton, 2000); Christopher Bayly, *The Making of the Modern World, 1780–1914* (Oxford, 2004).

16. This is actually the position that Cooper takes. Other examples are Bernhard Rieger and Martin Daunton, eds., *Meanings of Modernity: Britain from the Late Victorian Era to World War Two* (Oxford, 2001); Micah Nava and Alan O'Shea, eds., *Modern Times: A Century of English Modernity* (London, 1996). Kathleen Wilson does something similar for the eighteenth century in her edited book, *The New Imperial History: Culture, Identity and Modernity in Britain and Empire, 1660–1840* (Cambridge, 2004).

17. "Conservative Modernity," *New Formations* 28 (1996); Alison Light, *Forever England: Feminity, Literature and Conservatism between the Wars* (London, 1991); Antoinette Burton, ed., *Gender, Sexuality and Colonial Modernities* (London, 1999); Laura Doan and Jane Garrity, eds., *Sapphic Modernities: Sexuality, Women and National Culture* (London, 2004); David Gilbert, David Matless, and Brian Short, eds., *Geographies of British Modernity* (Oxford, 2003); Penny Tinkler and Cheryl Krasnick Warsh, "Feminine Modernity in Interwar Britain and North America," *Journal of Women's History* 20, no. 3 (2008).

18. A partial exception is Peter Mandler, ed., *Liberty and Authority in Victorian Britain* (Oxford, 2006). However, Mandler's emphasis remains on the political and Britain's precocious and peculiarly elaborated civil society, 17–19.

19. See Quentin Skinner, *Liberty before Liberalism* (Cambridge, 1998); J. G. A. Pocock, "The Varieties of Whiggism from Exclusion to Reform: A History of Ideology and Discourse," in *Virtue, Commerce, and History: Essays on Political Thought and History, Chiefly in the Eighteenth Century* (Cambridge, 1985); Porter, *The Creation of the Modern World*; Richard Bellamy, ed., *Victorian Liberalism: Nineteenth Century Thought and Practice* (London, 1990).

20. In a now-voluminous literature, see Carole Pateman, *The Sexual Contract* (Cambridge, 1988); Leonore Davidoff and Catherine Hall, *Family Fortunes: Men and Women of the English Middle Class, 1780–1850* (London, 1988); Antoinette Burton, *Burdens of History: British Feminists, Indian Women, and Imperial Culture, 1865–1915* (Chapel Hill, 1994); Mary Poovey, *Uneven Developments: The Ideological Work of Gender in Mid-Victorian Britain* (Chicago, 1998); Philippa Levine, ed., *Gender and Empire* (Oxford, 2004); Sarah Knott and Barbara Taylor, eds., *Women, Gender, and Enlight-*

enment (New York, 2005); Clare Midgeley, *Feminism and Empire: Women Activists in Imperial Britain, 1790–1865* (London, 2007).

21. Polanyi, *The Great Transformation;* Stefan Collini, Donald Winch, and John Burrow, *That Noble Science of Politics: A Study in Nineteenth-Century Intellectual History* (Cambridge, 1983); Gertrude Himmelfarb, *The Idea of Poverty: England in the Early Industrial Age* (New York, 1984); Boyd Hilton, *The Age of Atonement: The Influence of Evangelicalism on Social and Economic Thought, 1785–1865* (Oxford, 1992); Emma Rothschild, *Economic Sentiments: Adam Smith, Condorcet, and the Enlightenment* (Cambridge, MA, 2001); Gareth Stedman Jones, *An End to Poverty? A Historical Debate* (New York, 2004); Catherine Gallagher, *The Body Economic: Life, Death and Sensation in Political Economy and the Victorian Novel* (Princeton, 2006); Mary Poovey, *Genres of the Credit Economy: Mediating Value in Eighteenth- and Nineteenth-Century Britain* (Chicago, 2008); Frank Trentmann, *Free Trade Nation: Commerce, Consumption and Civil Society in Modern Britain* (Oxford, 2008).

22. Pincus, *1688;* Donald Winch, *Classical Political Economy and Colonies* (Cambridge, MA, 1965); Donald Winch, *Riches and Poverty: An Intellectual History of Political Economy in Britain, 1750–1834* (Cambridge, 1996); Bernard Semmel, *The Rise of Free Trade Imperialism: Classical Political Economy, the Empire of Free Trade and Imperialism, 1750–1850* (Cambridge, 1970).

23. For recent examples, see Anthony Howe, *Free Trade and Liberal England, 1846–1946* (Oxford, 1996); Trentmann, *Free Trade Nation.*

24. The classic texts here are John Vincent, *The Formation of the Liberal Party* (London, 1966); Peter Clarke, *Lancashire and the New Liberalism* (Cambridge, 1971); and George Dangerfield, *The Strange Death of Liberal England* (New York, 1935).

25. Eugenio Biagini and Alastair Reid, eds., *Currents of Radicalism* (Cambridge, 1991); Parry, *The Rise and Fall of Liberal Government;* Myriam Boussahba-Bravard, ed., *Suffrage outside Suffragism: Britain, 1880–1914* (Basingstoke, 2007).

26. Andrew Barry, Thomas Osborne, and Nikolas Rose, *Foucault and Political Reason: Liberalism, Neo-Liberalism, and Rationalities of Government* (London, 1996); Nikolas Rose, *Powers of Freedom: Reframing Political Thought* (Cambridge, 1999); Patrick Joyce, *The Rule of Freedom: Liberalism and the Modern City* (London, 2003).

27. The Foucauldians would of course see this commitment to freedom in terms of the presence, not absence, of government—aptly captured by Joyce's *The Rule of Freedom.*

28. A debate nicely apparent in the work on liberalism and imperialism, see Uday Mehta, *Liberalism and Empire: A Study in Nineteenth-Century British Political Thought* (Chicago, 1995); Thomas Metcalf, *Ideologies of the Raj* (Cambridge, 1997); Sankar Muthu, *Enlightenment against Empire* (Princeton, 2003); Jennifer Pitts, *A Turn to Empire: The Rise of Imperial Liberalism in*

Britain and France (Princeton, 2006); Andrew Sartori, "The British Empire and Its Liberal Mission," *Journal of Modern History* 78, no. 3 (2006): 623–42.

29. Dangerfield, *The Strange Death of Liberal England.*

30. For a classical restatement of this identification at the Europe-wide level, see Jürgen Kocka, "The Middle Classes in Europe," *Journal of Modern History* 67 (1995): 783–806.

31. A position elaborated well in Mary Poovey, *The Making of a Social Body: British Cultural Formation, 1830–1865* (Chicago, 1995), 14; and beautifully dissected by Ian Burney, "Bone in the Craw of Modernity," *Journal of Victorian Culture* 4, no. 1 (1999): 104–16.

32. E. P. Thompson, "The Peculiarities of the English," *Socialist Register* (1965). Subsequent references to this essay are to the reprinted version in Thompson, *The Poverty of Theory and Other Essays* (London, 1978). Perry Anderson, "The Origins of the Present Crisis," *New Left Review* 23 (1964): 50.

33. Thompson, "Peculiarities," 57.

34. Anderson, "Origins," 43.

35. Thompson, "Peculiarities," 59–64.

36. A phrase used by Robert Looker, "Shifting Trajectories: Perry Anderson's Account of the Pattern of English Historical Development," in *The Development of British Capitalist Society: A Marxist Debate*, ed. C. Barker and D. Nicholls (Manchester, 1988), 8.

37. Their imprint—and that of the debate as a whole—is apparent in many of the themes discussed in this introduction: the persistence of the ancien régime, the pace and social effects of industrialization, and the character of intellectual life. Geoff Eley and David Blackbourn's *The Peculiarities of German History* (Oxford, 1984) drew its inspiration directly from the terms of the earlier British debate, even if its subject was the German *Sonderweg*, or special path.

38. One variant of this is the focus on the Atlantic world or the development of a transnational "Anglo-world" of settlers from the eighteenth century. For two recent examples in voluminous literatures, see David Armitage and Michael Braddick, eds., *The British Atlantic World, 1500–1800* (New York, 2009); James Belich, *Replenishing the Earth: The Settler Revolution and the Rise of the Anglo-World, 1783–1939* (Oxford, 2009).

39. The literatures here are again voluminous, but see, e.g., Joyce Appleby, *Liberalism and Republicanism in the Historical Imagination* (Boston, 1992); Andrew Kalyvas and Ira Katznelson, eds., *Liberal Beginnings: Making a Republic for the Moderns* (Cambridge, 2008).

40. Such an approach has analogies with Cooper's argument that the history of capitalism "needs to be pulled apart rather than mushed together" and Timothy Mitchell's call to eschew binaries in historical explanation and acknowledge "the mixed way things happen." Cooper, *Colonialism in Question*, 125; Timothy Mitchell, *Rule of Experts: Egypt, Techno-Politics, Modernity* (Berkeley, 2002), 52.

41. Mike Davis, *Late Victorian Holocausts* (London, 2001); Ranajit Guha,

Elementary Aspects of Peasant Insurgency in Colonial India (Durham, NC, 1999); Stephen Howe, *Ireland and Empire* (Oxford, 2001); R. Ross, *Beyond the Pale: Essays on the History of Colonial South Africa* (Middletown, CT, 1993).

42. Nasser Hussain, *The Jurisprudence of Emergency: Colonialism and the Rule of Law* (Ann Arbor, 2003).

43. In a vast literature, see Robert Gildea, *Barricades and Borders: Europe, 1800–1914* (Oxford, 2003); Geoff Eley, *Forging Democracy: The History of the Left in Europe, 1850–2000* (Oxford, 2002); Mark Mazower, *Dark Continent: Europe's Twentieth Century* (London, 2000); David L. Hoffman and Yanni Kotsonis, eds., *Russian Modernity: Politics, Knowledge, Practices* (London, 2000); Roger Griffin, *Modernism and Fascism* (London, 2007).

44. Stuart Hall and Martin Jacques, eds., *New Times: The Changing Face of Politics in the 1990s* (London, 1989); David Harvey, *A Brief History of Neo-Liberalism* (Oxford, 2005); Andrew Gamble, Steve Ludlam, Andrew Taylor, and Stephen J. Wood, eds., *Labour, the State, Social Movements, and the Challenge of Neo-Liberal Globalisation* (New York, 2009).

45. There is no properly international conspectus of the topic, but neo-liberalism appears to have taken root in France and Germany, for instance, only since the 1990s.

CHAPTER 2

This chapter is part of a longer project on Macaulay and the writing of history to be published in 2011 as *Macaulay and Son: Writing Home, Nation and Empire.* I am grateful to the ESRC for the support they have provided, RES 063–27–0009. Thanks to Simon Gunn, James Vernon, Sally Alexander, and Stuart Hall for their comments.

1. George Otto Trevelyan, *The Life and Letters of Lord Macaulay* (London, 1881), 507–9.

2. Thomas Babington Macaulay, *The History of England from the Accession of James II (1848–61),* 3 vols. (London, 1906), 1:10.

3. There is a wealth of material on Macaulay. See in particular Thomas Pinney, ed., *The Letters of Thomas Babington Macaulay,* 6 vols. (Cambridge, 1974–81); William Thomas, ed., *The Journals of Thomas Babington Macaulay,* 5 vols. (London, 2008); Trevelyan, *Life and Letters;* John Clive, *Thomas Babington Macaulay: The Shaping of the Historian* (London, 1973); William Thomas, *The Quarrel of Macaulay and Croker: Politics and History in the Age of Reform* (Oxford, 2000).

4. Cited in J. T. Ward, *The Factory Movement, 1830–1855* (London, 1962), 58.

5. Cited in Arthur Stanley Turberville and Frank Beckwith, "Leeds and Parliamentary Reform, 1820–32," *Publications of the Thoresby Society* 61, pt. 1 (1943): 1–88, 66.

6. Thomas Babington Macaulay, *Speeches on Politics and Literature by Lord Macaulay* (London, 1909), 141.

7. Russell, cited in Peter Mandler, *Aristocratic Government in the Age*

of Reform: Whigs and Liberals, 1830–1852 (Oxford, 1990), 4; Ian Newbould, *Whiggery and Reform, 1830–1841* (Basingstoke, 1990). See also J. P. Parry, "Liberalism and Liberty," in *Liberty and Authority in Victorian Britain*, ed. Peter Mandler (Oxford, 2006), 71–100.

8. Robert Q. Gray, *The Factory Question and Industrial England, 1830–1860* (Cambridge, 1996), 210–11.

9. Macaulay, *Speeches*, 340.

10. Herbert Butterfield, *The Englishman and His History* (London, 1970 [1944]), 2.

11. Leslie Stephen, *Hours in a Library*, 3 vols. (London, 1909), 2:336–37.

12. Clive, *Macaulay*.

13. Joseph Hamburger, *Macaulay and the Whig Tradition* (Chicago, 1976).

14. J. W. Burrow, *A Liberal Descent: Victorian Historians and the English Past* (Cambridge, 1981), 92.

15. James Vernon, "Narrating the Constitution: The Discourse of 'the Real' and the Fantasies of Nineteenth-Century Constitutional History," in *Re-Reading the Constitution: New Narratives in the Political History of England's Long Nineteenth Century*, ed. James Vernon (Cambridge, 1996).

16. Thomas, *The Quarrel*, 5.

17. Herbert Butterfield, *The Whig Interpretation of History* (London, 1931), 9.

18. Robert E. Sullivan, *Macaulay: The Tragedy of Power* (Cambridge, MA, 2009), 241.

19. See also J. W. Burrow, *Whigs and Liberals: Continuity and Change in English Political Thought* (Oxford, 1988); William Thomas, *The Philosophical Radicals: Nine Studies in Theory and Practice, 1817–1841* (Oxford, 1979); Stefan Collini, Donald Winch, and John Burrow, *That Noble Science of Politics: A Study in Nineteenth-Century Intellectual History* (Cambridge, 1983); Biancamaria Fontana, *Rethinking the Politics of Commercial Society: The "Edinburgh Review," 1802–1832* (Cambridge, 1985).

20. See especially Mrinalini Sinha, *Spectres of Mother India: The Global Restructuring of an Empire* (Durham, NC, 2006).

21. Uday Singh Mehta, *Liberalism and Empire: A Study in Nineteenth-Century British Liberal Thought* (Chicago, 1999), 1.

22. Jennifer Pitts, *A Turn to Empire: The Rise of Imperial Liberalism in Britain and France* (Princeton, 2005), 2.

23. Andrew Sartori, "The British Empire and Its Liberal Mission," *Journal of Modern History* 78 (September 2006): 623–42. Sartori's book *Bengal in Global Concept Culture: Culturalism in the Age of Capital* (Chicago, 2008) aims to embed an intellectual history in its local specificity, situating Bengali culturalism as a specific set of practices in the context of a reaction against a dominant liberal ideological paradigm.

24. Partha Chatterjee, *The Nation and Its Fragments: Colonial and Postcolonial Histories* (Princeton, 1993), xi, 10. On the wedding of equality and exclusion in the liberal state, see Saidiya V. Hartman, *Scenes of Subjection:*

Terror, Slavery, and Self-Making in Nineteenth-Century America (New York, 1997). See also Catherine Hall, *Civilising Subjects: Metropole and Colony in the English Imagination* (Cambridge, 2002).

25. Thomas C. Holt, *The Problem of Freedom: Race, Labor, and Politics in Jamaica and Britain, 1832–1938* (Baltimore, 1992).

26. Patrick Joyce, *The Rule of Freedom: Liberalism and the Modern City* (London, 2003), 1.

27. Thanks to Jon Lawrence for drawing my attention to this.

28. Thomas Babington Macaulay, "The Earl of Chatham," in *Literary and Historical Essays Contributed to the Edinburgh Review*, 2 vols. (Oxford, 1913), 2:789.

29. Macaulay, *History*, 3:561.

30. For a longer discussion of these issues, see Catherine Hall, "At Home with History: Macaulay and the 'History of England,'" in *At Home with the Empire: Metropolitan Culture and the Imperial World*, ed. Catherine Hall and Sonya O. Rose (Cambridge, 2006).

31. Macaulay, *Speeches*, 124.

32. Uma Satyavolu Rau, "The National/Imperial Subject in T. B. Macaulay's Historiography," *Nineteenth Century Contexts* 23 (2001): 89–119.

33. Macaulay, "Gladstone on Church and State," in *Literary and Historical Essays*, 2:367.

34. Balachandra Rajan, *Under Western Eyes: India from Milton to Macaulay* (Durham, NC, 1999).

35. For a longer discussion, see Catherine Hall, "Making Colonial Subjects: Education in the Age of Empire," *History of Education* 37, no. 6 (November 2008): 773–87.

36. Biancamaria Fontana, 'Whigs and Liberals: The *Edinburgh Review* and the 'Liberal Movement' in Nineteenth-Century Britain," in *Victorian Liberalism: Nineteenth-Century Political Thought and Practice*, ed. Richard Bellamy (London, 1990), 48.

37. Judith Newton, "Sex and Political Economy in the *Edinburgh Review*," in *Starting Over: Feminism and the Politics of Cultural Critique* (Ann Arbor, 1994), 97–124.

38. Stephen, *Hours*, 2:348.

39. *Letters*, 5:42.

40. *Letters*, 4:15.

41. Macaulay, "Southey's Colloquies on Society," in *Literary and Historical Essays*, 1:129.

42. Ibid., 134.

43. *Journals*, 2, 10 April 1849.

44. Hayden White, "Historical Writing as a Bourgeois Science," in *The Content of the Form: Narrative Discourse and Historical Representation* (Baltimore, 1987).

45. For a discussion of this shift, see Karen O'Brien, "Emigration, Empire and History: From Enlightenment to Liberalism," in *Race, Nation and Empire:*

Making Histories, 1750 to the Present, ed. Catherine Hall and Keith McClelland (Manchester, 2010).

46. P. R. Ghosh, "Macaulay and the Heritage of the Enlightenment," *English Historical Review* 112, no. 446 (April 1997): 358–95. Ghosh argues that the form of the *History* severely constrained Macaulay.

47. *History,* 1:218.

48. Ibid., 219.

49. Ibid., 221.

50. Ibid., 218.

51. Ibid., 242.

52. *Journals,* 5, 12 August 1858.

53. *History,* 1:247.

54. Ibid., 248.

55. Ibid., 249.

56. Ibid.

57. Ibid., 304–5.

58. Ibid., 277–81.

59. Ibid., 286.

60. Ibid., 286–87.

61. Ibid., 290.

62. Ibid., 287.

63. Ibid., 319.

64. Ibid., 328.

65. Ibid., 327–28.

66. Ibid., 328–29.

67. *Journals,* 5, 29 October 1858.

CHAPTER 3

1. Uday S. Mehta, *Liberalism and Empire: A Study in Nineteenth-Century British Liberal Thought* (Chicago, 1999); Partha Chatterjee, *The Nation and Its Fragments: Colonial and Postcolonial Histories* (Princeton, 1993), chap. 1; Ranajit Guha, *Dominance without Hegemony: History and Power in Colonial India* (Cambridge, MA, 1997), esp. 60–72; Thomas R. Metcalf, *Ideologies of the Raj* (Cambridge, 1995).

2. Jennifer Pitts, *A Turn to Empire: The Rise of Imperial Liberalism in Britain and France* (Princeton, 2005), 62–63, and chap. 3 more generally; cf. Mehta, *Liberalism and Empire,* chap. 5.

3. This is the argument of Pitts, *Turn to Empire.* Also see Andrew Sartori, "The British Empire and Its Liberal Mission," *Journal of Modern History* 78 (2006): 623–42; Catherine Hall, Keith McClelland, and Jane Rendall, *Defining the Victorian Nation: Race, Gender and the British Reform Act of 1867* (Cambridge, 2000).

4. Kathleen Wilson, *The Island Race: Englishness, Empire and Gender in the Eighteenth Century* (London, 2003), 213 n. 74.

5. Richard Price, *Making Empire: Colonial Encounters and the Creation of Imperial Rule in Nineteenth-Century Africa* (Cambridge, 2008).

6. Sartori, "British Empire," 624.

7. Douglas Hay and Paul Craven, eds., *Masters, Servants, and Magistrates in Britain and Empire* (Chapel Hill, 2004), esp. editors' introduction; "Unfree Labour in the Development of the Atlantic World," special issue, *Slavery and Abolition*, ed. Paul E. Lovejoy and Nicholas Rogers, 15, no. 2 (1994).

8. Robert J. Steinfeld, *Coercion, Contract, and Free Labor in the Nineteenth Century* (Cambridge, 2001), 68 (quotation), chaps. 2 and 6.

9. David Brion Davis, "Reflections on Abolitionism and Ideological Hegemony," in *The Anti-Slavery Debate: Capitalism and Abolitionism as a Problem in Historical Interpretation*, ed. Thomas Bender (Berkeley, 1992), 170–71.

10. Moon-Ho Jung, *Coolies and Cane: Race, Labor, and Sugar in the Age of Emancipation* (Baltimore, 2006), 14.

11. Madhavi Kale, *Fragments of Empire: Capital, Slavery, and Indian Indentured Labor in the British Caribbean* (Philadelphia, 1998), 4–9, chap. 1, for Gladstone; see also Thomas C. Holt, *The Problem of Freedom: Race, Labor, and Politics in Jamaica and Britain, 1832–1938* (Baltimore, 1992); Hugh Tinker, *A New System of Slavery: The Export of Indian Labour Overseas, 1830–1920* (London, 1974); Walton Look Lai, *Indentured Labor, Caribean Sugar: Chinese and Indian Migrants to the British West Indies, 1838–1918* (Baltimore, 1993); cf. Clare Anderson, "Convicts and Coolies: Rethinking Indentured Labour in the Nineteenth Century," *Slavery and Abolition* 30 (2009): 93–109.

12. Christopher L. Brown, "Empire without Slaves: British Concepts of Emancipation in the Age of the American Revolution," *William and Mary Quarterly*, 3rd ser., 56 (1999): 273–306; more generally, see Seymour Drescher, *The Mighty Experiment: Free Labor and Slavery in British Emancipation* (Oxford, 2002).

13. My discussion draws on James Epstein, "In Search of Free Labour: Trinidad and the Abolition of the British Slave Trade," in *Gender, Labour, War, and Empire: Essays on Modern Britain*, ed. Philippa Levine and Susan Grayzel (London, 2008).

14. I have in mind Michel Foucault's concept of genealogy, in "Nietzsche, Genealogy, History," republished in D. F. Bouchard, ed., *Language, Counter-Memory, Practice: Selected Essays and Interviews* (Ithaca, 1977), 139–64. See also David Scott, "Colonial Governmentality," *Social Text*, no. 43 (1995): 191–220.

15. James Millette, *Society and Politics in Colonial Trinidad* (Port of Spain and London, 1985), 15–19; Bridget Brereton, *A History of Modern Trinidad, 1783–1962* (Kingston, 1981), chap. 2.

16. *Parliamentary History of England*, 36 (London, 1820), cols. 854–81; Patrick C. Lipscomb, "Party Politics, 1801–1802: George Canning and the Trinidad Question," *Historical Journal* 12 (1969): 442–66; Millette, *Society and Politics in Colonial Trinidad*, 78–87, for the background to debate.

17. C. A. Bayly, "The British and Indigenous People, 1760–1860: Power,

Perception, and Identity," in *Empire and Others: British Encounters with Indigenous Peoples, 1600–1850*, ed. Martin Daunton and Rick Halpern (Philadelphia, 1999), 22–23.

18. James Stephen, *The Crisis of the Sugar Colonies . . . which are subjoined Sketches of a Plan for Settling the Vacant Lands of Trinidada* (London, 1802), 157.

19. British Library, Add. Ms. 37,884, Canning to Windham, 23 May 1802, fols. 292–96.

20. Public Records Office, National Archives, Colonial Office (hereafter PRO, CO) 295/3, Hobart to the Commissioners for Trinidad, 16 October 1802, fols. 2–10.

21. PRO, CO 295/2, Hobart to Picton, 18 February 1802, fols. 40–45; Picton to Hobart, 12 April 1802; CO 295/10, report of February 1804, fols. 28–35.

22. PRO, CO 295/6, Charles Yorke to Addington, 28 January 1803, Alexander MacDonald to Yorke, 14 and 29 January 1803, MacDonald to Addington, 1 January 1803, "Proposals for Establishing a Colony of Highlanders in the Island of Trinidad," fols. 26–39.

23. Scottish Records Office, Forfeited Estates E730/32, quoted in A. J. Youngson, *After the Forty-Five: The Economic Impact on the Scottish Highlands* (Edinburgh, 1973), 36.

24. Earl of Selkirk, *Observations on the Present State of the Highlands of Scotland* (London, 1805), 3.

25. Patrick Colquhoun, *The State of Indigence, and the Situation of the Casual Poor in the Metropolis Explained* (London, 1799), 19–20.

26. Patrick Colquhoun, *A Treatise on Indigence; Exhibiting a General View of the National Resources for Productive Labor; with Propositions for Ameliorating the Conditions of the Poor* (London, 1806), 122; original emphasis.

27. See Gertrude Himmelfarb, *The Idea of Poverty: England in the Early Industrial Age* (New York, 1984), 77–85, which contrasts Colquhoun's "softer" reform vision to that of Bentham.

28. PRO, CO 295/6, Colquhoun to Sullivan, 12 February 1803, fols. 44–50; original emphasis.

29. Donna T. Andrew, *Philanthropy and Police: London Charity in the Eighteenth Century* (Princeton, 1989), chap. 6.

30. Saree Makdisi, *Romantic Imperialism: Universal Empire and the Culture of Modernity* (Cambridge, 1998), 78–80.

31. Karen Ordahl Kupperman, "Fear of Hot Climates in Anglo-American Colonial Experience," *William and Mary Quarterly*, 3rd ser., 41 (1984): 213–40; Michael Duffy, *Soldiers, Sugar, and Seapower: The British Expeditions to the West Indies and the War against Revolutionary France* (Oxford, 1987), chap. 14.

32. Cf. Andrew Mackillop, "For King, Country, and Regiment? Motive and Identity within Highland Soldiering," in *Fighting for Identity: Scottish Military Experience, c. 1550–1900*, ed. Steve Murdoch and A. Mackillop (Leiden, 2002), 185–211.

33. PRO, CO 295/3, Hobart to Commissioners, 16 October 1802, enclosure, "Suggestions with Respect to the Population and Settlement of Land in Trinidad," fols. 13–20; CO 296/4, enclosure no. 20, fols. 69–73.

34. See Alan Lester, *Imperial Networks: Creating Identities in Nineteenth-Century South Africa and Britain* (London, 2001), 5–7.

35. PRO, CO 295/6, "Memorandum relating to the introduction of Chinese Settlers into the West Indies," 7 April 1803, fol. 156, explicitly underscores concerns about slave insurrection.

36. PRO, Board of Trade [hereafter BT], "Hints for the Cultivation of Trinidad,"16 July 1802, and Layman's "Supplement to Hints for the Cultivation of Trinidad," 28 August 1802. For a fuller discussion, see B.W. Higman, "The Chinese in Trinidad, 1806–1838," *Caribbean Studies* 12 (1972): 21–44.

37. Layman, *Outline of a Plan*, 33–35, 44–47.

38. Ibid., 11–12; original emphasis. See Drescher, *Mighty Experiment*, chap. 2, for Smith and free labor ideology.

39. Mary Poovey, *A History of the Modern Fact: Problems of Knowledge in the Sciences of Wealth and Society* (Chicago, 1998).

40. Layman, *Outline of a Plan*, 11–20.

41. PRO, CO 296/4, enclosure no. 24, fol. 80.

42. PRO, BT 6/70, 28 August 1806, and also Barham's "Proposal to Government for the Purposes of Introducing Natives of the East as Free Labourers to Jamaica," 8 January 1807.

43. *Substance of the Debates on a Resolution for Abolishing the Slave Trade* (London, 1806), 57–58.

44. Layman, *Outline of a Plan*, 21, 80, 86.

45. Ibid., 22–24.

46. According to Cook, there was "nothing which a Chinese will not do for pay." James Cook, *A Compendious History of Captain Cook's First and Second Voyages* (London, 1784), 141.

47. Robert Townsend Farquhar, *Suggestions Arising from the Abolition of the African Slave Trade, for supplying the demands of the West India Colonies* (London, 1807), 47; also his "Observations," PRO, BT 6/70.

48. Layman, *Outline of a Plan*, 82; original emphasis.

49. PRO, CO 295/3, Staunton to John Roberts, 18 December 1802, fols. 200–204.

50. PRO, CO 295/6, MacQueen to Sullivan, April 1803, fols. 148–49; Hobart to MacQueen, 21 April 1803, fols. 152–55.

51. PRO 295/14, Hislop to Windham, 7 October 1806, fol. 165, and 26 October, 169–71; BT 6/70, MacQueen to Windham, 17 October 1806.

52. PRO, CO 295/14, fols. 194–96, and extracts of the minutes of Trinidad's Council, fols. 175–83; *Barbados Mercury*, 4 November 1806.

53. PRO CO 295/17, Gloster to Marryat, 3 April 1807, fols. 154–55; original emphasis.

54. Drescher, *Mighty Experiment*, chap. 6, 108–11.

55. Layman, *Outline of a Plan*, 88–91.

56. E.g., PRO, CO 295/6, MacQueen to [Sullivan], April 1803, fols. 148–49.

57. PRO, CO 295/16, Hislop to Governor General of Bengal in Council, 14 March 1807, fols. 100–103.

58. Layman, *Outline of a Plan*, 70–73.

59. British Library, Add. Ms. 37,886, Barham to William Windham, 14 February 1807, fols. 48–50.

60. Price, *Making Empire*, 6.

CHAPTER 4

I would like to thank Simon Gunn, James Vernon, and Peter Weston for helpful comments on an earlier draft. Keith Nield discussed this essay with me on a couple of occasions with his customary rigor. He died shortly after it went to press. It is dedicated to his memory.

1. Karl Marx and Friedrich Engels, *The Communist Manifesto*, ed. Gareth Stedman Jones (London, 2002), 223. Cited hereafter as *Communist Manifesto*.

2. Marshall Berman, *All That Is Solid Melts into Air. The Experience of Modernity* (London, 1983), 19–21. See also Perry Anderson, "Marshall Berman: Modernity and Revolution," in *A Zone of Engagement* (London, 1992), 25–55.

3. Despite its significance for Marx, this concept has been relatively neglected. There is no entry under "reserve army of labour" in *The New Palgrave: Marxian Economics*, ed. J. Eatwell, M. Millgare, and P. Newman (London, 1990). It receives little or no attention in such authoritative surveys of Marx as Ernest Mandel's *Marxist Economic Theory*, trans. B. Pearce (London, 1968); G. A. Cohen's *Karl Marx's Theory of History: A Defence* (Oxford, 1978); and John Elster's *Making Sense of Marx* (Cambridge, 1985).

4. *Despatches for the New York Tribune: Selected Journalism of Karl Marx*, ed. James Ledbitter (Harmondsworth, 2007), 113.

5. Ibid.

6. *Morning Chronicle*, 7 February 1853. This seems to be the most detailed account of the case in the London newspapers. Marx was a regular reader of the *Morning Chronicle* at this time.

7. Henry Mayhew, *London Labour and the London Poor*, 4 vols. (New York, 1968 [1861–62]), I, xv.

8. Karl Marx, *Capital: A Critique of Political Economy*, vol. 1, trans. Ben Fowkes (Harmondsworth, 1976), 831. Subsequent references are abbreviated as *Capital* I.

9. See, e.g., *Northern Star*, 4 and 11 January 1851. Engels had 35 articles published in the *Northern Star* between 1843 and the end of 1849. *Democratic Review* 1 (January 1850): 293–95; (February 1850): 344–48. Engels contributed 11 articles to the *Democratic Review* in spring 1850. *Red Republican* 1 (1850): 8, 16, 32, 40, 48, 79, 88, 174.

10. J. G. Eccarius, "Die Schneiderei in London oder der Kampf des grossen und des kleinen Capitals," *Neue Rheinische Zeitung. Politisch-ökonomische*

Revue, nos. 5–6 (November 1850). This article, which Marx may have had a hand in drafting, has not been translated into English.

11. Marx, editorial comment on J.G. Eccarius, "Tailoring in London or the Struggle between Big and Small Capital," *Neue Rheinische Zeitung. Politisch-ökonomische Revue,* nos. 5–6 (1850); *Collected Works of Marx and Engels,* vol. 10 (London, 1978), 486. This 50-volume edition is subsequently cited as *MECW.* The collected writings of Marx and Engels are being made available online by the excellent Marx and Engels Internet Archive (www.marxists.org/archive/marx/index.htm).

12. *Communist Manifesto,* 252.

13. *MECW,* 11:147.

14. See esp. Peter Stallybrass, "Marx and Heterogeneity: Rethinking the Lumpenproletariat," *Representations* 31 (Summer 1990): 69–95.

15. E.P. Thompson, *The Poverty of Theory and other Essays* (London, 1978), 163–67. For two parallel critiques of Marx, see Andre Gorz, *Farewell to the Working Class: An Essay on Post-Industrial Socialism,* trans. M. Sonenscher (London, 1982), esp. chap. 1; and Michael Lebowitz, *Beyond Capital: Marx's Political Economy of the Working Class,* 2nd ed. (Basingstoke, 2003); and the debate in the journal *Historical Materialism* 14, no. 2 (2006).

16. Nicholas Thoburn, "Difference in Marx: The Lumpenproletariat and the Proletarian Unnamable," *Economy & Society* 31, no. 3 (August 2002): 434–60.

17. Friedrich Engels, *The Condition of the Working Class in England,* ed. V. Kiernan (Harmondsworth, 2009), 119.

18. Engels provides an extended critique of Malthus in his "Outlines of a Critique of Political Economy," published by Marx in the *Deutsch-Französische Jahrbüche* in spring 1844. See *MECW,* 3:418 ff.

19. *MECW,* 6:424, 432.

20. Ibid., 9:226.

21. Ibid. 9:228.

22. *Capital* I, 797.

23. Ibid.

24. Ibid., 792.

25. Ibid., 375–76.

26. Ibid., 796.

27. Ibid., 617–18.

28. Ibid., 818.

29. Mayhew, *London Labour,* I, 339–40.

30. *Capital* I, 92.

31. Ibid., 364.

32. Ibid., 377.

33. Ibid., 378.

34. Ibid., 414.

35. Ibid., 279–80.

36. Ibid., 476–77.

37. Ibid., 615.

38. Raphael Samuel, "Comers and Goers," in *The Victorian City: Images and Realities*, ed. H.J. Dyos and Michael Wolff (London, 1976), 1:123–60.

39. *Morning Chronicle*, 18 April 1848.

40. *Preston Guardian*, 15 July 1848.

41. H.A. Shannon, "Migration and the Growth of London, 1841–91," *Economic History Review* 5, no. 2 (1935): 79–86.

42. *Northern Star*, 31 July 1841.

43. *Morning Chronicle*, 27 December 1843.

44. "The Criminality of the Metropolis," *Ragged School Union Magazine* 2 (July 1850): 19.

45. *Jackson's Oxford Journal*, 25 March 1848.

46. In one of his *New York Tribune* articles of 1853 Marx detailed the case of Henry Morgan, a needle maker tramping the roads looking for work, found dead in a barn. *Despatches for the New York Tribune*, 111–12.

47. Giorgio Agamben, *Homo Sacer: Sovereign Power and Bare Life*, trans. D. Heller-Roazen (Stanford, 1998).

48. *MECW*, 8:218.

49. *Proceedings of the Select Committee on District Asylums (Metropolis)* 388 (1846), xxiv. See also the *Times*, 5 June 1846.

50. *Northern Star*, 11 November 1848.

51. On this point, see John Marriott, *The Other Empire: Metropolis, India and Progress in the Colonial Imagination* (Manchester, 2003).

52. Mayhew, *London Labour*, I, 1–3.

53. Karl Marx, *Grundrisse: Foundations of the Critique of Political Economy (Rough Draft)*, trans. M. Nicolaus (Harmondsworth, 1973), 100.

54. Ibid., 101.

55. *Capital* I, 90.

CHAPTER 5

1. Michel Foucault, *Discipline and Punish: The Birth of the Prison*, trans. Alan Sheridan (London, 1991).

2. Chris Otter, *The Victorian Eye: A Political History of Light and Vision in Victorian Britain, 1800–1910* (Chicago, 2008); Tom Crook, "Sanitary Inspection and the Public Sphere in Late-Victorian and Edwardian Britain: A Case Study in Liberal Governance," *Social History* 32 (2007): 369–93.

3. Lauren M.E. Goodlad, *Victorian Literature and the Victorian State: Character and Governance in a Liberal Society* (Baltimore, 2003).

4. Sissela Bok's study of the ethics of secrecy suggests that the "defining trait" of secrecy is intentional concealment. Sissela Bok, *Secrets: On the Ethics of Concealment and Revelation* (New York, 1983), 6.

5. Stefanos Geroulanos, "Theoscopy: Transparency, Omnipotence and Modernity," in *Political Theologies: Public Religions in a Post-Secular World*, ed. Hent de Vries and Lawrence E. Sullivan (New York, 2006), 641–42.

6. Giorgio Agamben, *Homo Sacer: Sovereign Power and Bare Life*, trans. Daniel Heller-Roazen (Stanford, 1998).

7. Giorgio Agamben, *State of Exception*, trans. Kevin Attell (Chicago, 2005), 11–22.

8. Patrick Joyce, *The Rule of Freedom: Liberalism and the Modern City* (London, 2003), chap. 3.

9. Bernard Porter, *Plots and Paranoia: A History of Political Espionage in Britain, 1790–1988* (London, 1989), 43–45.

10. "Post-Office Espionage," *North British Review* 2 (1844): 270–71.

11. "Report from the Secret Committee on the Post-Office; together with the Appendix," *Parliamentary Papers*, vol. 14 (1844), 14.

12. "Report from the Secret Committee of the House of Lords Relative to the Post-Office," *Parliamentary Papers*, vol. 14 (1844), 3.

13. "Report from the Secret Committee on the Post-Office," 3.

14. See also David Vincent, *The Culture of Secrecy: Britain, 1832–1998* (Oxford, 1998), chaps. 1 and 2.

15. Thomas Laqueur, *Solitary Sex: A Cultural History of Masturbation* (New York, 2003).

16. Ibid., 245.

17. Jacques Derrida, *Of Grammatology*, trans. Gayatri Chakravorty Spivak (Baltimore, 1997), pt. 2, chap. 2.

18. Alan Hunt, "The Great Masturbation Panic and the Discourse of Moral Regulation in Nineteenth- and Early Twentieth-Century Britain," *Journal of the History of Sexuality* 8 (1998): 575–615.

19. See, e.g., Charles Edward Paget, *Healthy Schools* (London, 1884), 42–43.

20. Clement Dukes, *Health at School* (London, 1887), 93.

21. Laqueur, *Solitary Sex*, 420.

22. Pierre Manent, *A World Beyond Politics? A Defense of the Nation-State*, trans. Marc LePain (Princeton, 2006), chaps. 3 and 4.

23. This is a relatively well known tension, of course. See, e.g., Norberto Bobbio, *Liberalism and Democracy*, trans. Martin Ryle and Kate Soper (London, 2005); and Hannah Arendt, *The Human Condition* (Chicago, 1958), chap. 2.

24. For more elaborate discussions of this tension, see Michael Walzer, "Citizenship," in *Political Innovation and Conceptual Change*, ed. Terrence Ball, James Farr, and Russell L. Hanson (Cambridge, 1989), 211–19; and J. G. A. Pocock, "The Ideal of Citizenship since Classical Times," in *Theorizing Citizenship*, ed. Ronald Beiner (New York, 1995), 29–52.

25. John Gray, ed., *John Stuart Mill: On Liberty and Other Essays* (Oxford, 1991), 355.

26. Anon., *The Ballot: Five Letters by Vigil* (London, 1871), 8.

27. George Jacob Holyoake, *A New Defence of the Ballot, In Consequence of Mr. Mill's Objections to It* (London, 1868), 3–4.

28. For a full discussion of the intense complexity that characterizes the development and diffusion of secret balloting procedures, see Malcolm Crook and Tom Crook, "Reforming Voting Practices in a Global Age: The Making

and Remaking of the Modern Secret Ballot in Britain, France and America, c. 1600–c. 1950," *Past and Present* (forthcoming).

CHAPTER 6

1. See Patrick Joyce, *The Rule of Freedom: Liberalism and the Modern City* (London, 2003), 4.

2. On liberalism and the archive, see Patrick Joyce, "The Politics of the Liberal Archive," *History of the Human Sciences* 12, no. 2 (1999): 35–49.

3. See, e.g., Mitchell Dean, *Governmentality* (London, 1999).

4. See, on this, Joyce, *Rule of Freedom*, 19.

5. Jacques le Goff, *History and Memory*, trans. Steven Rendall and Elizabeth Claman (Cambridge, 1992).

6. Thomas Osborne, "The Ordinariness of the Archive," *History of the Human Sciences* 12, no. 2 (1999): 51–64.

7. See, for more nuanced detail on this, chap. 11 in this volume.

8. John D. Cantwell, *The Public Record Office, 1838–1958* (London, 1991); cf. E. Hallam, "Nine Centuries of Keeping the Public Records," in *The Records of the Nation: The Public Record Office, 1838–1988*, ed. Geoffrey Martin and Peter Spufford (London, 1990).

9. Ian Hacking, "Bio-Power and the Avalanche of Printed Numbers," *Humanities in Society* 5 (1982): 279–95.

10. See, e.g., William Stubbs, *Historical Introductions to the Rolls Series*, ed. A. Hassall (London, 1902).

11. R.G. Collingwood, *The Idea of History* (Oxford, 1946); cf. Mark Cousins, "The Practice of Historical Investigation," in *Post-Structuralism and the Question of History*, ed. Derek Attridge, Geoff Bennington, and Robert Young (Manchester, 1987).

12. Osborne, "Ordinariness of the Archive."

13. Le Goff, *History and Memory*.

14. Philippa Levine, *The Amateur and the Professional* (Cambridge, 1986).

15. Reinhardt Koselleck, *The Practice of Conceptual History*, trans. T. S. Presner et al. (Stanford, 2002).

16. See, for the most concise version, Michel Foucault, *The Birth of Bio-Politics*, trans. Graham Burchell (London, 2008), 317–25.

17. Peter Miller and Nikolas Rose, *Governing the Present* (Cambridge, 2008); cf. Jacques Donzelot, *The Policing of Families* (London, 1979).

18. Ian Hacking, *The Taming of Chance* (Cambridge, 1990); Giovanna Procacci and Arpad Szakoczai, *La scoperta della società* (Rome, 2003).

19. Foucault, *The Birth of Bio-Politics*, 321; cf. Colin Gordon, "Governmental Rationality—An Introduction," in *The Foucault Effect*, ed. Graham Burchell, Colin Gordon, and Peter Miller (Hemel Hempstead, 1991)—still the best introduction to this literature.

20. Michel Foucault, *Security, Territory, Population*, trans. Graham Burchell (London, 2007), 48.

21. See, for an overview and critical discussion, James Vernon, "Narrating the Constitution," in *Re-Reading the Constitution*, ed. James Vernon (Cambridge, 1996).

22. William Stubbs, *Constitutional History*, vol. 1 (Oxford, 1873), v.

23. Michel Foucault, *Society Must Be Defended*, trans. David Macey (London, 2003), 66.

24. F. W. Maitland, ed., *The Constitutional History of England* (Cambridge, 1908), 537.

25. William Stubbs, *Lectures on Early English History*, ed. A. Hassall (London, 1906), 194.

26. Ibid., 37.

27. Vernon, "Narrating the Constitution," 217–18; cf. E. A. Freeman, *The History of the Norman Conquest of England*, vol. 1 (Oxford, 1877), x.

28. Vernon, "Narrating the Constitution," 217–18.

29. Maitland, *Constitutional History*, 539.

30. Stubbs, *Lectures on Early English History*, 4.

31. Ibid., 197.

32. Ibid., 273.

33. Freeman, *History of the Norman Conquest*, 69–71; cf. C. Hill, "The Norman Yoke," in *Puritanism and Revolution* (London, 1965), where Stubbs is erroneously mentioned as a signatory to the Norman Yoke idea.

34. Stubbs, *Lectures on Early English History*, 3.

35. Ibid., 18–19.

36. William Stubbs, *Seventeen Lectures on the Study of Mediaeval and Modern History* (Oxford, 1887), 238 ff.

37. Ibid., 255.

38. Ibid., 2.

39. See Levine, *The Amateur and Professional*, 136.

40. J. W. Burrow, *A Liberal Descent: Victorian Historians and the English Past* (Cambridge, 1981), 131; cf. Stefan Collini, Donald Winch, and James W. Burrow, *That Noble Science of Politics: A Study in Nineteenth-Century Intellectual History* (Cambridge, 1983), 200.

41. Levine, *Amateur and Professional*, 151.

42. See Reinhardt Koselleck, "*Begriffsgeschichte* and Social History," in *Futures Past: On the Semantics of Historical Time*, trans. Keith Tribe (Cambridge, MA, 1990); cf. Thomas Osborne, "History, Theory, Disciplinarity," in *The Social in Question*, ed. Patrick Joyce (London, 2002).

CHAPTER 7

I would like to thank the editors and Kay Anderson for their helpful comments on an early draft of this chapter.

1. Cited in Kay Anderson, *Race and the Crisis of Humanism* (London, 2007), 120.

2. Cited in Anderson, *Race*, 120–21.

3. There are strong parallels between Anderson's account and my own in Tony Bennett, *Pasts beyond Memory: Evolution, Museums, Colonialism* (London, 2004). I draw both on this and a more general discussion of the role of habit in modern social, political, and cultural theory—see Tony Bennett, "Culture, History, Habit," CRESC Working Paper no. 64 (www.cresc.ac.uk)—for aspects of the argument developed in this chapter.

4. See Uday S. Mehta, "Liberal Strategies of Exclusion," in *Tensions of Empire: Colonial Cultures in a Bourgeois World*, ed. Frederick Cooper and Ann Laura Stoler (Berkeley, 1997), 59–86; Mariana Valverde, "'Despotism' and Ethical Liberal Governance," *Economy and Society* 25, no. 3 (1996): 357–72; and Melanie White, "The Liberal Character of Ethnological Governance," *Economy and Society* 34, no. 3 (2005): 474–94.

5. Nikolas Rose, "Authority and the Genealogy of Subjectivity," in *Detraditionalisation: Critical Reflections on Authority and Identity*, ed. Paul Heelas, Scott Lash, and Paul Morris (Oxford, 1996), 301.

6. Patrick Joyce, *The Rule of Freedom: Liberalism and the Modern City* (London, 2003), 118.

7. Ibid., 120.

8. John Stuart Mill, *A System of Logic, Ratiocinative and Deductive. Being a Connected View of the Principles of Evidence and the Methods of Scientific Investigation* (London, 1967).

9. Melanie White, "Liberal Character," 474–94.

10. James Tulley, "Governing Conduct: Locke on the Reform of Thought and Behaviour," in *Conscience and Casuistry in Early Modern Europe*, ed. E. Leites (Cambridge, 1989), 12–71.

11. Immanuel Kant, *Anthropology from a Pragmatic Point of View*, trans. Robert L. Louden (Cambridge, 2006 [1798]), xiii.

12. Ibid., 40.

13. Ibid.; original emphasis.

14. Ibid.

15. Sankar Muthu, *Enlightenment against Empire* (Princeton, 2003), 128.

16. John Stuart Mill, *On Liberty, Representative Government, the Subjection of Women: Three Essays* (London, 1969), 74–75.

17. Colin Campbell, "Detraditionalisation, Character and the Limits to Agency," in Heelas, Lash, and Morris, *Detraditionalisation*.

18. Mill, *Liberty*, 73.

19. Ibid., 83.

20. Reinhart Koselleck, *The Practice of Conceptual History: Timing History, Spacing Concepts* (Stanford, 2002).

21. Mill, *Liberty*, 15.

22. Ibid., 16.

23. See Stefan Collini, *Liberalism and Sociology: L. T. Hobhouse and Political Argument in England, 1880–1914* (Cambridge, 1979); and *Public Moralists: Political Thought and Intellectual Life in Britain, 1850–1930* (Oxford,

1991). See also Mike Hawkins, *Social Darwinism in European and American Thought, 1860–1945* (Cambridge, 1997).

24. Walter Bagehot, *Physics and Politics: Or Thoughts on the Application of the Principles of "Natural Selection" and "Inheritance" to Political Society* (London, 1873).

25. Henry Maudsley, *Life in Mind and Conduct* (London, 1902).

26. Lloyd Morgan, *Habit and Instinct* (London, 1896).

27. Laura Otis, *Organic Memory: History and Body in the Late Nineteenth and Early Twentieth Centuries* (Lincoln, 1994), 3–10.

28. Georges Canguilhem, *Knowledge of Life* (New York, 2008), 103–5.

29. Otis, *Organic Memory*, 3; original emphasis.

30. Ibid., 6.

31. Félix Raivaisson, *Of Habit* (London, 2008 [1838]).

32. Catherine Malabou, "Addiction and Grace," preface to Ravaisson, *Of Habit*, vii.

33. Raivaisson, *Of Habit*, 59.

34. Ibid.

35. Ibid.

36. Herbert Spencer, *The Principles of Psychology* (London, 1996 [1855]).

37. Mariana Valverde, *Diseases of the Will: Alcohol and the Dilemmas of Freedom* (Cambridge, 1998).

38. Maudsley, *Life*, 37.

39. Ibid.

40. Ibid., 38.

41. Ibid., 47.

42. Ibid., 226–27.

43. Ibid., 231.

44. I follow convention here in using Spencer's spelling rather than the corrected form, *Arrernte*, since my concern is with the operation of this category in nineteenth-century Eurocentric discourses.

45. Baldwin Spencer and Frank J. Gillen, *The Native Tribes of Central Australia* (London, 1899).

46. I have discussed the transformations in Spencer's views regarding the improvability of Aborigines in greater detail in Tony Bennett, "Making and Mobilising Worlds: Assembling and Governing the Other," in *Material Powers: Culture, History and the Material Turn*, ed. Tony Bennett and Patrick Joyce (London, 2010), 188–208.

47. George W. Stocking Jr., *Victorian Anthropology* (New York, 1987).

48. Edward Tylor, *Primitive Culture*, 2 vols. (London, 1871).

49. Patrick Wolfe, *Settler Colonialism and the Transformation of Anthropology: The Politics and Poetics of an Ethnographic Event* (London, 1999), 131.

50. John Lubbock, *Pre-Historic Times as Illustrated by Ancient Remains, and the Manners and Customs of Modern Savages* (London, 1865).

51. While some aspects of Pitt Rivers's account are similar to Darwin's account, published a year earlier (1874), of the relations between the intellec-

tual faculties and habit in man and the lower animals, the differences are more telling. Although Darwin also refers to Spencer and Lubbock and although he admits that "some intelligent actions, after being performed during several generations, become converted into instincts and are inherited" (Charles Darwin, *The Descent of Man, and Selection in Relation to Sex* [Chicago, 1952], 288), this is a long way from the general theories of the relations between habit and instinct characterizing Spencer's neo-Lamarckian account.

52. Henry Pitt Rivers (published under Col. A. H. Lane Fox), "On the Principles of Classification Adopted in the Arrangement of his Anthropological Collection Now Exhibited in the Bethnal Green Museum," *Journal of the Anthropological Institute of Great Britain and Ireland* 4 (1875): 296.

53. Ibid., 298.

54. Ibid., 299.

55. Ibid., 300; original emphasis.

56. Bagehot, *Physics and Politics*, 113.

57. Ibid., 143–45.

58. Wolfe, *Settler Colonialism*.

59. Michel Foucault, *Society Must Be Defended: Lectures at the Collège de France, 1975–76* (New York, 2003), 256.

60. Ibid., 257.

61. Pitt Rivers, "Principles of Classification," 308.

62. Maudsley, *Life*, 231–32.

63. John Clarke, "Programmatic Statements and Dull Empiricism: Foucault's Neo-Liberalism and Social Policies," *Journal of Cultural Economy* 2, nos. 1–2 (2009): 229–33.

64. Tim Rowse, *White Flour, White Power: From Rations to Citizenship in Central Australia* (Cambridge, 1998).

65. See, for detailed discussions, Anna Haebich, *Broken Circles: Fragmenting Indigenous Families, 1800–2000* (Fremantle, 2000); and Russell McGregor, *Imagined Destinies: Aboriginal Australians and the Doomed Race Theory, 1880–1939* (Melbourne, 1997).

66. See, e.g., Jane Lydon, *Eye Contact: Photographing Indigenous Australians* (Durham, NC, 2005).

67. See Bennett, "Making and Mobilising," for a fuller discussion.

68. Elkin, cited in McGregor, *Imagined Destinies*, 199.

CHAPTER 8

1. For a model historicized application of this approach, see Patrick Joyce, *The Rule of Freedom: Liberalism and the Modern City* (London, 2003). For the specific cultural territory considered here, see Peter Bailey, "Theatres of Entertainment/Spaces of Modernity: Rethinking the British Popular Stage, 1890–1914," *Nineteenth Century Theatre* 26, no. 1 (Summer 1998): 5–24.

2. Matthew Browne, *Views and Opinions* (London, 1866), 280; W. E. Gladstone, "Locksley Hall and the Jubilee," *Nineteenth Century* 21 (1887): 1–18;

Peter Bailey, *Leisure and Class in Victorian England: Rational Recreation and the Contest for Control, 1830–1880*, 2nd ed. (London, 1987).

3. John Morley, *Studies in Conduct* (London, 1867), 1–10; Henry Haweis, *Thoughts for the Times* (London, 1872), 288; Samuel Smiles, *Self-Help: The Art of Achievement Illustrated by Accounts of the Lives of Great Men* (London, 1968 [1859]), 215.

4. Peter Bailey, "Languages of Pleasure in Britain's Belle Epoque," *Revue française de civilization Britannique* 14, no. 2 (Spring 2007): 81–95.

5. On holidays and "time off," see Douglas A. Reid, "Playing and Praying," in *Cambridge Urban History of Britain*, vol. 3, *1840–1950*, ed. Martin Daunton (Cambridge, 2000), 745–807; on income, Jose Harris, *Private Lives, Public Spirit: A Social History of Britain, 1870–1914* (Oxford, 1993), 33.

6. Reverend W. C. Lake, in *The Use and Abuse of the World*, ed. J. E. Kempe (London, 1873), 39–56.

7. Lise Shapiro Sanders, *Consuming Fantasies: Labor, Leisure, and the London Shopgirl, 1880–1920* (Columbus, OH, 2006).

8. Charles Booth, *Life and Labour of the People in London*, "Notes on Social Influences," 1903, quoted in James Walvin, *Leisure and Society, 1830–1950* (London, 1978), 63.

9. J. A. Hobson, *Evolution of Modern Capitalism* (New York, 1926 [1894]), 432–35; H. E. Meller, *Leisure and the Changing City, 1870–1914* (London, 1976).

10. Ian Britain, *Fabianism and Culture: A Study in British Socialism and the Arts* (Cambridge, 1982); Chris Waters, *British Socialists and the Politics of Popular Culture* (Stanford, 1990).

11. C. F. G. Masterman, ed., *The Heart of the Empire* (London, 1902), 7–8; C. F. G. Masterman, *Condition of England* (London, 1909), 162; W. T. Stead, "Impressions of the Theatre," *Review of Reviews*, September 1906, 255–58.

12. John Stokes, *In the Nineties* (Chicago, 1989), 3–8; Joseph Donohue, *Fantasies of Empire: The Empire Theatre of Varieties and the Licensing Controversy of 1894* (Iowa City, 2005); *Daily Chronicle*, 6 August 1895; *Speaker: A Review of Politics, Letters, Science and the Arts* (later the *Nation*), 6 August 1895.

13. Grant Allen, *Fortnightly Review*, n.s., 1 (March 1894): 377–92.

14. Richard Le Gallienne, *The Romantic Nineties* (London, 1951 [1925]).

15. Jonathan Rose, *The Edwardian Temperament, 1895–1910* (Athens, OH, 1986); Bill Brown, *The Material Unconscious: American Amusement, Stephen Crane, and the Economies of Play* (Cambridge, MA, 1996).

16. Andrew Horrall, *Popular Culture in London, c. 1890–1918: The Transformation of Entertainment* (Manchester, 2001).

17. Dagmar Kift, *The Victorian Music Hall: Culture, Class and Conflict* (Cambridge, 1996), provides the most comprehensive scholarly treatment. See also Peter Bailey, ed., *Music Hall: The Business of Pleasure* (Milton Keynes, 1986); J. S. Bratton, ed., *Music Hall: Performance and Style* (Milton Keynes, 1986); Dave Russell, "Varieties of Life: The Making of the Edwardian Music

Hall," in *The Edwardian Theatre: Essays on Performance and the Stage*, ed. Michael Booth and Joel H. Kaplan (Cambridge, 1996), 61–85; Andrew Crowhurst, "The Music Hall, 1885–1912: The Emergence of a National Entertainment Industry in Britain" (Ph.D. diss., Cambridge University, 1991); Tracy C. Davis, *The Economics of the British Stage, 1800–1914* (Cambridge, 2000); Paul Maloney, *Scotland and the Music Hall, 1850–1914* (Manchester, 2003).

18. *Performer*, 27 April 1911.

19. Andrew Crowhurst, "London's 'Music Hall War': Trade Unionism in an Edwardian Service Industry," *London Journal* 2, no. 21 (1996): 149–63; *Performer*, 1 January 1914.

20. Peter Bailey, "Custom, Capital and Culture in the Victorian Music Hall," in *Popular Culture and Custom in Nineteenth-Century England*, ed. Robert D. Storch (London, 1982), 180–208; and "Audiences and Ambience in the Mid-Victorian Music Hall" (unpublished paper, London Group of Historical Geographers, Institute of Historical Research, University of London, October 2006).

21. Victor Glasstone, *Victorian and Edwardian Theatres: An Architectural and Social Survey* (London, 1975); John Earl, "Building the Halls," in Bailey, *Music Hall*, 1–32: Brian Mercer Walker, ed., *Frank Matcham, Theatre Architect* (Belfast, 1980); Jonathan Crary, *Suspensions of Perception: Attention, Spectacle, and Modern Culture* (Cambridge, MA, 1999), 253–55; Chris Otter, *The Victorian Eye: A Political History of Light and Vision in Britain, 1800–1910* (Chicago, 2008), 74.

22. Max Beerbohm, "At the Tivoli," *Saturday Review*, 3 December 1898, anticipating scholarly claims for the reenchantment of modernity. See Joshua Landy and Michael Saler, *The Re-Enchantment of the World: Secular Magic in a Rational Age* (Stanford, 2009).

23. In Manchester in 1918 Matcham's Hippodrome was an august enough site for conferring the freedom of the city on various notables, including Lloyd George; see Cyril Ehrlich and Brian Mercer Walker, "Enterprise and Entertainment: The Economic and Social Background," in Walker, *Frank Matcham*, 28. On the design and symbolism of public buildings in the late-century "moral city," see Joyce, *Rule of Freedom*, 148–71. Matcham's interiors anticipated the "atmospherics" of interwar modernist cinemas; see Bruce Peter, *Form Follows Fun: Modernism and Modernity in British Pleasure Architecture, 1925–1940* (London, 2007).

24. Tony Bennett, *The Birth of the Museum: History, Theory, Politics* (London, 1995), 59–88. For self-policing at classical music concerts, see Simon Gunn, *The Public Culture of the Victorian Middle Class: Ritual and Authority in the English Industrial City, 1840–1914* (Manchester, 2000), 137, 142–46. See also Richard Butsch, *The Making of American Audiences: From Stage to Television, 1750–1990* (New York, 2000); Gary S. Cross and John K. Walton, *The Playful Crowd: Pleasure Places in the Twentieth Century* (New York, 2005).

25. For a comparable site of "scopic promiscuity" and "mutable social space"

akin to the early halls, see Lynda Nead, *Victorian Babylon: People, Streets, and Images in Nineteenth-Century London* (New Haven, 2000), on Cremorne Pleasure Gardens, forced out of business by moral reformers in the 1870s.

26. Bailey, "Audiences and Ambience." On sanitation, see Kift, *Victorian Music Hall*, 61; Tracy C. Davis, "'Filthy-Nay-Pestilential': Sanitation and Victorian Theatres," in *Exceptional Spaces: Essays in Performance and the Stage*, ed. Della Pollock (Chapel Hill, 1997), 161–86; Joyce, *Rule of Freedom*, 73–75, on "civic toilette." Of the Granville in Fulham, John Earl remarks, "It was as washable a theatre as could ever be imagined"; see his "The London Theatres," in Walker, *Frank Matcham*, 36–61.

27. *Era*, 21 July 1861; *Entr'acte*, 5 November 1870. See the widely used slogan of Lewis's pioneer department store in Liverpool in the midcentury, Asa Briggs, *Friends of the People: Lewis's of Liverpool* (London, 1956).

28. *Era*, 4 April 1873; *Leeds Mercury*, 8 January 1876.

29. Peter Bailey, "A Community of Friends: Business and Good Fellowship in London Music Hall Management, c. 1860–1885," in Bailey, *Music Hall*, 33–52. For other worlds of sociable obligation, motivated by the grant and pursuit of favor, see Avner Offer, "Between the Gift and the Market: The Economy of Regard," *Economic History Review* 50, no. 3 (1997): 450–76.

30. Charles Morton, "A Few Words from the Proprietor to His Patrons and the Public," 1857, pamphlet reprinted in John Earl and John Stanton, *The Canterbury Hall and Theatre of Varieties* (Cambridge, 1982), 55–58.

31. On Holland, see Peter Bailey, *Popular Culture and Performance in the Victorian City* (Cambridge, 1998), 80–96, 101–27. For Gladstone, free trade, and consumption, see Martin Daunton, *Wealth and Welfare: An Economic and Social History of Britain, 1851–1951* (Oxford, 2007), 8–9. Publicans and caterers were nonetheless predictably Tory in their party politics.

32. *Gladstone Diaries*, ed. H. C. G. Matthew (Oxford, 1986), vol. 9, 21 July 1877.

33. Catherine Hall, Keith McClelland, and Jane Rendall, *Defining the Victorian Nation: Class, Race, Gender and the British Reform Act of 1867* (Cambridge, 2000), 57–70; Patrick Joyce, *Visions of the People: Industrial England and the Question of Class, 1840–1914* (Cambridge, 1991), 308–9; *Times*, 30 August 1860.

34. Walter Benjamin identified "an ironic utopia" in the midcentury Paris of Offenbach and operettas, "Paris: Capital of the Nineteenth Century" (1935), reprinted in Benjamin, *Reflections* (New York, 1978), 146–62.

35. On Hackney Empire, see Earl, "Building the Halls," 27–31.

36. Felix Barker, *The House That Stoll Built: The Story of the Coliseum* (London, 1957); Crowhurst, "Oswald Stoll: A Music Hall Pioneer," *Theatre Notebook* 49, no. 1 (1995): 27–49. Both the Coliseum and Hackney Empire are still in use. For other aspects of music hall and Britain's empire, see Penny Summerfield, "Patriotism and Empire: Music-Hall Entertainment, 1870–1914," in *Imperialism and Popular Culture*, ed. John M. Mackenzie (Manchester, 1986), 17–48; Donohue, *Fantasies of Empire*.

37. Bailey, "Languages of Pleasure," 89–93; *Daily Telegraph*, 14 September 1903; Lionel Monckton and Ivan Caryll, *Our Miss Gibbs*, Lord Chamberlain's Plays, British Library Manuscripts Room.

38. M. Mostyn Bird, *Women at Work*, 1911, cited in Sanders, *Consuming Fantasies*, 38.

39. Peter Bailey, "'Naughty But Nice': Musical Comedy and the Rhetoric of the Girl," in Booth and Kaplan, *Edwardian Theatre*, 36–60; Judith R. Walkowitz, "'The Vision of Salome': Cosmopolitanism and Erotic Dancing in Central London, 1908–1918," *American Historical Review* 108, no. 2 (April 2003): 337–76.

40. Arnold Bennett, *Buried Alive* (Harmondsworth, 1976 [1908]), 87–89. For the "public habitat of images" in the world of modern consumption, see Nikolas Rose, *The Power of Freedom: Reframing Political Thought* (Cambridge, 1999), 85–89.

41. Peter Clark, *British Clubs and Societies, 1580–1800: The Origins of an Associational World* (Oxford, 2002). On the radical origins of the free and easy, see John Brewer, "Commercialisation and Politics," in N. McKendrick, J. Brewer, and J. H. Plumb, *Birth of a Consumer Society: The Commercialisation of Eighteenth-Century England* (London, 1982), 228–29; on the late Victorian version, Joyce, *Rule of Freedom*, 206–7.

42. Bailey, "Custom, Capital and Culture." For the unexamined history of the "Free Halls," the lowest tier of the independents, see *Magnet* (Leeds), a penny weekly for the trade, 1866–1926.

43. Peter Bailey, "Conspiracies of Meaning: Music Hall and the Knowingness of Popular Culture," *Past and Present* 44 (August 1994), reprinted in Bailey, *Popular Culture and Performance*, 128–50; Lenin to Maxim Gorky, quoted in Nigel Fountain, *Lost Empires: Theatres Past, Present and Future* (London, 2005), 100.

44. Penny Summerfield, "The Effingham Arms and the Empire: Deliberate Selection in the Evolution of Music Hall in London," in *Popular Culture and Class Conflict*, ed. Eileen Yeo and Stephen Yeo (Brighton, 1981), 209–40. For the provinces where protests were more evident and much of the opposition came from Liberal councillors, see, on Bradford, Kift, *Victorian Music Hall*, 122–24; "The Passing of the Free Halls," *Magnet*, a decade-long lament from the mid-1890s onward; *Burnley Express*, 7 October 1893; *Nottingham Evening News*, 17 February 1903.

45. For public protests against the disadvantaging of the popular audience in the late Victorian theatre amid parallel changes in configuration and management, plus a critique of a Foucauldian reading, see Jim Davis and Victor Emeljanow, *Reflecting the Audience: London Theatregoing, 1840–1880* (Iowa City, 2001), 160–61, 221, 228–29.

46. Barry Faulk, *Music Hall and Modernity: The Late Victorian Discovery of Popular Culture* (Columbus, OH, 2004).

47. Browne, *Views and Opinions*, 280; Lyons, quoted in Erika Rappaport, *Shopping for Pleasure: Women in the Making of London's West End* (Prince-

ton, 2000), 95. In the telling euphemism of the streets, prostitutes were known as "free traders."

48. *Era*, 8 October 1892.

49. For terminal *kulturpessimismus*, see Theodor Adorno and Max Hork-heimer, *Dialectic of Enlightenment* (London: Verso, 1979 [1947]), 144: "Fun is a medicinal bath which the pleasure industry never fails to prescribe, making laughter the instrument of the fraud practised on happiness." For a reevalua-tion of Adorno and the mass culture critique, see James W. Cook, "The Return of the Culture Industry," in *The Cultural Turn in U.S. History*, ed. James W. Cook, Lawrence B. Glickman, and Michael O'Malley (Chicago, 2008), 291–317. On the later transformation of fun from expectation to virtual self-obligation, see the psychologist Martha Wolfenstein's "The Emergence of Fun Morality," in *Mass Leisure*, ed. Eric Larrabee and Rolf Meyersohn (Glencoe, IL, 1958), 86.

CHAPTER 9

1. Stephen Legg, *Spaces of Colonialism: Delhi's Urban Governmentali-ties* (Oxford, 2007); Prashant Kidambi, *The Making of an Indian Metropolis: Colonial Governance and Public Culture in Bombay, 1890–1920* (Aldershot, 2007); Swati Chattopadhyay, *Representing Calcutta: Modernity, Nationalism and the Colonial Uncanny* (Oxford, 2005).

2. Frederick Cooper, *Colonialism in Question* (Berkeley, 2005), 113–49.

3. Largely overlooked in Andrew Sartori's otherwise useful review of recent literature, "The British Empire and Its Liberal Mission," *Journal of Modern History* 78 (September 2006).

4. As urged in Frederick Cooper and Ann Laura Stoler, eds., *Tensions of Empire: Colonial Cultures in a Bourgeois World* (Berkeley, 1997), 4.

5. Much of the literature is indebted to Foucault's suggestive reading of urban form and the governance of conduct, first sketched in Michel Foucault, *Society Must Be Defended* (London, 2004), 250–51; elaborated at length in Michel Foucault, *Security, Territory, Population* (Basingstoke, 2007); and developed productively in Timothy Mitchell, *Colonising Egypt* (Cambridge, 1988); Legg, *Spaces of Colonialism*; Patrick Joyce, *The Rule of Freedom: Liberalism and the Modern City* (London, 2003). See also Chris Otter, *The Victorian Eye: A Political History of Light and Vision in Britain, 1800–1910* (Chicago, 2009).

6. See Hall's reading of Macaulay in Catherine Hall, "At Home with His-tory: Macaulay and the History of England," in *At Home with the Empire: Metropolitan Culture and the Imperial World*, ed. Catherine Hall and Sonya O. Rose (Cambridge, 2006), 44–47.

7. The literature is enormous. See Nicholas Dirks, *The Scandal of Empire* (Cambridge, MA, 2006), esp. 87–131; Kathleen Wilson, *The Island Race: Englishness, Empire and Gender in the Eighteenth Century* (London, 2003). For the latter period, see Catherine Hall, *Civilising Subjects: Metropole and Colony in the English Imagination, 1830–1867* (Cambridge, 2002); Simon

Gikandi, *Maps of Englishness: Writing Identity in the Culture of Colonialism* (New York, 1996); Bill Schwarz, "The Expansion and Contraction of England," in *The Expansion of England*, ed. Bill Schwarz (London, 1996).

8. In these important ways, liberalism, like history, possesses a significant colonial genealogy. See Uday Singh Mehta, *Liberalism and Empire: A Study in Nineteenth-Century British Liberal Thought* (Chicago, 1999), esp. chap. 3.

9. See Henry Mayhew, *London Labour and the London Poor*, 4 vols. (London, 1851–62); G. R. Sims, *How the Poor Live* (London, 1883); Andrew Mearns, *The Bitter Cry of Outcast London* (London, 1893). Sims's oft-cited introduction, inviting the reader "into a dark continent that is within easy walking distance of the General Post Office," concludes by noting, "It is the increased civilization of this marvelous age which has made life a victory only for the strong, the gifted, the specially blest, and left the weak, the poor, the ignorant to work out in their proper persons the theory of the survival of the fittest to its bitter end" (6).

10. See, e.g., Jonathan Schneer, *London 1900: The Imperial Metropolis* (New Haven, 1999); Felix Driver and David Gilbert, *Imperial Cities* (Manchester, 1999), esp. chapters by Smith, Ryan, and Hassam; see also G. Alex Bremner, "Nation and Empire in the Government Architecture of Mid-Victorian London: The Foreign and India Office Reconsidered," *Historical Journal* 48, no. 3 (2005).

11. As Dennis has noted, the city was both a product of modernity and a powerful contributor to its development. See Richard Dennis, *Cities in Modernity: Representations and Productions of Metropolitan Space, 1840–1930* (Cambridge, 2008).

12. In addition to their economic and strategic functions, transport and communications networks, as well as architectural and urban form, served important representational and performative roles. This process of colonial envisioning was subsequently appropriated as part of the nationalist critique of British rule. See Manu Goswami, *Producing India: From Colonial Economy to National Space* (Chicago, 2004), esp. 73–102.

13. Frere's purpose was to realize in India the national architecture of England, both as a means of demonstrating to the colonized the magnificence of England's architecture and as a way of ensuring that the colonist remained true to his English roots. See Ian Baucom, *Out of Place: Englishness, Empire, and the Location of Culture* (Princeton, 1999), 77–86.

14. For the comparable shared and overlapping rationales that underscored both modernist and historicist architecture, see Joyce, *Rule of Freedom*, 169–71.

15. Mehta, *Liberalism and Empire, passim*; Bikhu Parekh, "Liberalism and Colonialism: A Critique of Locke and Mill," in *The Decolonization of Imagination*, ed. Bikhu Parekh and Jan Neuerveen Pieterse (London, 1995).

16. For an account of the slippage between colonial and Indian readings of Bombay, see Pruti Chopra, "Refiguring the Colonial City: Recovering the Role of Local Inhabitants in the Construction of Colonial Bombay, 1854–1918," *Buildings and Landscapes* 14 (2007).

17. Thomas R. Metcalf, *Ideologies of the Raj*, vol. 3, pt. 4, of *The New Cambridge History of India* (Cambridge, 1997).

18. Again, the literature is enormous. See, e.g., Gyan Prakash, *Another Reason: Science and the Imagination of Modern India* (Princeton, 1999); Partha Chatterjee, *The Nation and Its Fragments: Colonial and Postcolonial Histories* (Princeton, 1993).

19. Veena Oldenburg, *The Making of Colonial Lucknow, 1856–1877* (Oxford, 1999).

20. More than half a century earlier, George Trevelyan had argued in favor of remaking Delhi as the center of British power in India: "Should we not appropriate the traditional associations of the place and make them contribute to the renown of our power. . . . It might be called Fort Victoria, as a counterpart to Fort William and an emblem of the final establishment of our power in the interior of India." Trevelyan, quoted in G. Alex Bremner, "Nation and Empire," 719 n. 58. See also Narayani Gupta, *Delhi between Two Empires, 1803–1930* (Oxford, 1981); Robert Grant Irving, *Indian Summer: Lutyens, Baker, Imperial Delhi* (New Haven, 1982); Thomas R. Metcalf, *An Imperial Vision: Indian Architecture and Britain's Raj* (Oxford, 2002); Anthony D. King, *Colonial Urban Development* (London, 1976).

21. The viceroy wrote that Delhi was "still a name to conjure with. It is intimately associated in the minds of the Hindus with sacred legends which go back even beyond the dawn of history. . . . To the Mohamedans, it would be a source of unbounded gratification to see the ancient capital of the Moguls restored to its proud position as the seat of the Empire." Irving, *Indian Summer*, 28.

22. Legg, *Spaces of Colonialism*, 1.

23. Following his appointment to the New Delhi project, Herbert Baker wrote to Lutyens emphasizing his view that the new city was to be "imperial . . . not Indian, nor English, nor Roman." The foremost advocate of the "Indic" model, E. B. Havell, argued that "the judicious application of Western science and mechanical invention" would rescue "lost Indian vitality." Havell's argument was partly directed against the "Europeanisation" brought about by "Macaulayism": the "philistine war of extermination" against Hinduism. Though it was Lutyens's classicism that defined New Delhi, the "Macaulaysim" derided by Havell exercised little influence on the planners and administrators of the new city. Though Havell's Indic styles were intended to mark a new and more consensual form of empire than that envisaged by Macaulay, they were equally proscribed by the logic of difference on which late-colonial rationalities of rule depended. Metcalf, *An Imperial Vision*, 218.

24. On the development of the city's plan, see Irving, *Indian Summer*, 91–116.

25. Irving, *Indian Summer*, 72–73.

26. Neatly reflected in aerial photographs of the old and new city. See Legg, *Spaces of Colonialism*, frontis. Joyce, *Rule of Freedom*, 257.

27. Stanfordham was concerned that the viceroy's residence should not be

"dominated by the Jumma Masjid and the Fort nor dwarfed by the Ridge." In thus triumphing over India's terrain and superseding her previous imperial rulers, the new city was to inscribe Britain's imperial hegemony.

28. Hosagrahar H. Jyoti, "City as Durbar: Theater and Power in Imperial Delhi," in *Forms of Dominance: On the Architecture and Urbanism of the Colonial Enterprise*, ed. N. Al Sayad (Amesbury, 1992), 97–98; Bernard S. Cohn, "Representing Authority in Victorian India," in *The Invention of Tradition*, ed. Eric Hobsbawm and Terence Ranger (Cambridge, 1992).

29. See Robert Byron's account of New Delhi, discussed in Jyoti, "City as Durbar," 96–99. Much the same philosophy was evident in a host of other colonial cities: as Mitchell has noted, the new colonial cities of the late nineteenth century were "unambiguously expressive." The durbar may be less significant as the progenitor of New Delhi than as a reflection of how widely diffused ideas about performativity and spectacle were in colonial logic. See Mitchell, *Colonising Egypt*, esp. 34–62, 161–79.

30. Though these disciplinary and regulatory interventions rarely delivered the desired improvements in behavior. Thus a raft of bylaws were enacted in the late 1930s as part of an attempt to control and moderate behavior within the capital. Scott's analysis of the myopic nature of "high modernist" planning—overlooked in Cooper's critique of Scott—is helpful here. See James C. Scott, *Seeing Like a State: How Certain Schemes to Improve the Human Condition Have Failed* (New Haven, 1998).

31. This also resulted in the poor traveling the greatest distance to work, often on foot, mitigating against economic efficiency and productivity, as well as quality of life.

32. In the elite, white quarters of New Delhi's Kingsway, the ratio of police to inhabitants was approximately 1:392, whereas in the clerk's quarters the ratio was 1:544, compared to a citywide ratio of 1:420, significantly lower than in the old city, where it was 1:1041. Legg, *Spaces of Colonialism*, 87.

33. As was to be the case in New Delhi during the 1930s, these measures were a response to repeated disruptions of colonial public order, especially evident in Bombay during the 1890s. See Kidambi, *The Making of an Imperial Metropolis*, 136–55.

34. Narayani Gupta, "Military Security and Urban Development," *Modern Asian Studies* 5, no. 1 (1971).

35. Such limits are also exposed in much of the military and strategic planning, which derived from the notion of moral effect and was based on the assumption that colonial law would operate "mainly through fear." The capacity for illiberal repression in colonial governance was not exceptional or contradictory but was in fact fundamental to the rationality of colonial rule, which stressed that illiberal techniques be used to discipline those who had not inculcated the liberal habits of self-regulation. Violence was therefore central to the logic of colonial policing, expressed not as moments of legal exception or negation but as moments in which the law took on a different logic. See Legg, *Spaces of Colonialism*, 98. See also Mariana Valverde, "Despotism and Liberal Gover-

nance," *Economy and Society* 25 (1996). For related discussions in a variety of contexts, see Megan Vaughan, *Curing Their Ills: Colonial Power and African Illness* (Berkeley, 1991); David Arnold, *Colonizing the Body: State Medicine and Epidemic Disease in Nineteenth-Century India* (Berkeley, 1993); U. Kalpagam, "Colonial Governmentality and the Economy," *Economy and Society* 29, no. 3 (2000); Ann Laura Stoler, *Race and the Education of Desire: Foucault's "History of Sexuality" and the Colonial Order of Things* (Durham, 1995).

36. H. Jyoti, "City as Durbar"; also H. Jyoti, "Mansions to Margins: Modernity and the Domestic Landscapes of Historic Delhi, 1847–1910," *Journal of the Society of Architectural Historians* 60 (2001). This form of transculturation could operate in both directions: from the late nineteenth century Gothic features were incorporated into "native" architecture, reflecting the dissemination and appropriation of architectural styles across racial and colonial cleavages. See Chopra, "Refiguring the Colonial City," 117–18.

37. Legg, *Spaces of Colonialism*, 51–52.

38. Echoing Edmund Burke's attacks on empire's degenerative effects, Dadabhai Naoroji's critique of the poverty wrought on India by the "UnBritish" nature of nineteenth-century colonial rule illustrates some of the ways in which liberal, universalist ideals were appropriated by nationalist critics of British imperialism. However, it was not liberalism that provided the most effective grounds for the nationalist critique of imperialism but rather either modernism (which, for Nehru, the British were failing to deliver) or antimodernism (as for Gandhi, for whom modernism was the root cause of India's subjugation). See Andrew Sartori, "Emancipation as Heteronomy: The Crisis of Liberalism in Later Nineteenth-Century Bengal," *Journal of Historical Sociology* 17, no. 1 (2004); also Chattopadhyay, *Representing Calcutta*, 136–78.

39. See Legg, *Spaces of Colonialism*, 70.

40. Compare Chopra, "Refiguring the Colonial City" on Bombay, with Chris Otter, "Cleansing and Clarifying: Technology and Perception in Nineteenth-Century London," *Journal of British Studies* 43, no. 1 (January 2004).

41. Consider, for example, the capacity of liberal subjects to imbibe "improving knowledge": the "regulated restlessness" that Bennett has identified as key to the pedagogic effect of the museum could realize its liberal potentialities only for those deemed capable of progressive and prudential self-improvement. See Tony Bennett, "Regulated Restlessness: Museums, Liberal Government and the Historical Sciences," *Economy and Society* 26, no. 2 (1997). In spite of the demonstrable evidence to the contrary—some of which is noted above—Indians were frequently deemed incapable of such change. Once again, the categories and institutional mechanisms by which liberal governmentality was defined and made operational are dependent on those who are excluded from liberalism's claims to universality. Objectified by the "exhibitionary complex," colonial subjects were thought to lack the capacity for "liberal" self-improvement. As Nick Dirks has noted, "Early anthropology [thus] grew out of modern history, becoming the history of those without history as well as the prehistory of those now mired in history" (*Castes of Mind*, 181–97).

42. Homi K. Bhabha, *The Location of Culture* (London, 1994); M. Sinha, *Colonial Masculinity: The 'Manly Englishman' and the 'Effeminate Bengali' in the Late Nineteenth Century* (Manchester, 1995).

43. Joyce, *Rule of Freedom*, 252–53.

44. Indicatively, when Indian princes began to buy up property in the hill stations, the imperial government moved to prevent further intrusions on sanitary grounds, citing the "hordes of ragamuffins" that followed the princes. See D. Kennedy, *The Magic Mountains* (Berkeley, 1996), 198.

45. In Latour's terms, the denial of these hybrids mirrors the moderns' denial of the work of mediation. Bruno Latour, *We Have Never Been Modern* (Cambridge, MA, 1993), esp. 39–43, 49–90. While Cooper is right to insist that modernity cannot help us to narrate historical causality, it was frequently to modernity that colonialism took recourse in justifying its existence. See Cooper, *Colonialism in Question*, 133–34.

46. See Legg, *Spaces of Colonialism*, 93; Bhabha, *The Location of Culture*.

47. See Richard Saumarez Smith, "Rule-by-Records and Rule-by-Reports: Complementary Aspects of the British Imperial Rule of Law," *Contributions to Indian Sociology* 19, no. 1 (1985).

48. Gavin Rand, "'Martial Races' and 'Imperial Subjects': Violence and Governance in Colonial India, 1857–1914," *European Review of History— Revue europeenne d'Histoire* 13, no. 1 (2006)

49. Bremner, "Nation and Empire," 736–37. For more on the "face" of imperial London, see Schneer, *London 1900*, 17–36.

50. Recruiting officers were advised to avoid enlisting from India's cities, where it was felt only "inferior specimens" could be procured.

51. Though the Nehruvian vision of a technically modern India rather than Gandhi's favored village communities emerged as the dominant strain of the nationalist critique, we should be cautious not to assume that the modernist order of nationalist succession was inevitable. See Prakash, *Another Reason*; Goswami, *Producing India*; Chatterjee, *Nation and Its Fragments*.

52. Alternative locations were considered, but, according to the chief engineer of Punjab, P. L. Verma, "none of the existing cities of the Punjab possessed sufficient magnificence and glamour to make up for the psychological loss of Lahore suffered by the strife-stricken but proud Punjabis." See Vikramaditya Prakash, *Chandigarh's Le Corbusier: The Struggle for Modernity in Post- colonial India* (Seattle, 2002), 7. On the "failures" of high-modernist planning, see Scott, *Seeing Like a State*.

53. Prakash, *Chandigrah's Le Corbusier*; Ravi Kalia, *Chandigarh: The Making of an Indian City* (Oxford, 1987). Paradoxically, Le Corbusier's vision of India mirrored elements of Gandhi's: both men envisaged India's civiliza- tion as largely uncorrupted by modern life. Though their prescriptions for the future were plainly at odds, there is thus significant overlap in their visions of India's "humane and profound civilization." See Prakash, *Chandigrah's Le Corbusier*, 9.

54. See, e.g., Roger Griffin, *Modernism and Fascism: A Sense of a Begin-*

ning under Mussolini and Hitler (London, 2007), 43–69. Though I do not wish to push this point too far, if the "new beginning" laid out in urban form in New Delhi and Chandigarh was fundamentally different from Nazi attempts to remake the biopolitical order in the 1930s and 1940s, the role of "the modern" in animating both liberal and distinctly illiberal attempts to refashion the world is still striking. For related arguments in this direction, see Z. Bauman, *Modernity and the Holocaust* (Ithaca, 2001); Detlev Peukert, "The Genesis of the Final Solution from the Spirit of Science," in *Re-Evaluating the Third Reich*, ed. Thomas Childers and Jane Caplan (New York, 1993).

CHAPTER 10

I would like to thank David Feldman and the editors of this volume for their helpful comments on earlier drafts of this chapter.

1. See Perry Anderson, "Origins of the Present Crisis," *New Left Review* 23 (January–February 1964): 19–45; and "Components of the National Culture," *New Left Review* 50 (July–August 1968): 3–57, though here the emphasis is on Britain's failure to follow the "correct" path to modernity more than on the reasons for the persistence of conservatism.

2. E. P. Thompson, *The Making of the English Working Class* (London, 1963); Nicholas Rogers, *Crowds, Culture, and Politics in Georgian Britain* (Oxford, 1998); Charles Tilly, *Popular Contention in Great Britain, 1758–1834* (Cambridge, MA, 1995).

3. Boyd Hilton, *A Mad, Bad and Dangerous People? England, 1783–1846* (Oxford, 2006), esp. chap. 5.

4. Michael E. Rose, "Settlement, Removal and the New Poor Law," in *The New Poor Law*, ed. Derek Fraser (London, 1976).

5. Boyd Hilton, *The Age of Atonement: The Influence of Evangelicalism on Social and Economic Thought, 1785–1865* (Oxford, 1988), 100–108.

6. See especially J. W. Burrow, *Whigs and Liberals: Continuity and Change in English Political Thought* (Oxford, 1988).

7. Kim Lawes, *Paternalism and Politics: The Revival of Paternalism in Early Nineteenth-Century Britain* (Basingstoke, 2000); Joanna Innes, "Forms of 'Government Growth,' 1780–1830," in *Structures and Transformations in Modern British History: Essays for Gareth Stedman Jones*, ed. David Feldman and Jon Lawrence (Cambridge, 2011).

8. Peter Mandler, *Aristocratic Government in the Age of Reform: Whigs and Liberals, 1830–1852* (Oxford, 1990); also Hilton, *Mad, Bad and Dangerous People?* 519–24, 611.

9. Burrow, *Whigs and Liberals*, 2–8, 20; also J. W. Burrow, *A Liberal Descent: Victorian Historians and the English Past* (Cambridge, 1981).

10. Jon Parry, *The Politics of Patriotism: English Liberalism, National Identity and Europe, 1830–1886* (Cambridge, 2006).

11. Peter Mandler, *The English National Character: The History of an Idea from Edmund Burke to Tony Blair* (New Haven, 2006), esp. 3, 17–26, 32–33.

12. Dror Wahrman, *The Making of the Modern Self: Identity and Culture in Eighteenth-Century England* (New Haven, 2004); Mandler, *English National Character*, 18, 23.

13. Mary Poovey, *Making a Social Body: British Cultural Formation, 1830–1864* (Chicago, 1995), 14–15.

14. Raymond Williams, *Culture and Society, 1780–1950* (London, 1963 [1958]), 314–15; original emphasis.

15. Bill Schwarz, "The Language of Constitutionalism: Baldwinite Conservatism," in *Formations of Nation and People* (London, 1984); and "Ancestral Citizens: Reflections on British Conservatism," in *Conservative Modernity*, ed. Cora Kaplan and David Glover, *New Formations* 28 (1996).

16. K.D.M. Snell, *Parish and Belonging: Community, Identity and Welfare in England and Wales, 1700–1950* (Cambridge, 2006); Marc Brodie, *The Politics of the Poor: The East End of London, 1885–1914* (Oxford, 2004).

17. Patrick Joyce, *Work, Society and Politics: The Culture of the Factory in Later Victorian England* (Brighton, 1980); J.A. Mangan, *Athleticism in the Victorian and Edwardian Public School: The Emergence and Consolidation of an Educational Ideology* (London, 2000); Jon Lawrence, "Labour and the Politics of Class, 1900–1940," in Feldman and Lawrence, *Structures and Transformations*.

18. Philip Salmon, *Electoral Reform at Work: Local Politics and National Parties, 1832–1841* (Woodbridge, 2002), 7–8.

19. Catherine Hall, Keith McClelland, and Jane Rendall, eds., *Defining the Victorian Nation: Class, Race, Gender and the Reform Act of 1867* (Cambridge, 2000); and on the specific valorization of ratepayers as a class, Robert Saunders, "The Politics of Reform and the Making of the Second Reform Act, 1848–1867," *Historical Journal* 50 (2007): 571–91, at 586–91.

20. Pat Hudson, *Regions and Industries: A Perspective on the Industrial Revolution in Britain* (Cambridge, 1989).

21. Malcolm Crook and Tom Crook, "The Advent of the Secret Ballot in Britain and France, 1789–1914: From Public Assembly to Private Compartment," *History* 92 (2007): 449–71; Bruce L. Kinzer, *The Ballot Question in Nineteenth-Century English Politics* (New York, 1982).

22. Hall, McClelland, and Rendall, *Defining the Victorian Nation*, esp. McClelland's "England's Greatness, the Working Man"; Anna Clark, *The Struggle for the Breeches: Gender and the Making of the British Working Class* (Berkeley, 1995), and her "Gender, Class, and the Constitution: Franchise Reform in England, 1832–1928," in *Re-Reading the Constitution: New Narratives in the Political History of England's Long Nineteenth Century*, ed. James Vernon (Cambridge, 1996).

23. Nicoletta F. Gullace, *"The Blood of Our Sons": Men, Women and the Renegotation of British Citizenship during the Great War* (Basingstoke, 2002), 184–94.

24. Susan Pedersen, "Gender, Welfare, and Citizenship in Britain during the Great War," *American Historical Review* 95 (1990): 983–1006.

25. Alan Deacon, *In Search of the Scrounger: The Administration of Unemployment Insurance in Britain, 1920–1931* (London, 1976).

26. Susan Pedersen, *Eleanor Rathbone and the Politics of Conscience* (New Haven, 2004), 216.

27. Something I only discovered because she was horrified to find that I had reproduced in print her lifelong claim never to have voted Labour; Lawrence, *Speaking*, 2. He was in every other respect the antithesis of the patriarchal tyrant.

28. D. J. Rossiter, R. J. Johnston, and C. J. Pattie, *The Boundary Commissioners: Redrawing the UK's Map of Parliamentary Constituencies* (Manchester, 1999), 39–40, 52–53, 62.

29. Alex Windscheffel, *Popular Conservatism in Imperial London, 1868–1906* (Woodbridge, 2007); Matthew Roberts, "Constructing a Tory World-View: Popular Politics and the Conservative Press in Late-Victorian Leeds," *Historical Research* 79, no. 203 (2006): 115–43; and "'Villa Toryism' and Popular Conservatism in Leeds, 1885–1902," *Historical Journal* 49 (2006): 217–46.

30. Keith Middlemas, *Politics and Industrial Society: The Experience of the British System since 1911* (London, 1979), 120–213; L. P. Carpenter, "Corporatism in Britain, 1930–1945," *Journal of Contemporary History* 11 (1976): 3–25.

31. Christopher Harvie, *The Lights of Liberalism: University Liberals and the Challenge of Democracy, 1860–86* (London, 1976); Margot C. Finn, *After Chartism: Class and Nation in English Radical Politics, 1848–1884* (Cambridge, 1993); Miles Taylor, *The Decline of British Radicalism, 1847–1860* (Oxford, 1995).

32. Harvie, *Lights of Liberalism;* Mandler, *English National Character,* 106–22, 141; Burrow, *Whigs and Liberals,* chap. 6.

33. Michael Sanderson, *Education, Economic Change and Society in England, 1780–1870* (London, 1983), 23, 33–38, 59–60.

34. Michael Sanderson, *Educational Opportunity and Social Change in England* (London, 1987), 18–38, 75–77.

35. Paul Johnson, "Class Law in Victorian England," *Past and Present* 141 (1993): 147–69.

36. David Vincent, *The Culture of Secrecy: Britain, 1832–1998* (Oxford, 1998).

37. Christopher Hilliard, *To Exercise Our Talents: The Democratization of Writing in Britain* (Cambridge, MA, 2006), 144–46.

38. David Thomas, David Carlton, and Anne Etienne, *Theatre Censorship: From Walpole to Wilson* (Oxford, 2007), 112–22.

39. See TNA, HO45/10744/454 and /459, where Home Office officials revisit a decision not to prosecute a socialist for incitement to violence, arguing that the unrest in Glasgow in January 1919 has "altered the position"; Alastair Reid, 'The Dialectics of Liberation: The Old Left, the New Left and the Counterculture," in Feldman and Lawrence, *Structures and Transformations.*

40. *Times,* 21 October and 2 November 1960; C. H. Rolph, ed., *The Trial of Lady Chatterley: Regina v. Penguin Books Limited* (London, 1961), 17, 195, 228.

41. Rolph, *Trial*, 37, 195.

42. Hence the rather dismissive account of the British case in Charles Rembar, *The End of Obscenity* (London, 1969), 152–60; Rembar had led the case for the defense in the U.S. trial of *Lady Chatterley* in 1959.

43. Mark Jarvis, *Conservative Governments, Morality and Social Change in Affluent Britain, 1957–64* (Manchester, 2004); Lawrence Black, *The Political Culture of the Left in Affluent Britain, 1951–1964: Old Labour, New Britain?* (Basingstoke, 2003).

44. Bernard Porter, *The Absent-Minded Imperialists: What the British Really Thought about Empire* (Oxford, 2004).

45. David Edgerton, *Warfare State: Britain, 1920–1970* (Cambridge, 2006).

46. Jon Lawrence, *Electing Our Masters: The Hustings in British Politics from Hogarth to Blair* (Oxford, 2009); see also Lawrence, *Speaking*, chap. 7.

47. Jon Lawrence, "The Transformation of British Public Politics after the First World War," *Past and Present* 190 (2006): 185–216; Lawrence, *Electing Our Masters*, chap. 4.

48. Martin Francis, "The Labour Party: Modernisation and the Politics of Restraint," in *Moments of Modernity: Reconstructing Britain, 1945–1964,* ed. Becky Conekin, Frank Mort, and Chris Waters (London, 1999); and "Tears, Tantrums and Bared Teeth: The Emotional Economy of Three Conservative Prime Ministers, 1951–1963," *Journal of British Studies* 41 (2002): 354–87.

49. Francis, "Politics of Restraint," 153, 155.

50. Schwarz, "Language of Constitutionalism"; Philip Williamson, *Stanley Baldwin: Conservative Leadership and National Values* (Cambridge, 1999).

51. Raymond Williams, *The Long Revolution* (London, 1965 [1961]), 333–34.

52. Joyce, *Work, Society and Politics*, 272–303; Jon Lawrence, "Class and Gender in the Making of Urban Toryism, 1880-1914," *English Historical Review* 108 (1993): 629–52.

53. David Howell, *British Workers and the Independent Labour Party, 1888–1906* (Manchester, 1983), 373–88; Martin Pugh, "The Rise of Labour and the Political Culture of Conservatism 1890–1945," *History* 87, no. 288 (2002): 514–37; Gregg McClymont, "Socialism, Puritanism, Hedonism: The Parliamentary Labour Party's Attitude to Gambling, 1923–31," *Twentieth Century British History* 19 (2008): 288–313.

54. Chris Waters, *British Socialists and the Politics of Popular Culture, 1884–1914* (Manchester, 1990); Stuart MacIntyre, "British Labour, Marxism and Working-class Apathy in the Nineteen Twenties," *Historical Journal* 20 (1977): 479–96; Jeremy Nuttall, *Psychological Socialism: The Labour Party and Qualities of Mind and Character, 1931 to the Present* (Manchester, 2006), esp. 52–58; Black, *Political Culture of the Left*.

55. Raphael Samuel, "Born-Again Socialism," in *Out of Apathy: Voices of the New Left 30 Years On*, ed. Robin Archer et al. (London, 1989), 55.

56. Douglas Jay, *The Socialist Case* (London, 1937), 317, discussed in Nuttall, *Psychological Socialism*, 58–59.

57. Pat Thane, "Labour and Welfare," in *Labour's First Century*, ed. Dun-

can Tanner, Pat Thane, and Nick Tiratsoo (Cambridge, 2000), 99–103; Rodney Lowe, "The Road from 1945," 5, and John Macnicol, "From 'Problem Family' to 'Underclass,' 1945–95," both in *Welfare Policy in Britain: The Road from 1945,* ed. Helen Fawcett and Rodney Lowe (Basingstoke, 1999).

58. Robert Moore, *Pitmen, Preachers and Politics: The Effects of Methodism in a Durham Mining Community* (Cambridge, 1974), 186.

59. Lawrence, "Labour and the Politics of Class."

60. Winston Churchill, "The Conservative Case for a New Parliament," *Listener,* 19 February 1948, 302–3, reprinted by Conservative Central Office as *Set the People Free: A Broadcast Talk* (London, 1948); Ina Zweiniger-Bargielowska, *Austerity in Britain: Rationing, Controls and Consumption, 1939–1955* (Oxford, 2000).

61. Marcus Collins, "The Fall of the English Gentleman: The National Character in Decline, c. 1918–1970," *Historical Research* 75, no. 187 (2002): 90–111; Jim Tomlinson, *The Politics of Decline: Understanding Post-War Britain* (Harlow, 2000).

62. Philip Williamson, "The Modern British State and Religion: National Days of Prayer in Britain, 1830–1956" (unpublished paper read at Cambridge University Modern British History seminar, October 2005); Matthew Grimley, "The Religion of Englishness: Puritanism, Providentialism, and 'National Character,' 1918–1945," *Journal of British Studies* 46 (2007): 884–906.

63. "Choosing the Next Prime Minister: Ability versus Birth," ABMS 3/134, Mark Abrams Papers, Churchill Archives Centre, Cambridge.

64. Anthony Howard and Richard West, *The Making of the Prime Minister* (London, 1965).

65. John H. Goldthorpe, "The Current Inflation: Towards a Sociological Account," in *The Political Economy of Inflation,* ed. Fred Hirsch and John H. Goldthorpe (Cambridge, MA, 1978), esp. 196–201. As with his wider "affluent worker" thesis, this argument hinged on an exaggerated picture of "traditional" behavior—nondeferential wage bargaining was hardly new (I am grateful to Ross McKibbin for this reference).

66. Mandler, *English National Character,* chap. 5.

67. Conekin, Mort, and Waters, *Moments of Modernity.*

68. Stuart Hall, *The Hard Road to Renewal: Thatcherism and the Crisis of the Left* (London, 1988).

CHAPTER 11

1. *Hansard,* 24 February 2009, col. 153.

2. The fullest account of the event is to be found in F. B. Smith, "British Post Office Espionage 1844," *Historical Studies* 4 (1970). See also A. P. Donajgrodzki, "Sir James Graham at the Home Office," *Historical Journal* 20, no. 1 (1977); Bernard Porter, *Plots and Paranoia* (London, 1989), 76–78; Howard Robinson, *Britain's Post Office* (Cambridge, 1953), 47, 55, 91–92; Edward Troup, *The Home Office,* 2nd ed. (London, 1926), 109–10; David Vincent, "Communi-

cations, Community and the State," in *Artisans, Peasants and Proletarians, 1760–1860,* ed. Clive Emsley and James Walvin (London, 1985), 166–86.

3. *Hansard,* 3rd ser., LXXV, 14 June 1844, col. 892. For an example of what he was talking about, see the account of contemporary practice in Russia: R. Hingley, *The Russian Secret Service* (London, 1970), 3–35.

4. *Hansard,* 3rd ser., LXXV, 24 June 1844, col. 1264.

5. Henry Taylor, *The Statesman* (New York, 1956 [1836]), 89.

6. *Your Right to Know: Freedom of Information* (December 1997), Cm 3818, Preface.

7. Scotland is covered by its own Freedom of Information (Scotland) Act of 2002, which contains a similar veto clause, 52(2).

8. Information Commissioner's Office, 11 June 2009, 1.

9. Maurice Frankel, "In the Public Eye," *Guardian,* 14 December 2004. A class exemption covers all material falling within a particular category, irrespective of its content.

10. "Interview with Maurice Frankel, Director of the Campaign for the Freedom of Information," Freedom of Information, http://freedomofinformation.co.uk.

11. Information Commissioner's Office, *Freedom of Information Act 2000 (Section 50), Decision Notice 19 February 2008,* 2.

12. Presumably in response to this information, the commissioner ruled that sensitive material in the cabinet record could be "redacted," or blacked out, from the publicly released material.

13. Information Commissioner's Office, *Decision Notice 19 February 2008,* 9.

14. Ibid.

15. Cited in *Hansard,* 24 February 2009, col. 154.

16. Campaign for Freedom of Information, "Iraq Veto Decision 'Extremely Retrograde,'" 24 February 2009, www.cfoi.org.uk/foi240209pr.html.

17. Perhaps the nearest proxy for such a table is Transparency International's annual *Corruption Perception Index,* which it has compiled since 1995. In the 2008 index Britain slipped from twelfth to sixteenth place. It is perhaps no accident that New Zealand and Sweden, which top the register, were also among the first countries to pass a Freedom of Information Act.

18. See the comments of John Stewart Mill, who earned his living as Examiner of Indian Correspondence. *Report of the Select Committee of the House of Lords on the East India Company's Charter* (1852), PP 1852–53, vol. XXX, 305.

19. See, e.g., Richard Thomas, "The Experience of Other Countries," in *Open Government,* ed. Richard A. Chapman and Michael Hunt (London, 1989).

20. David Vincent, *The Culture of Secrecy: Britain, 1832–1998* (Oxford, 1998), 4.

21. Information Commissioners' Office, *Annual Report Summary 2008/09* (Wilmslow, Cheshire, 2009), 4–5.

22. Ibid., 9.

23. *Hansard*, 24 February 2009, col. 154.

24. E.g., Richard Norton-Taylor, "Oh the Irony of Jack Straw's Stand," www.Guardian.co.uk (24 February 2009).

25. *Papers on the Reorganisation of the Civil Service (1855)*, PP 1854–55, XX, 116.

26. Ibid.

27. Kurt H. Wolff, ed. and trans., *The Sociology of Georg Simmel* (Toronto, 1950), 348.

28. Andrew Barry, Thomas Osborne, and Nikolas Rose, introduction to *Foucault and Political Reason: Liberalism, NeoLiberalism and Rationalities of Government* (London, 1996), 8.

29. David Vincent, *The Rise of Mass Literacy: Reading and Writing in Modern Europe* (Cambridge, 2000), chap. 1.

30. Standard accounts of the organization are given in George A. Codding, *The Universal Postal Union* (New York, 1964); Manikath A. K. Menon, *The Universal Postal Union* (New York: March 1965).

31. Charles Marvin's leak is discussed in Edward Hertslet, *Recollections of the Old Foreign Office* (London, 1901), 191–92; John A. C. Tilley and Stephen Gaselee, *The Foreign Office* (London, 1933), 129–40; D. Hooper, *Official Secrets* (London, 1987), 19–21; Jonathan Aitken, *Officially Secret* (London, 1971), 7–15.

32. The phrase was used by Lord Tenterden, Permanent Secretary at the Foreign Office following the leak of a secret treaty in 1878 by a temporary copyist. PRO FO/363/3, Tenterden Papers, Tenterden to Salisbury, 15 June 1878.

33. *Departmental Committee on Section 2 of the Official Secrets Act 1991* [Franks] (London, 1971), Cmnd 5104, vol. 1, 121.

34. PP 1889, VI.

35. Bernard Crick, *The Reform of Parliament* (London, 1964), xii.

36. Lord Fulton, *The Civil Service*, vol. 1, *Report of the Committee, 1966–68* (London, 1968), Cmnd. 3638, 91.

37. Cited by Richard Thomas, "Freedom of Information and Privacy—The Regulatory Role of the Information Commissioner," speech to the Centre for Regulated Industries, 9 January 2008 (Information Commissioners' Office, 2008), 9.

38. Thomas, "Freedom of Information and Privacy," 7–8.

39. Nikolas Rose, *Powers of Freedom: Reframing Political Thought* (Cambridge, 1999), 18.

40. Information Commissioner's Office, *Annual Report Summary 2008/09*, 6.

41. Department for Constitutional Affairs, *The Freedom of Information Act 2000*, www.dca.gov.uk/foi/foiact2000.htm; Campaign for Freedom of Information, *A Short Guide to the Freedom of Information Act and Other New Access Rights*, 28 January 2005.

42. Information Commissioner's Office, *Annual Report Summary 2008/ 09*, 5.

43. Campaign for Freedom of Information, "'Severe Delays' in Investigating Freedom of Information Complaints 'Undermining' FOI Act," 3 July 2009; Information Commissioner's Office, "ICO Response to Report by the Campaign for Freedom of Information," 3 July 2009.

44. Thomas, "Freedom of Information and Privacy," 10.

45. Ibid., 15; Information Commissioner's Office, *Annual Report Summary 2008/09*, 10.

46. Interception of Communications Act 1985, Security Services Act 1989, and Official Secrets Act 1989.

47. *Hansard*, 24 February 2009, col. 153.

48. Tony Blair, *A Journey* (London, 2010), 516–17.

49. *Hansard*, 24 June 1844, col. 1274.

50. Ibid., col. 1275.

51. Ibid., col. 1274.

52. Ibid., cols. 1276–77.

CHAPTER 12

The author would like to thank John Brooke, Simon Gunn, Geoffrey Parker, Kristina Sessa, and James Vernon, and two anonymous reviewers, for their generous help and advice on earlier drafts of this chapter. Thanks to John and Geoffrey in particular for allowing me to read extracts from their forthcoming books.

1. Karl Marx and Friedrich Engels, *The Communist Manifesto* (New York, 1998 [1848]), 53; Karl Marx, *Free Trade: A Speech Delivered before the Democratic Club, Brussels, Belgium, January 9, 1848*, trans. Florence Wischnewetzky (Boston, 1888), 25.

2. Patrick Joyce, *The Rule of Freedom: Liberalism and the Modern City* (London, 2003).

3. John Sheail, *An Environmental History of Twentieth-Century Britain* (New York, 2002); B. W. Clapp, *An Environmental History of Britain* (New York, 1994); James Winter, *Secure from Rash Assault: Sustaining the Victorian Environment* (Berkeley, 1999); Harriet Ritvo, *The Dawn of Green: Manchester, Thirlmere, and Modern Environmentalism* (Chicago, 2009); T. C. Smout, *Nature Contested: Environmental History in Scotland and North England since 1600* (Edinburgh, 2000); Richard Grove, *Green Imperialism: Colonial Expansion, Tropical Island Edens and the Idea of Environmentalism, 1600–1860* (Cambridge, 1995); Ian Simmons, *An Environmental History of Great Britain: From 10,000 Years Ago to the Present* (Edinburgh, 2001).

4. Stephen Mosley, "Common Ground: Integrating Social and Environmental History," *Journal of Social History* 39, no. 3 (Spring 2006): 915.

5. Isaiah Berlin, "Two Concepts of Liberty," in Berlin, *Liberty, Incorporating Four Essays on Liberty*, ed. Henry Hardy (Oxford, 2002), 121.

6. Karl Polanyi, *The Great Transformation: The Political and Economic Origins of Our Time*, new ed. (Boston, 2001).

7. Peter Mandler, "Introduction: State and Society in Victorian Britain," in *Liberty and Authority in Victorian Britain*, ed. Peter Mandler (Oxford, 2006), 16.

8. John Bellamy Foster, *Marx's Ecology: Materialism and Nature* (New York, 2000), 195.

9. W. S. Jevons, *The Coal Question: An Inquiry Concerning the Progress of the Nation, and the Probable Exhaustion of our Coal-mines*, 3rd ed. rev. (New York, 1965 [1906]), 2.

10. Vaclav Smil, *Energy in World History* (Boulder, CO, 1994), 161.

11. Roy Church, *The History of the British Coal Industry*, vol. 3, *1830–1913: Victorian Pre-eminence* (Oxford, 1986), 759.

12. Jevons, *Coal Question*, 2.

13. Smil, *Energy*, 161–64.

14. "Tours in the Russian Provinces," *Quarterly Review* 67 (March 1841): 373.

15. Edward Jeffrey, *Coal and Civilization* (New York, 1925), 2–6.

16. Ibid., 13.

17. E. A. Wrigley, *Continuity, Chance and Change: The Character of the Industrial Revolution in England* (Cambridge, 1988).

18. Smil, *Energy*, 158; Edmund Burke III, "The Big Story: Human History, Energy Regimes, and the Environment," in *The Environment and World History*, ed. Edmund Burke III and Kenneth Pomeranz (Berkeley, 2009), 35.

19. John Holland, *The History and Description of Fossil Fuel, the Collieries, and Coal Trade of Great Britain* (London: Cass, 1968 [1841]), 372–73.

20. Cited in Church, *Coal Industry*, 62.

21. Holland, *Fossil Fuel*, 385. See also Frederick Clifford, *A History of Private Bill Legislation* (London, 1887), II, 392.

22. Church, *Coal Industry*, 36.

23. Jevons, *Coal Question*, 301.

24. Wrigley, *Continuity, Chance and Change*, 55.

25. Robert Bald, *A General View of the Coal Trade of Scotland, Chiefly That of the River Forth and Mid-Lothian* (Edinburgh, 1812), 201. Jevons, *Coal Question*, 444–45.

26. Church, *Coal Industry*, 30.

27. Michael Freeden, *Railways and the Victorian Imagination* (New Haven, 1999), 152–53. Philip Bagwell, *The Transport Revolution* (London, 1988), 157–70.

28. Bagwell, *Transport Revolution*, 177–81.

29. Freeden, *Railways*, 36, 29.

30. *Morning Chronicle*, 19 June 1824, cited in Christine MacLeod, *Heroes of Invention: Technology, Liberalism and British Identity, 1750–1914* (Cambridge, 2007), 104.

31. Cited in Daniel Headrick, *The Tools of Empire: Technology and European Imperialism in the Nineteenth Century* (Oxford, 1981), 182.

32. James Vernon, *Hunger: A Modern History* (Cambridge, MA, 2007), 50–54.

33. William Bone, "Coal and Health," *Nineteenth Century and After* 86 (August 1919): 337.

34. Ernest Darwin Simon and Marion Fitzgerald, *The Smokeless City* (London, 1922), 19.

35. Peter Thorsheim, *Inventing Pollution: Coal, Smoke, and Culture in Britain since 1800* (Athens, OH, 2006), 59.

36. Stephen Mosley, *The Chimney of the World: A History of Smoke Pollution in Victorian and Edwardian Manchester* (Cambridge, 2001), 34.

37. Church, *Coal Industry*, 781.

38. Mosley, *Chimney of the World*, 50.

39. Thorsheim, *Inventing Pollution*, 30. On climate, see John Brooke, *A Rough World: Human History and a Volatile Earth* (Cambridge, forthcoming).

40. Colin Townsend, Michael Begon, and John Harper, *Essentials of Ecology*, 2nd ed. (Malden, MA, 2003), 51.

41. Mosley, *Chimney of the World*, 176.

42. Jeffrey, *Coal and Civilization*, 12–13; Church, *Coal Industry*, 31.

43. William Eassie, *Healthy Houses: A Handbook to the History, Defects, and Remedies of Drainage, Ventilation, Warming, and Kindred Subjects* (New York, 1872), 181.

44. Mosley, *Chimney of the World*, 159–60.

45. Jevons, *Coal Question*, 412; original emphasis.

46. Rowland Hill, "High Price of Coal: Suggestions for Neutralizing Its Evils," *Journal of the Royal Statistical Society* 36 (December 1873): 565–70.

47. Asa Briggs, *Victorian Things* (London, 1988), 304.

48. Thomas Hughes, *Networks of Power: Electrification in Western Society, 1880–1930* (Baltimore, 1983), 140–74.

49. Christian Petersen, *Bread and the British Economy, c. 1770–1870*, ed. Andrew Jenkins (Aldershot, 1995), 212.

50. E. J. T. Collins, "Dietary Change and Cereal Consumption in Britain in the Nineteenth Century," *Agricultural History Review* 232 (1975): 97–115.

51. E. J. T. Collins, "The 'Consumer Revolution' and the Growth of Factory Foods: Changing Patterns of Bread and Cereal-Eating in Britain in the Twentieth Century," in *The Making of the Modern British Diet*, ed. Derek Oddy and Derek Miller (London, 1976), 29.

52. John Klippart, *The Wheat Plant: Its Origin, Culture, Growth, Development, Composition, Varieties, Diseases, Etc. Etc.* (Cincinnati, 1860), ix.

53. Frank Trentmann, *Free Trade Nation: Commerce, Consumption, and Civil Society in Modern Britain* (Oxford, 2008), 2; Anthony Howe, *Free Trade and Liberal England, 1846–1946* (Oxford, 1997), 5.

54. Petersen, *Bread*, 97–124.

55. E. P. Thompson, "The Moral Economy of the English Crowd in the Eighteenth Century," *Past and Present* 1 (1971): 76–136. For a critique of the overuse of the "moral economy" concept, see Frank Trentmann, "Before Fair

Trade: Empire, Free Trade and the Moral Economies of Food in the Modern World," in *Food and Globalization: Consumption, Markets and Politics in the Modern World*, ed. Alexander Nützenadel and Frank Trentmann (Oxford, 2008), 266–69.

56. T. B. Macaulay, "Total Repeal of the Corn Laws—Mr. Villiers's Motion. February 21, 1842," in Macaulay, *Speeches*, II (New York, 1853), 71.

57. Robert Peel, "Reflexions on the Present State of the Corn Laws," cited in Howe, *Free Trade*, 41.

58. John H. Perkins, *Geopolitics and the Green Revolution: Wheat, Genes and the Cold War* (Oxford, 1997), 45; Avner Offer, *The First World War: An Agrarian Interpretation* (Oxford, 1989), 93.

59. Cited in Dan Morgan, *Merchants of Grain* (New York, 1979), 36–37.

60. Royal Commission on Agriculture, Minutes of Evidence, BPP, 1882, xix, Giffen evidence, Q 64,839, cited in E. J. T. Collins, "Food Supplies and Food Policy," in *The Agrarian History of England and Wales*, vol. 7, *1850–1914*, ed. E. J. T. Collins (Cambridge, 2000), pt. 1, 50.

61. Harriet Friedmann, "State Policy and World Commerce: The Case of Wheat, 1815 to the Present," in *Foreign Policy and the Modern World System*, ed. Pat McGowan and Charles W. Kegley Jr. (London, 1983), 137; Offer, *First World War*, 97; Karl Gunnar Persson, *Grain Markets in Europe, 1500–1900: Integration and Deregulation* (Cambridge, 1999), 91–92.

62. Alexander Nützenadel, "A Green International? Food Markets and Transnational Politics, c. 1850–1914," in Nützenadel and Trentmann, *Food and Globalization*, 155–57.

63. Wilfred Malenbaum, *The World Wheat Economy, 1885–1939* (Cambridge, MA, 1953), 104.

64. Rollin Smith, *Wheat Fields and Markets of the World* (Saint Louis, 1908), 4.

65. Offer, *First World War*, 220.

66. Joachim Radkau, *Nature and Power: A Global History of the Environment*, trans. Thomas Dunlap (Cambridge, 2008), 40–41.

67. Karl Marx, *Capital: A Critique of Political Economy, Vol. III*, trans. David Fernbach (London, 1991), 949.

68. Foster, *Marx's Ecology*, 156.

69. Rolf Sieferle, *The Subterranean Forest: Energy Systems and the Industrial Revolution* (Cambridge, 2001), 134–35; Vaclav Smil, *Enriching the Earth: Fritz Haber, Carl Bosch, and the Transformation of World Food Production* (Cambridge, MA, 2001), 131.

70. David Grigg, *The World Food Problem*, 2nd ed. (Oxford, 1993), 124–25.

71. Eutrophication is a process whereby excessive nutrients in water generate superabundant algal (or other plant) growth, leading to diminished oxygen and reduced or extinguished animal life.

72. Petersen, *Bread*, 55.

73. Ibid.

74. Ibid., 155.

75. Raj Patel, *Stuffed and Starved: The Hidden Battle for the World Food System* (New York, 2007), 295.

76. William Cronon, *Nature's Metropolis: Chicago and the Great West* (New York, 1992), 98–135.

77. Michael Atkin, *Agricultural Commodity Markets: A Guide to Futures Trading* (London, 1989), 56.

78. Nützenadel, "Green International?" 162.

79. Peter Dondlinger, *The Book of Wheat: An Economic History and Practical Manual of the Wheat Industry* (London, 1908), 283–84.

80. Offer, *First World War*, 100.

81. R. H. Biffen, "Mendel's Laws of Inheritance and Wheat Breeding," *Journal of Agricultural Science* 1 (1905), cited in Perkins, *Green Revolution*, 57.

82. Perkins, *Green Revolution*, 250.

83. Tom Coultate, *Food, the Chemistry of Its Components*, 4th ed. (Cambridge, 2002), 173.

84. Siegfried Giedion, *Mechanization Takes Command: A Contribution to Anonymous History* (New York, 1948), 198.

85. Arbuthnot Lane (1928), cited in James Whorton, *Inner Hygiene: Constipation and the Pursuit of Health in Modern Society* (Oxford, 2000), 208.

86. Mike Davis, *Late Victorian Holocausts: El Niño Famines and the Making of the Third World* (London, 2001); Vernon, *Hunger*, 30–40, 44–48.

87. J. A. Hobson, *The Social Question* (Bristol, 1996), 208.

88. See Trentmann, "Before Fair Trade."

89. William Crookes, "The World's Wheat Supply," in *The Wheat Problem; Based on Remarks Made in the Presidential Address to the British Association at Bristol in 1898. Revised, with an Answer to Various Critics* (London, 1900), 16.

90. Crookes, "Replies to My Critics," in Crookes, *Wheat Problem*, 146.

91. Radkau, *Nature and Power*, 258. On the early modern period, see John F. Richards, *The Unending Frontier: An Environmental History of the Early Modern World* (Berkeley, 2003).

92. Frank Uekötter, *The Green and the Brown: A History of Conservation in Nazi Germany* (Cambridge, 2006), 62–63, 68.

93. Luc Ferry, *The New Ecological Order*, trans. Carol Volk (Chicago, 1995), 89, 102–3.

94. Michael Bess, *The Light-Green Society: Ecology and Technological Modernity in France, 1960–2000* (Chicago, 2003), 130–40; Raymond Dominick, *The Environmental Movement in Germany: Prophets and Pioneers, 1871–1971* (Bloomington, IN, 1992), 111.

95. N. N. Kliuev, ed., *Rossiia i ee regiony: Vneshnye i vnutrennie ekologicheskie ugrozy* (Moscow, 2001), 42, cited in Douglas Weiner, "The Predatory Tribute-Taking State: A Framework for Understanding Russian Environmental History," in Burke and Pomeranz, *Environment and World History*, 293.

96. Judith Shapiro, *Mao's War against Nature: Politics and the Environment in Revolutionary China* (New York, 2001), 64; Paul Josephson, *Resources*

under Regimes: Technology, Environment, and the State (Cambridge, MA, 2005), 132.

97. Shapiro, Mao's War, 21–65.

98. Sergio Díaz-Briquets and Jorge Pérez-Lopéz, Conquering Nature: The Environmental Legacy of Socialism in Cuba (Pittsburgh, 2000); Josephson, Resources under Regimes, 133–44.

99. Kenneth Pomeranz, "Introduction," in Burke and Pomeranz, Environment and World History, 7.

100. Ibid., 10; Kenneth Pomeranz, "The Transformation of China's Environment, 1500–2000," in Burke and Pomeranz, Environment and World History, 119–120; Polanyi, Great Transformation, 71–80; Radkau, Nature and Power, 202.

101. Richards, Unending Frontier, 11. On global ecological pressures in the seventeenth century, see Geoffrey Parker, The Global Crisis: Climate, War, and Collapse in the Seventeenth-Century World (New Haven, 2011).

102. On the fiscal-military state, see John Brewer, The Sinews of Power: War, Money, and the English State, 1688–1783 (Cambridge, MA, 1990).

103. For a more nuanced account of this shift than I can give here, see Philip Harling and Peter Mandler, "From 'Fiscal-Military' State to Laissez-Faire State, 1760–1850," Journal of British Studies 32 (January 1993): 44–70.

104. Radkau, Nature and Power, 202–4.

105. Ibid., 193–94; Kenneth Pomeranz, The Great Divergence: China, Europe, and the Making of the Modern World Economy (Princeton, 2000).

106. Brooke, Rough World, chap. 9.

107. David Harvey, A Brief History of Neoliberalism (Oxford, 2005).

108. Jennifer Clapp, Toxic Exports: The Transfer of Hazardous Wastes from Rich to Poor Countries (Ithaca, NY, 2001); Nik Heynen, James McCarthy, Scott Prudham, and Paul Robbins, eds., Neoliberal Environments: False Promises and Unnatural Consequences (New York, 2007),

109. Florian Charvolin, L'Invention de l'environnement en France: Chroniques anthropologiques d'une institutionnalisation (Paris, 2003); Bess, Light-Green Society, 232–33; Dominick, Environmental Movement, 138–39.

110. Sheail, Environmental History, 272, 188.

111. Pierre Rosanvallon, The New Social Question: Rethinking the Welfare State, trans. Barbara Harshav (Princeton, 2000).

112. Jacques Donzelot, L'Invention du social: Essai sur le déclin des passions politiques (Paris, 1984).

113. Margaret Thatcher, "Speech at the Second World Climate Conference," 6 November 1990, www.margaretthatcher.org/speeches/displaydocument.asp ?docid = 108237 (accessed 4 August 2009).

114. Bess, Light-Green Society.

115. See, e.g., Joel Mokyr, "Editor's Introduction: The New Economic History and the Industrial Revolution," in The British Industrial Revolution: An Economic Perspective, ed. Joel Mokyr (Boulder, CO, 1993), 1–127; Robert Allen, The British Industrial Revolution in Global Perspective (Cambridge, 2009).

116. Alice Conklin, *A Mission to Civilize: The Republican Idea of Empire in France and West Africa, 1895–1930* (Stanford, 1997); Persson, *Grain Markets*, 135–36.

117. This process was not straightforwardly secular, however. See Crosbie Smith, *The Science of Energy: A Cultural History of Energy Physics in Victorian Britain* (Chicago, 1998), 110–11.

118. See, e.g., Kenneth Deffeyes, *Hubbert's Peak: The Impending World Oil Shortage* (Princeton, 2001).

CHAPTER 13

1. *An Inquiry into the Nature and Causes of The Wealth of Nations*, ed. Edwin Cannan (New York: Modern Library, 1937 [1776]), IV: 2, pt. 4, 223.

2. For my more extended discussion of these developments, see *A History of the Modern Fact: Problems of Knowledge in the Sciences of Wealth and Society* (Chicago, 1998), esp. chap. 7. For the distinction between precision and accuracy, see *A History of the Modern Fact*, chap. 1.

3. See Philip Mirowski, *Machine Dreams: Economics Becomes a Cyborg Science* (Cambridge, 2002), esp. chap. 4.

4. See Rakesh Khurana, *From Higher Aims to Hired Hands: The Social Transformation of American Business Schools and the Unfulfilled Promise of Management as a Profession* (Princeton, 2007), esp. chap. 3.

5. By 1914 there were 25 university-based business schools in the United States. The number of MBAs these schools granted reflects their growing popularity: in 1919, 110 MBAs were granted; by 1949, this number had risen to 3,897 (during the same thirty-year period, the U.S. population increased by only 50 percent). See Khurana, *From Higher Aims*, 195. In Britain, the old universities remained skeptical about business education far longer. Oxford University, for example, did not open its business school (the Said Business School) until 1996.

6. It is important to note that the early curricula of U.S. business schools did not center on economics, which many considered too theoretical for business training; but the principles of scientific management, which featured prominently in the curriculum of the Harvard Business School (among others) were considered as rigorous, rational, and disinterested as training in any other "scientific"—or fully professionalized—subject. Economic principles became the cornerstone of America's elite business schools in the period between 1950 and 1980, following the recommendations of the Ford Foundation, which advised B-schools to hire more discipline-trained faculty and to emphasize quantification. See Khurana, *From Higher Aims*, esp. chaps. 6 and 7.

7. The scholarly literature on this subject is extensive. Among the most helpful studies are Michael Hudson, *Super Imperialism: The Origins and Fundamentals of U.S. World Dominance*, 2nd ed. (London, 2003); Alex Rosenson, "The Terms of the Anglo-American Financial Agreement," *American Economic Review* 37, no. 1 (1947): 178–87; and David Kynaston, *The City of London: Illusions of Gold, 1914–1945* (London, 1999).

8. My thanks to Anush Kapadia for helping with this formulation and parts of the analysis that follows (private communication).

9. Peter L. Bernstein, *Capital Ideas Evolving* (New York, 1997), xviii.

10. George Soros, *The Crisis of 2008 and What It Means: The New Paradigm for Financial Markets* (New York, 2008; rpt., 2009), Kindle electronic edition, section titled "The Flaw in Equilibrium Theory," loc. 797.

11. Peter L. Bernstein, *Capital Ideas: The Improbable Origins of Modern Wall Street* (New York, 1992), 57–58.

12. Bernstein, *Capital Ideas*, 132–33. Khurana argues that the idealism with which the first promoters of U.S. university-based business schools had associated managerial science had evaporated by 1970. From that time forward, Khurana argues, U.S. business schools began to adopt curricula exclusively designed to support the capitalist market, including courses in financial analysis. See *From Higher Aims*, pt. 3.

13. Bernstein writes that financial managers' hostility to relying on mathematical formulations began to change around 1971. See *Capital Ideas*, 202. Khurana argues explicitly that the inclusion of more economists in business school faculties and the formulation, then adoption, of the efficient market hypothesis helped transform business schools from training grounds for general managers into "institutions that trained professional investors and financial engineers" (*From Higher Aims*, 311). In Khurana's powerful argument, this transformation marked the betrayal of the idealism behind locating business schools in universities in favor of a narrow opportunism that stressed only self-interest. See *From Higher Aims*, chaps. 7 and 8.

14. On agency theory, see Khurana, *From Higher Aims*, 309–12. The relationship between this economic theory and the liberal model of the subject is complex and deserves further elaboration.

15. See Malcolm Gladwell, "'The Sure Thing': How Entrepreneurs Really Succeed," *New Yorker*, 18 January 2010, 28.

16. On the role of hostile takeovers in shaping corporate culture, see Justin Fox, *The Myth of the Rational Market: A History of Risk, Reward, and Delusion on Wall Street* (New York, 2009), 166–77; on the influence of "the number," see Fox, *Myth*, 274–79.

17. See Fox, *Myth*, 227–28. According to Fox, the crash demonstrated conclusively "that the definition of risk accepted among finance scholars—and, increasingly, on Wall Street—was inadequate. In this worldview, risk was seen as a natural phenomenon, a scatter graph of potential outcomes that could be kept within bounds and manipulated mathematically. It was usually assumed for the sake of convenience that the bounds were those of the bell curve, the enormously useful properties of which had paved the way for modern portfolio theory, risk-adjusted performance assessment of money managers, and the options-pricing models behind the work done at Leland O'Brien Rubinstein" (228). This example leads Fox to offer his most explicit theoretical statement of what Soros calls reflexivity: "Financial markets are not natural phenomenon. They are man-made—made by men and women whose business is gazing into

an uncertain, risky future. The act of managing risk in such an environment alters that environment, creating a never-stable feedback loop" (229).

18. Soros, *The Crash of 2008*, loc. 1532–50.

19. See Charles R. Morris, *The Two Trillion Dollar Meltdown: Easy Money, High Rollers, and the Great Credit Crash* (New York, 2008), for a discussion of the bewildering variety of derivative products.

20. William D. Cohan, *House of Cards: A Tale of Hubris and Wretched Excess on Wall Street* (New York, 2009); Lawrence G. McDonald, *A Colossal Failure of Common Sense: The Inside Story of the Collapse of Lehman Brothers* (New York, 2009); David Wessel, *In Fed We Trust: Ben Bernanke's War on the Great Panic* (New York, 2009); Erin Avredlund, *Too Good to Be True: The Rise and Fall of Bernie Madoff* (New York, 2009).

21. See, e.g., Martha Poon, "From New Deal Institutions to Capital Markets: Consumer Risk Scores and the Marketing of Subprime Mortgage Finance," *Accounting, Organizations and Society* 35, no. 5 (2009): 654–74.

22. Michel Callon, "An Essay on Framing and Overflowing: Economic Externalities Revisited by Sociology," in *The Laws of the Market*, ed. Michel Callon (Oxford, 1998), 244–69.

Contributors

PETER BAILEY is Emeritus Professor of History at the University of Manitoba and Visiting Professor in the Department of History at Indiana University. He is the author of *Popular Culture and Performance in the Victorian City* (1998) and other works on the history of leisure, popular culture, gender, and sexuality.

TONY BENNETT is Research Professor in Social and Cultural Theory and Director of Research at the University of Western Sydney and Visiting Professor at the Open University in the United Kingdom. His recent publications include *Handbook of Cultural Analysis* (2008, edited with John Frow), *Culture, Class, Distinction* (2009, coauthored with Mike Savage, Elizabeth Silva, Alan Warde, Modesto Gayo-Cal, and David Wright), and *Material Powers: Culture, History, and the Material Turn* (2009, coedited with Patrick Joyce).

TOM CROOK is Lecturer in Modern British History at Oxford Brookes University. He is currently working on two book projects: a study of Victorian public health and English modernity *(Time, Power and the Social Body: Public Health and English Modernity, 1830–1914)*; and a study of secrecy and modernity *(Powers of Secrecy: Modernity and the Obscure)*.

JAMES EPSTEIN teaches history at Vanderbilt University. Most recently, he is the author of *In Practice: Studies in the Language and Culture of Popular Politics in Modern Britain* (2003). He is currently writing a book on Britain and Trinidad in the age of revolution, provisionally titled *Negotiating Empire*.

SIMON GUNN is Professor of Urban History at the University of Leicester. His recent books include *History and Cultural Theory* (2006) and *The Public Culture of the Victorian Middle Class* (2000). He is joint editor of *Urban History* and is currently researching the transformation of British cities since 1945.

CATHERINE HALL is Professor of Modern British Social and Cultural History at University College London. Her first book, *Family Fortunes: Men and*

261

Women of the English Middle Class 1780–1850 (1987, 2002), was jointly written with Leonore Davidoff. Since the 1990s she has been working on questions of race, nation, empire, and identity, publishing *Civilising Subjects: Metropole and Colony in the English Imagination, 1830–1867* (2002) and a collection edited with Sonya Rose, *At Home with the Empire: Metropolitan Culture and the Imperial World* (2006). Her current research focuses on Macaulay and the writing of history.

PATRICK JOYCE is Emeritus Professor of History at the University of Manchester and Visiting Professor of Sociology at the London School of Economics. He is the author of *Work, Society and Politics: The Culture of the Factory in Later Victorian England* (1981), *Visions of the People: Industrial England and the Question of Class, 1840–1914* (1991), *Democratic Subjects* (1995), and *The Rule of Freedom: Liberalism and the Modern City* (2003).

JON LAWRENCE is Senior Lecturer in Modern British History at the University of Cambridge and a fellow of Emmanuel College. His most recent book is *Electing Our Masters: The Hustings in British Politics from Hogarth to Blair* (2009). Among his other publications are *Speaking for the People* (1998) and *Party, State and Society: Electoral Behaviour in Britain since 1820* (1997, with Miles Taylor).

THOMAS OSBORNE is Professor of Social and Cultural Theory at the University of Bristol. He is the author of *Aspects of Enlightenment: Social Theory and the Ethics of Truth* (1998) and *The Structure of Modern Cultural Theory* (2008), as well as a wide range of articles in the fields of social theory, the history of the human sciences, the sociology of literature, and intellectual history.

CHRIS OTTER is Assistant Professor in the Department of History at Ohio State University. He is the author of *The Victorian Eye: A Political History of Light and Vision in Britain, 1800–1910* (2008).

MARY POOVEY is Samuel Rudin University Professor in the Humanities and Director of the Institute for the History of the Production of Knowledge at New York University. Most recently, she is the author of *Genres of the Credit Economy: Mediating Value in Eighteenth- and Nineteenth-Century Britain* (2008). She has also written *A History of the Modern Fact: Problems of Knowledge in the Sciences of Wealth and Society* (1998) and *Making a Social Body: British Cultural Formation, 1830–1864* (1995).

GAVIN RAND is Lecturer in the Department of History at the University of Greenwich. He has researched and published on colonialism and the military in nineteenth-century India.

JOHN SEED is Honorary Research Fellow at Roehampton University London, where he taught from 1983 to 2010. He is the author of *Dissenting Histories: Religious Division and the Politics of Memory in Eighteenth-Century England* (2008) and *Marx: A Guide for the Perplexed* (2010).

JAMES VERNON is Professor of History at the University of California, Berkeley. He is the author of *Politics and the People* (1993) and *Hunger: A Modern History* (2007) and editor of *Re-Reading the Constitution* (1996). He is on the editorial boards of *Social History, Representations,* and *Twentieth Century British History.*

DAVID VINCENT is Professor of Social History at the Open University. His books include *The Culture of Secrecy: Britain, 1832–1998* (1998) and *The Rise of Mass Literacy: Reading and Writing in Modern Europe* (2000). He is currently working on the history of privacy.

Index

Made in the USA
Columbia, SC
01 August 2021